ASHISH JOSHI

LITIGATING FAMILY VIOLENCE

A Practitioner's Handbook

ABA
AMERICAN BAR ASSOCIATION
Litigation Section

Cover design by Amanda Fry/ABA Design

Printed in the United States of America.

30 29 28 27 26 5 4 3 2 1

Library of Congress Cataloging-in-Publication Data

Names: Joshi, Ashish author | American Bar Association. Section of Litigation issuing body
Title: Litigating family violence : a practitioner's handbook / Ashish S. Joshi.
Description: Chicago : American Bar Association, Litigation Section, 2026. | Includes bibliographical references and index. | Summary: "Practical, trauma-informed guidance for legal practitioners"— Provided by publisher.
Identifiers: LCCN 2026015807 (print) | LCCN 2026015808 (ebook) | ISBN 9781639057436 paperback | ISBN 9781639057443 ebook
Subjects: LCSH: Family violence—Law and legislation—United States | Family violence—United States—Prevention | Child abuse—Law and legislation—United States | Parental alienation syndrome—United States | LCGFT: Handbooks and manuals
Classification: LCC KF9322 .J67 2026 (print) | LCC KF9322 (ebook)
LC record available at https://lccn.loc.gov/2026015807
LC ebook record available at https://lccn.loc.gov/2026015808

Discounts are available for books ordered in bulk. Special consideration is given to state bars, CLE programs, and other bar-related organizations. Inquire at Book Publishing, ABA Publishing, American Bar Association, 321 N. Clark Street, Chicago, Illinois 60654-7598.

www.shopABA.org

For Payal, yet again.

CONTENTS

FOREWORD

Hon. Tiffany Williams Brewer (Ret.)

Family violence cases are among the most emotionally complex and legally challenging matters a litigator can face. As a former litigator, judge, and lifelong advocate for children's rights, I have witnessed firsthand the toll that family violence takes not only on survivors but also on the structure and function of the family unit—especially on children. The legal system, in its effort to provide justice, must confront the reality that domestic violence is not an isolated event but often part of a long-standing pattern of coercive control, power imbalance, and trauma. When children are involved, the stakes are even higher.

It is from this lens—one shaped by decades of service in the courtroom, in chambers, and in the broader legal community—that I commend *Litigating Family Violence: A Practitioner's Handbook* to you. Published by the American Bar Association Litigation Section, this handbook is not merely a reference; it is a critical tool in the hands of practitioners who are charged with advocating for the most vulnerable among us. Whether you are a seasoned family law attorney or just beginning your journey into civil litigation involving intimate partner violence, this resource will deepen your understanding of both the legal doctrines and the human dimensions at play.

This book comes at a pivotal time. Across the country, family courts continue to wrestle with how best to respond to allegations of family violence, especially when layered against custody disputes, post-divorce conflict, and concerns for a child's safety and well-being. The need for practical, trauma-informed, and legally sound guidance has never been more urgent.

The chapters in this volume bring together the wisdom of an experienced practitioner who understands the nuances of litigating family violence in civil contexts domestically and internationally. The guidance offered to dispel misinformation around family abuse and coercive behaviors is groundbreaking and transformative for practitioners. Particularly valuable are the insights on the use of guardians ad litem, the importance of screening tools, and the evolving case law that shapes how courts across the states are responding to family violence.

By also centering children's needs and perspectives in our legal processes, this book seeks to strengthen families by maximizing safety and upholding dignity and the right to be heard. This book echoes that principle, reminding us that in the often-chaotic world of family litigation, our highest obligation is to those whose futures depend on the integrity of our legal advocacy.

INTRODUCTION

Blood, Bruises, and Brainwashing: An Introduction to Family Violence

Family courts, legal practitioners, and professionals affiliated with family courts confront family violence on a regular basis and with an increasing frequency. The universality of family violence crosses all boundaries and barriers: geography, race, culture, language, gender, and sexuality.

Experts frame family violence as the hypernym of violent and abusive incidents or a pattern of behavior within families, with potential hyponyms that include domestic violence, intimate partner violence, sexual violence, coercive control violence, financial abuse, legal abuse, elder abuse, pet abuse, and child psychological maltreatment, which could include parental alienating behaviors depending on their pattern, frequency, and severity.[1] See Figure 1.[2]

The term *family violence* has been conceptualized and defined in more ways than one. The Organisation for Economic Cooperation and Development (OECD) defines family violence, also known as domestic violence, as "any violent act inflicted by one family member onto another," a term encompassing both child abuse and intimate partner violence (IPV).[3] As defined, the term includes physical, sexual, emotional, and economic violence, as well as neglect.[4]

1. Robin M. Deutsch et al., *Guest Editors' Introduction to the 2024 Special Issue on Family Violence and Parenting*, 62(1) FAM. CT. REV. 11–14 (Jan. 2024), DOI: 10.1111.fcre.12761.

2. Adapted from Deutsch et al., *supra* note 1.

3. Jennifer Harman et al., *Parental Alienating Behaviors: An Unacknowledged Form of Family Violence*, 144(12) PSYCH. BULL., 1275-99, 1277 (2018), citing Organisation for Economic Cooperation and Development (2013), SF3.4: Family violence, https://www.oecd.org/els/soc/SF3_4_Family_violence_Jan2013.pdf.

4. *Id.* at 1277.

Figure 1

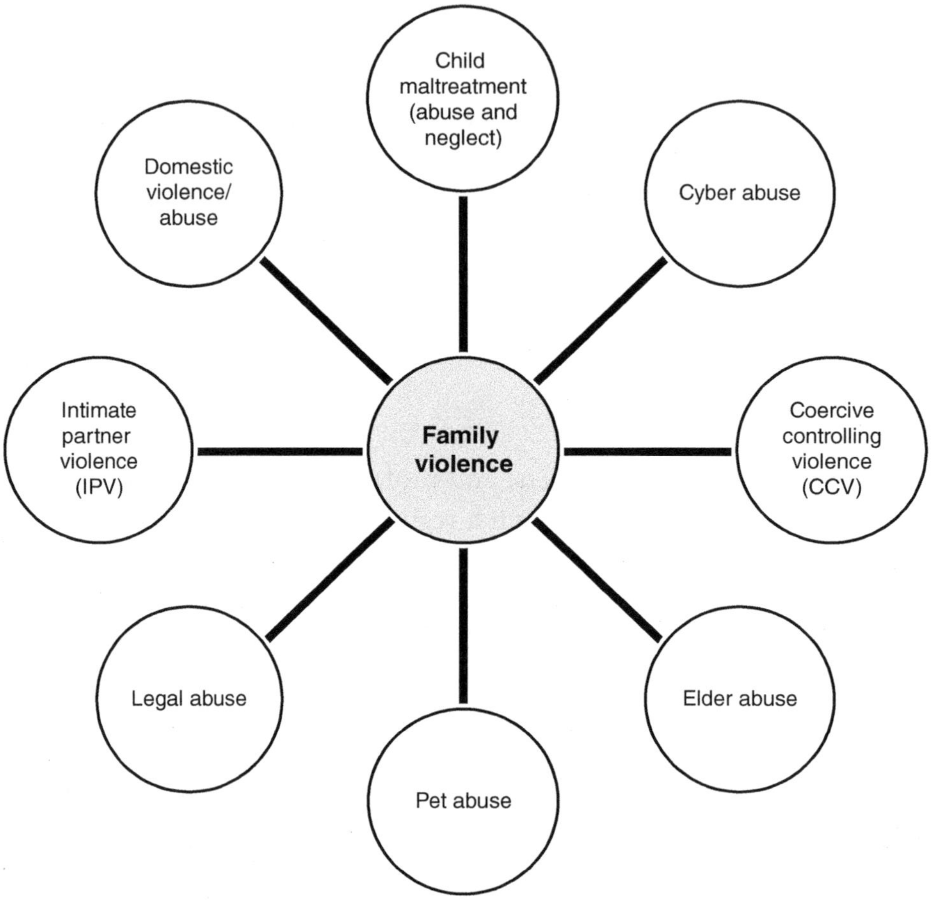

Family violence has been addressed at both federal and state levels. For instance, the U.S. Department of Justice's Office of Violence Against Women identifies physical, sexual, emotional, economic, or psychological actions or threats of actions as forms of violence that can intimidate, manipulate, humiliate, isolate, frighten, terrorize, coerce, threaten, blame, hurt, injure, or wound someone.[5] State laws have also defined family violence or some forms of it within their criminal or penal codes.[6]

---

5. U.S. Dep't of Just., Office of Violence Against Women (2017), Domestic Violence, https://www.justice.gov/ovw/domestic-violence (last updated Jan. 22, 2025).

6. Child Welfare Information Gateway, Definitions of Domestic Violence: State statutes current through August 2017. Washington DC: Department of Health and Human Services. https://www.childwelfare.gov/resources/definitions-domestic-violence/.

Common misconceptions and flawed assumptions continue to compromise outcomes in courts: such as, "if things were *really* bad, victims would just leave," or "a lack of visible injury means it is not serious," or "emotional abuse is just *words*." A study published by the United Nations Office on Drugs and Crime called home "the most dangerous place for women."[7] The study cited a stunning statistic: Fifty thousand women around the world were killed by their partners, spouses, or family members in just one year. Fifty thousand women killed in *one* year. And while there is a growing awareness that men, too, can be victims of family violence, the overwhelming number of victims—about 85 percent—are women and girls. Family violence is lethal: For every woman killed in the United States from domestic violence homicide, nearly nine are almost killed.[8]

This book aims to introduce family law practitioners and other professionals affiliated with family court proceedings to the dynamics of family violence, including its types and nuances. Chapter 1, Intimate Partner Violence, focuses on IPV, which is a specific form of domestic violence that occurs within romantic relationships, encompassing physical, sexual, psychological, and financial abuse, among other forms of aggression. It affects a significant portion of the population, with 41 percent of women and 26 percent of men reporting experiences of IPV in their lifetimes. IPV is not limited to physical acts but also includes coercive and controlling behaviors, and it can be perpetrated by both men and women across various demographics. Risk factors for IPV include substance abuse, low income, and exposure to violence in childhood.

IPV is a critical consideration in family law, particularly in child custody and parenting time disputes, where evidence of IPV can significantly influence court decisions related to child custody, parenting time and visitation, and, in some cases, determination of spousal support and the division of marital assets. Physical violence is a common aspect of IPV, where victims may suffer from traumatic brain injuries that are frequently undiagnosed due to a lack of visible injuries. Sexual violence, including rape, sexual assault, and revenge porn is also prevalent in IPV cases. Stalking, both traditional and through technology, is another component of IPV, often leading to fear and control over a victim.

7. UNODC, *Home, the Most Dangerous Place for Women* (2017).

8. Rachel Louise Snyder, No Visible Bruises: What We Don't Know About Domestic Violence Can Kill Us 6 (2019).

IPV also includes emotional and psychological abuse, including coercion and control, which are increasingly seen as serious forms of family violence. This type of abuse can have significant impacts on victims' cognitive and mental health and affect their parenting abilities. Economic abuse, where the abuser controls the victim's financial resources, is another form of IPV that can trap victims in abusive relationships. The Violence Against Women Act (VAWA) acknowledges the link between IPV and economic insecurity, highlighting the importance of financial independence for survivors.

Family courts often face challenges in cases involving bidirectional IPV, where both partners engage in abusive behaviors. In such cases, courts may attempt to identify the primary aggressor to make custody decisions. The severity of IPV can influence custody outcomes, with courts often favoring the parent less likely to continue violent behavior. IPV has profound effects on victims' parenting and on children's well-being, with exposure to IPV leading to various developmental and emotional issues in children.

Chapter 1 discusses how, in child custody disputes, allegations of IPV can overturn presumptions favoring joint custody or ample visitation. Many states have rebuttable presumptions against awarding custody to a parent with a history of IPV, requiring substantial evidence to overcome these presumptions. The presence of IPV in a relationship can complicate custody and visitation arrangements, necessitating clear and specific court orders to protect victims and children.

Victims of IPV often face challenges in leaving abusive relationships due to financial constraints, fear of retaliation, and concerns for their children's safety. False allegations of IPV can have serious consequences, affecting the credibility of genuine victims and complicating legal proceedings. Despite these challenges, IPV remains a significant issue in family law, requiring careful consideration and intervention to protect victims and children.

Chapter 2 is titled "Coercive Control: A Slow but Steady Stripping Away One's Sense of Self." Coercive control is a form of IPV that extends beyond physical abuse; it involves a pattern of behavior aimed at stripping away a victim's sense of self, liberty, and autonomy. This form of abuse is often overlooked because it does not leave visible marks like physical violence often does, yet it is equally damaging. Coercive control is characterized by psychological aggression, where the abuser monitors, controls, or threatens their partner, effectively imprisoning them in their own life.

The impact of coercive control is disproportionately felt by women and children, as well as marginalized groups such as racial minorities and the

LGBTQ+ community. Studies indicate that Black and American Indian/ Alaskan Native women experience higher rates of intimate partner violence. Similarly, individuals from lower socioeconomic backgrounds and those identifying as LGBTQ+ are more vulnerable to such abuse.

Coercive control manifests in various forms, including economic abuse, where the abuser controls the victim's financial resources, and emotional abuse, which involves tactics like gaslighting to undermine a victim's sense of reality. The abuser may also employ intimidation, threats, and isolation to maintain control. These behaviors are often subtle and insidious, making them difficult to prove in court. The legal system has been slow to recognize and address coercive control. While some jurisdictions have enacted laws to define and combat this form of abuse, enforcement remains a challenge. For instance, California law includes coercive control in its definition of domestic violence, allowing courts to issue orders to prevent such behavior. However, the effectiveness of these laws depends on the training and awareness of law enforcement and judicial officials.

Coercive control can have severe psychological effects on victims, leading to issues such as anxiety, depression, and post-traumatic stress disorder. It also poses significant risks to children, who may be used as tools by an abuser to exert control over a victim. This can have long-term detrimental effects on a child's well-being and development. In family law cases involving child custody disputes, coercive control is often intertwined with issues of parental alienation and child psychological maltreatment. Abusers may manipulate the legal system to continue exerting control over their victims, using tactics such as refusing to follow court orders, filing frivolous motions, or making false allegations. This can lead to prolonged legal battles that drain a victim's financial and emotional resources.

Despite the challenges, there is a growing recognition of the need to address coercive control within the legal framework. Advocates argue for clearer statutory definitions and better training for professionals to identify and respond to this form of abuse. The goal is to provide victims with the legal remedies they need to escape abusive relationships and rebuild their lives.

Chapter 3, Child Psychological Maltreatment: An Attack on a Child's Basic Need Fulfillment, addresses child psychological maltreatment (PM), which although pervasive and harmful remains under-recognized and misunderstood by professionals involved in child welfare and family court systems. PM is characterized by a parent or caregiver's attack on a child's fundamental needs for security, love, and attachment. PM can have both immediate and long-lasting consequences. Despite its prevalence, PM lacks a clear and consistent definition, complicating its recognition and intervention by child welfare professionals and caregivers. The Diagnostic and Statistical Manual of Mental Disorders (DSM-5) defines child psychological abuse as nonaccidental acts by a caregiver that result in significant psychological harm, excluding physical and sexual abuse. The American Professional Society on the Abuse of Children (APSAC) provides a foundational definition of PM, emphasizing caregiver behaviors that thwart a child's basic psychological needs and convey a sense of worthlessness or expendability. However, researchers have sought to expand upon this definition to include isolated incidents of extreme harm, arguing that a pattern of behavior should not be required to classify an act as PM.

Characteristics of perpetrators of PM often include undiagnosed personality disorders or a history of exposure to violence or abuse. These caregivers may lack empathy and fail to consider a child's needs, often prioritizing their own needs and experiences. Factors such as mental illness, cultural beliefs, unrealistic expectations, and addictions can contribute to a caregiver's inability to meet a child's needs. Some caregivers may fit the profile of a "traumatizing narcissist," who suppresses a child's individuality to maintain dominance. Chapter 3 discusses the phenomenon of enmeshment, a form of PM, which occurs when a parent and child form an unhealthy coalition that breaches generational boundaries, often resulting in role reversal where the child fulfills the parent's emotional needs. This dynamic is common in families facing systemic pressures such as poverty, illness, or high-conflict divorce. Effective treatment for enmeshment involves both parents and the child, with the enmeshed parent establishing boundaries and availing helpful resources to relieve the child of their emotional burden.

Enmeshment can manifest in various forms, including *parentification*, *adultification*, and *infantilization*. Parentification involves a child taking on caregiving roles for siblings or parents, which can lead to significant emotional and mental health issues. Instrumental or transactional parentification, where a child assists with practical tasks, is generally less harmful, while emotional parentification, where a child provides emotional support, can have severe negative impacts. Adultification occurs when a child is burdened with inappropriate responsibilities or information, undermining their security and development. Infantilization involves inhibiting a child's autonomy, often resulting in academic and social underachievement. Each form of enmeshment requires specific treatment interventions to address a child's anxiety and restore appropriate boundaries.

In child custody litigation, enmeshment dynamics can complicate proceedings, particularly when one parent engages in behaviors that alienate the child from the other parent or causes the child to align with a favored or enmeshed parent. Courts have recognized the unhealthy impact of enmeshment and have made custody decisions to protect a child's well-being. Chapter 3 further discusses other forms of PM, for example, *spurning*, a form of PM that involves verbal and nonverbal acts that degrade a child, often leading to long-term emotional harm; *terrorizing*, which includes behaviors that threaten or place a child in dangerous situations; and *exploiting and corrupting*, which involve encouraging a child to engage in inappropriate behaviors. These forms of PM can result in changes to custody and parenting time arrangements to safeguard children.

The impact of PM on children is profound; it affects their intrapersonal, emotional, social, educational, and physical development. PM is linked to mental health disorders, substance abuse, and social dysfunction. The severity of PM is influenced by factors such as the intensity and frequency of the behavior, the child's developmental stage, and the caregiver's willingness to change. Certain forms of PM, like spurning and terrorizing, are particularly damaging during early childhood and adolescence. Despite the challenges in determining the prevalence of PM, self-report data suggests it is more common than legal cases indicate, with a significant portion of children experiencing some form of PM in their lifetimes.

Interventions to address PM require a coordinated effort among child protective services, legal professionals, and mental health clinicians. A three-tiered approach is recommended, focusing on all children, those at risk and those experiencing maltreatment. Public awareness campaigns and training for caregivers and professionals are essential to prevent PM and to support children's rights. Existing interventions can be adapted to incorporate a multitier approach, emphasizing the importance of a child rights-informed public health strategy to proactively protect children from PM.

Chapter 4, Alienation and Brainwashing: Weaponizing Children, discusses the dynamics of parental alienation, including the tactics known as brainwashing and programming whereby a child is weaponized to reject the victim parent or is used as a proxy to perpetrate acts of abuse against the target parent. This chapter explores the complex issue of child alignment through alienation, a phenomenon that occurs when a child unjustifiably rejects a parent, due to the influence of the other parent. This situation is particularly prevalent in highly contentious and litigious cases of divorce and separation, where one parent may manipulate their child, intentionally or inadvertently, to reject the other parent without legitimate reasons. Parental alienation is characterized by a child's unwavering rejection of the targeted parent, often accompanied by a distorted belief that the parent is unworthy of love or is unsafe, unfit, and dangerous.

Parental alienation is not a new concept; it has been recognized in legal cases since the early 19th century and in scientific literature since the 1940s. Despite its long history, the term and its implications are not always well understood by legal and mental health professionals. Chapter 4 discusses the legal recognition of parental alienation, citing court cases across the United States and other jurisdictions where the phenomenon has been acknowledged and addressed. Courts have defined parental alienation as behaviors by one parent that damage a child's relationship with the other parent, whether intentional or not. The chapter also provides examples of court cases where parental alienation was identified and interventions were made to protect a child's relationship with the targeted parent.

The severity of parental alienation can vary, with symptoms ranging from mild to severe. Mild cases involve a child resisting contact but enjoying the relationship once it begins, while severe cases involve a child adamantly refusing contact, possibly hiding or running away from the rejected parent, or attacking the parent. The chapter emphasizes that parental alienation is a form of child abuse, with severe cases causing significant emotional and psychological harm to a child.

The chapter also distinguishes between parental alienation and estrangement, noting that estrangement occurs when a child's rejection of a parent is justified by the parent's abusive or neglectful behavior. In contrast, parental alienation involves rejection without legitimate justification. The chapter stresses the importance of thoroughly investigating allegations of abuse to differentiate between alienation and estrangement.

The chapter briefly addresses the controversy surrounding the term *Parental Alienation Syndrome*, which was introduced by Dr. Richard Gardner. While some criticize the term, the chapter argues that the focus should be on the behaviors of the alienating parent rather than the alleged syndrome. It highlights the consensus among courts and mental health professionals that parental alienating *behaviors* are a real phenomenon that causes significant harm to the targeted parent's relationship with the child.

Chapter 4 concludes with a discussion that underscores the importance of recognizing and addressing parental alienation in family court cases. It calls for legal and mental health professionals to understand the research supporting parental alienation and to take action to protect a child's relationship with both parents. It emphasizes that parental alienation is a valid construct that, when present, can cause long-term harm to a child and should be addressed with appropriate interventions.

Chapter 5, Stereotypes, Shame, and Silence: Intimate Partner Violence Against Men, explores the often-overlooked issue of IPV against men, highlighting societal stereotypes and biases that contribute to the silence surrounding male victimization. The chapter begins by referencing the high-profile case of Johnny Depp and Amber Heard, where Depp's claims of being a victim of domestic violence brought attention to the issue of male victimization in IPV cases. Heard's recorded statement in court mocking Depp's claim to be a victim of IPV underscored the societal belief that men cannot be victims of IPV, a notion that this chapter seeks to challenge.

Chapter 5 discusses the prevalence of IPV against men, noting that both men and women are capable of inflicting violence on their partners. Despite 30 years of research documenting this, men's experiences as victims have been largely ignored by courts and social institutions. This oversight is partly due to the historical focus on female victims and male perpetrators, which has shaped the research and policy landscape. The chapter argues that this perspective has led to a misdirection of social and legal policies, which often disregard data that contradicts the prevailing theory of male-dominated IPV.

Research indicates that women are at least as likely as men to engage in partner aggression, with some studies showing that women are the instigators in a significant percentage of cases. The chapter highlights a Centers for Disease Control survey that found women were the instigators in 71 percent of one-way partner aggression cases. It also notes that in help-seeking samples, female perpetrators used physical and psychological aggression at higher rates than their male partners. This data challenges the belief that women do not cause significant harm to men and that their violence is often inconsequential.

Chapter 5 further explores the implications of gender dynamics in IPV for the family law system, particularly in child custody and visitation decisions. It emphasizes the need for courts to understand the bidirectional nature of IPV and the similar motives and risk factors that drive it. It cites a global study that found most IPV is bidirectional and related to the same risk factors, with men comprising a significant portion of IPV victims. The chapter also addresses the motivations behind IPV, suggesting that it is driven by intimacy and psychopathology rather than gender. It cites studies on same-sex couples to support the argument that IPV is not specific to men and cannot be explained solely by gender roles. Instead, factors such as psychopathology, attachment issues, and substance abuse are identified as contributing to IPV.

IPV has a severe impact on male victims, noting that men often stay in abusive relationships due to emotional ties and concerns for their children. It discusses the barriers men face in seeking help, including societal stigma and the need to prove the severity of the violence they experience. The chapter calls for services that cater to a diverse range of populations, including men, to improve access to support for male victims. It concludes by emphasizing the importance of understanding IPV as a dyadic system, where interventions must address the dynamics within the couple. It stresses the need for courts to consider the impact of IPV on children and the family system when making custody determinations. Finally, the chapter calls for a shift in societal perceptions of masculinity and victimization to better support male victims of IPV.

Chapter 6, Fallacies, False Positives, and Fake News: Mis- and Disinformation About Family Violence, explores the pervasive myths, fallacies, and misconceptions surrounding family violence, including IPV, coercive control, and parental alienation. It highlights the challenges faced in litigation due to these misconceptions and the need for a careful examination of facts to address the issues effectively. The chapter discusses the historical debate on domestic violence, noting the disagreements between different schools of thought regarding its motivation and the criteria for identifying it. It emphasizes the role of mis- and disinformation and propaganda, which may compromise legal outcomes and treatment in cases involving family violence, particularly in divorce, child custody, and parenting time litigation.

The chapter references research, which identifies the global public health problem of abuse against women and the myths that minimize its extent. It notes that despite the acceptance of domestic violence as a social problem by mental health and legal professionals, misinformation continues to affect legal proceedings. Common myths include the belief that domestic violence is only physical, a private matter, or a temporary issue, and that victims can easily leave abusive environments if they want to. These misconceptions are often perpetuated in family courts, and supported by social media and ideologically driven groups, leading to significant harm to victims.

Chapter 6 also addresses the issue of parental alienation, a concept recognized by family courts as a form of emotional abuse. It explains that parental alienation involves behaviors by one parent that cause a child to unjustifiably reject the other parent. It highlights the importance of focusing on parental alienating behaviors rather than the abstract theory of parental alienation syndrome. It notes that courts have found it more effective to address specific behaviors that obstruct a child's relationship with a parent, rather than debating the existence of a psychological syndrome. Furthermore, the chapter discusses the challenges in distinguishing parental alienation from estrangement, emphasizing the need for a methodical approach in litigating cases involving alienation. It outlines the criteria for identifying parental alienation, including marshalling evidence of the alienating behaviors by the favored parent. The chapter also addresses the fallacy that parental alienation cannot be diagnosed because it is not included in the DSM-5, arguing that many recognized mental conditions that are widely accepted are not listed in the DSM. It provides examples of diagnoses that can be used in cases involving parental alienation, such as parent-child relational problem and child psychological abuse.

Chapter 6 concludes by emphasizing the societal challenges posed by mis- and disinformation about family violence. It warns that such misinformation can lead to compromised legal outcomes and deter victims from seeking help. It calls for family law practitioners to counter these myths and focus on behaviors that constitute abuse, rather than abstract theories and stereotypes, to ensure that family courts act in the best interests of the child.

Finally, Chapter 7, Practice Pointers: Tips on Representing Victims of Family Violence, offers my parting thoughts to practitioners who handle cases of family violence. Cases involving family violence are tough and hard-hitting. Interacting with and representing victims of family violence, especially minor children, takes its toll. Professionals who work in this field complain of burnout, being desensitized to domestic abuse and violence, and, on occasions, suffering from vicarious or secondary trauma. The chapter discusses the importance of using appropriate screening tools to not just collect all the necessary information when interviewing a victim who complains of having been subjected to family violence, but also to mitigate against biases and thinking errors, which are pervasive and against which no human is immune. It also emphasizes the importance of ensuring self-care and laying down boundaries when representing victims of family violence.

This book, like my previous book, *Litigating Parental Alienation: Evaluating and Presenting an Effective Case in Court* (ABA, 2021), would not have been possible without the help of my colleagues. I am thankful to Andrew Bossory, Elle Murphree, Melissa Blevins, and Rona Lohry for their assistance and support. I am also grateful for the help, encouragement, patience, and camaraderie of my wife, Payal, and the support of our two children, Arya and Arjun. Finally, I am thankful for the unconditional love and support of my parents, Kishori and Shailesh, who have always inspired me and continue to do so.

Chapter 1

Intimate Partner Violence

Intimate partner violence (IPV) is a unique subset of domestic violence that also includes non-intimate partner violence, which is violence between individuals who are not intimate partners but have a familial relationship, such as mother and adult son or brother and sister.[1] Broadly speaking, IPV is abuse or aggression that occurs in a romantic relationship.[2] It encompasses acts of violence by or against current and former spouses or dating couples, with or without a child in common. It occurs among heterosexual or same-sex couples and does not require sexual intimacy.[3] IPV includes physical violence, sexual violence, coercive controlling behaviors, psychological abuse or aggression, stalking, financial coercion or abuse, and other acts of aggression or abusive behavior.

About 41 percent of women and 26 percent of men report physical violence, sexual violence, or stalking from an intimate partner in their lifetime.[4] IPV often begins in adolescence, and 10 percent to 20 percent of children are exposed to IPV annually. An estimated 8.5 million women in the U.S. (7 percent) and more than 4 million men (4 percent) reported experiencing physical violence, rape, sexual assault, strangulation, or stalking from an intimate partner in their lifetime.[5]

---

1. Domestic Violence Coordinating Council, *Dynamics of Domestic Violence*, Delaware.gov, https://dvcc.delaware.gov/background-purpose/dynamics-domestic-abuse/ (last visited Nov. 27, 2023).

2. Centers for Disease Control, *About Intimate Partner Violence*, https://www.cdc.gov/intimate-partner-violence/about/?CDC_AAref_Val=https://www.cdc.gov/violenceprevention/intimatepartnerviolence/fastfact.html.

3. Domestic Violence Coordinating Council, *supra* note 1.

4. Centers for Disease Control, *supra* note 2.

5. Phyllis Holditch Niolon et al., Intimate Partner Violence Prevention: Resource for Action 8 (Ctrs. for Disease Control 2017).

IPV may include a single act or a series or acts or conduct forming a pattern of abusive behavior. Aside from physical and sexual violence, IPV also includes economically and psychologically controlling behaviors as well as coercion through "intimidation, intrusiveness, isolation and/or control."[6] It is a serious problem not just in the United States but also around the world. Relying on the National Intimate Partner and Sexual Violence Survey, the Centers for Disease Control and Prevention (CDC) has reported that forms of IPV, including sexual violence, have been commonly reported among the U.S. women and men in their lifetimes.[7] IPV is perpetrated in relationships regardless of race, gender, ethnicity, marital status, sexual orientation, economic status, or educational background.[8] Some studies suggest that IPV occurs equally between men and women, but research demonstrates that women continue to suffer more serious harm and consequences as a result of the violence.[9] However, it would be a mistake to see IPV as a "gendered" phenomenon where the acts of violence—physical, sexual, emotional, or psychological—are perpetrated only by men against women. As the forensic psychologist and researcher John Hamel, PhD, has demonstrated through his research, IPV varies in its occurrence, frequency, severity, causes, and impact, and contrary to common stereotypes is perpetrated by women as well as men.[10] It is by no means a homogenous or gendered phenomenon.

While IPV is typically carried out by a partner or spouse in an intimate relationship, it may also be carried out by extended family members or third parties who may aid, abet, or provide support for a perpetrator's abusive behavior toward a victim. Risk factors for IPV include alcohol

---

6. Ass'n of Family & Conciliation Cts., Guidelines for Examining Intimate Partner Violence: A Supplement to the AFCC Model Standards of Practice for Child Custody Evaluation 3 (2016).

7. Kathleen C. Basile, et al., *The National Intimate Partner and Sexual Violence Survey: 2016/2017 Report on Sexual Violence*. Atlanta, GA: National Center for Injury Prevention and Control, Centers for Disease Control and Prevention (June 2022), https://www.cdc.gov/nisvs/documentation/nisvsReportonSexualViolence.pdf.

8. Michael Saini et al., *Treating Children Exposed to Intimate Partner Violence Within the Context of Child Custody Disputes*, *in* Evidence-Informed Interventions for Court-Involved Families (Lyn R. Greenberg et al. eds., Oxford Univ. Press 2019).

9. *Id.* (citing John Archer, *Sex Differences in Aggression Between Heterosexual Partners: A Meta-Analytic Review*, 126(5) Psych. Bull. 651–80 (2000)).

10. John Hamel, *Perpetrator or Victim? A Review of Complexities of Domestic Violence Cases*, 12(2) J. Aggression, Conflict & Peace Rsch. 55–62 (2020).

or substance dependency or abuse, adolescence or young adulthood, low income, low educational attainment, unemployment, stress, anxiety, antisocial personality traits, beliefs or attitudes condoning violence in relationships, and belief in strict gender roles.[11] Childhood factors such as parental violence, child abuse/neglect, and poor parenting contribute to the risk factors.[12] Other factors include peer violence, delinquency, and hostile means of communication.[13]

There is an overlap between domestic violence and IPV. The U.S. Department of Justice's Office on Violence Against Women defines domestic violence, which includes IPV, as "a pattern of abusive behavior in any relationship that is used by one partner to gain or maintain power and control over another intimate partner."[14] It manifests in many harmful ways including "physical, sexual, emotional, economic, psychological, or technological actions or threats," as well as in "other patterns of coercive behavior that influence another person within an intimate partner relationship."[15] These abusive behaviors include those that "intimidate, manipulate, humiliate, isolate, frighten, terrorize, coerce, threaten, blame, hurt, injure, or wound" the other partner.[16]

IPV's role in family law and domestic relations cases cannot be overstated. In cases and controversies involving child custody and parenting time disputes, state courts consider evidence of IPV in making these decisions, with some characterizing it as "a factor of *primary importance*"[17] or "critical importance."[18] Also, in cases involving international child kidnapping, both federal and international law "direct[] that domestic violence is a factor that must be considered when determining whether to retain jurisdiction in the United States in an international custody case under the International Parental Kidnapping Act."[19] In fact, the "existence of domestic

---

11. Niolon et al., *supra* note 5.

12. *Id.*

13. *Id.*

14. U.S. Dep't of Just., Off. on Violence Against Women, *What Is Domestic Violence?*, https://www.justice.gov/ovw/domestic-violence (last updated Jan. 22, 2025).

15. *Id.*

16. *Id.*

17. Christopher K. v. Markaa S., 311 P.3d 1110, 1114 (Ariz. Ct. App. 2013) (emphasis added).

18. Kasprowicz v. Kasprowicz, 1998 ND 68, 575 N.W.2d 921 (N.D. Mar. 30, 1998).

19. Jeanne E.M. v. Lindey M.M., 734 N.Y.S.2d 837, 838 (N.Y. Fam. Ct. 2001).

violence would also support one country's refusal to return a child to the child's country of residence to resolve a custody dispute."[20]

Aside from issues related to child custody and parenting time, some states consider IPV or domestic violence as a factor in the equitable distribution of a marital estate or in making an award of spousal support and maintenance. For instance, California considers domestic violence when making awards of spousal support,[21] and there is a rebuttable presumption against such an award to an abusive spouse.[22] In Michigan, courts consider the past relations and conduct of the parties, which can include consideration of domestic violence.[23] As the Michigan Court of Appeals explained in one case, "[t]o the extent that the trial court considered alleged domestic violence in reaching its decision, the conduct and past relations of the parties is one of the specific factors a trial court is to consider when dividing the parties' assets."[24] In New York, "courts are permitted to award increased spousal support and maintenance to an abused spouse and the subject of domestic violence by the other."[25]

Legal Definition of IPV

Domestic violence, including IPV, is viewed by social scientists and researchers as a "serious public health problem," where a significant number of women and men report having experienced not just physical violence, sexual violence, and stalking behaviors but also acts of emotional and psychological coercion and abuse.[26] Given its protean nature and inherent difficulty in classifying human behavior into strict categories, IPV can be difficult to characterize. To address the problem, some states have created broad inclusive definitions. Arizona, for example, has a catch-all: It attempts to protect victims where the perpetrator is shown to have engaged "in a pattern of

---

20. *Id.*

21. CAL. FAM. CODE § 4320(i).

22. *Id.* § 4325.

23. *See* Gates v. Gates, 256 Mich. App. 420, 422; 664 N.W.2d 231 (2003); *see also* Parrish v. Parrish, 138 Mich. App. 546, 361 N.W.2d 366 (1984).

24. Anbuchozhan v. Arjunan, unpublished opinion of the Court of Appeals, issued Mar. 21, 2019 (Docket No. 344301), 2019 WL 1301822, at *3.

25. MR v. DR, 82 Misc. 3d 1213(A); 206 N.Y.S.3d 919 (2024). *See also* JN v. TN, 77 Misc. 3d 894, 182 N.Y.S.3d 497 (2022).

26. Hila Avieli, *False Allegations of Domestic Violence: A Qualitative Analysis of Ex-Partners' Narratives*, 37 J. FAM. VIOLENCE 1391, 1392 (2022).

behavior for which a court may issue an ex parte [without hearing] order to protect."[27] Similarly, Kentucky also takes a broad approach, defining "domestic violence and abuse" as "physical injury, serious physical injury, sexual abuse, assault or the infliction of fear of imminent physical injury, serious physical injury, sexual abuse, or assault between family members or members of an unmarried couple," as well as violence to animals "as a method of coercion, control, punishment, intimidation, or revenge."[28]

West Virginia also lists several acts that fall within domestic violence "between family or household member," including physical harm and apprehension thereof, sexual assault, "creating fear of physical harm by harassment, psychological abuse or threatening act," sexual abuse, and kidnapping and confining.[29] Some states define domestic violence or IPV by cross-referencing to criminal statutes that define criminal acts. For instance, in Washington, an act of domestic violence includes enumerated acts that are committed either by (1) one family or household member against another family or household member or (2) one intimate partner against another intimate partner.[30] The statute then lists more than 20 enumerated acts or crimes, such as assault, stalking, rape, murder, trespass, kidnapping, and "malicious mischief," which, if committed by and against a class of persons defined within the statute, would constitute domestic violence.[31] Florida's approach is similar.[32] Other states define domestic violence or IPV in a broad and inclusive manner, such as California, which defines "domestic violence" as "abuse committed against an adult or a minor who is a spouse, former spouse, cohabitant, former cohabitant, or person with whom the suspect has had a child or is having or has had a dating or engagement relationship."[33]

Types of IPV

IPV could be broadly classified into two categories: (1) physical and sexual violence and (2) emotional, psychological, and other nonphysical forms of violence.

---

27. Ariz. Rev. Stat. Ann. § 25-403.03(D).
28. Ky. Rev. Stat. Ann. § 403.720 (West).
29. W. Va. Code Ann. § 48-27-202 (West).
30. Wash. Rev. Code Ann. § 10.99.020(4) (West).
31. *Id.*
32. Fla. Stat. Ann. § 741.28 (West).
33. Cal. Penal Code § 13700(b) (West).

These categories are not mutually exclusive. In fact, in a significant number of cases more than one kind of abusive behavior is seen: A victim could be physically assaulted or beaten and subjected to controlling behavior, which could include emotional abuse or financial coercion. At times, abusers weaponize children by either threatening harm to the children should the victim leave the abuser or exposing the children to a pattern of physical and/or emotional violence whereby the children are desensitized to violence and normalize it.

Physical and Sexual Violence

A 2022 qualitative research study reported that "23.2% of women and 13.9% of men have experienced severe physical violence by an intimate partner."[34] Physical violence is the most common and widely accepted facet of domestic violence and IPV. Every jurisdiction acknowledges physical violence as a key ingredient of IPV. For instance, Louisiana defines "family violence" and "domestic violence" as including physical abuse,[35] and Oklahoma defines it to include "the threat of infliction of physical injury, any act of physical harm or the creation of a reasonable fear thereof."[36] Arizona's definition includes intentional, knowing, or reckless causing or attempting to cause serious physical injury, or putting "a person in reasonable apprehension of imminent serious physical injury."[37] The inclusion of "physical" violence within definitions of domestic violence appears to be universal.[38]

The CDC estimates that one in five women in the United States experience severe physical injuries, most commonly to the head, neck, and face, because of IPV. In 2022, the *New York Times* published an article on research

34. Avieli, *supra* note 26, at 1392.

35. La. Stat. Ann. § 9:364(A).

36. Okla. Stat. tit. 43, § 109(I)(2).

37. Ariz. Rev. Stat. Ann. § 25-403.03(D)

38. *See, e.g.* N.D. Cent. Code Ann. § 14-07.1-01(2) (West); Ky. Rev. Stat. Ann. § 403.720(2) (West); Wash. Rev. Code Ann. § 7.105.010(9) (West); Fla. Stat. Ann. § 741-28(2) (West); Idaho Code Ann. § 39-6303(1) (West); Ill. Comp. Stat. Ann. 750 § 60/103(1), (3) (West); Mo. Ann. Stat. § 455.010(1)(c), (5) (West); Ohio Rev. Code Ann. § 33.018(1)(a); Ohio Rev. Code Ann § 2919.25(A) (West); Mich. Comp. Laws Ann. § 768.27b(6)(a) (West); Del. Code Ann. 13 § 703A(a) (West); Alaska Stat. Ann. § 25.24.150(h) (West); Cal. Fam. Code § 6203(a)(1) (West); N.J. Stat. Ann. § 2C:25-19(a) (West); Utah Code Ann. § 77-36-1(4) (West); W. Va. Code Ann. § 48-27-202 (West).

that revealed a hidden epidemic of traumatic brain injury to women who were victims of domestic violence. Volunteers at domestic-violence shelters heard victims of physical violence report their "heads [being] pummeled with baseball bats and work boots":[39]

> In 1999, researchers at SUNY Stony Brook published a study in which they examined the case records of 26 women at a shelter and found that more than one-third of them reported head trauma. Most of them had been punched in the head. One had been hit with a broom handle, another stabbed in the head, another knocked out by a car door, another run over. All nine women reported symptoms like dizziness, hearing problems and blurred vision. Some developed seizures or strokes, which can surface years after strangulation. (Strangulation can inflict anoxic and hypoxic injuries, which occur when brain cells are damaged by oxygen deprivation.) Some also suffered confusion, fatigue, and memory loss.[40]

Researchers who work closely with the survivors of physical violence in intimate relationships speak of neurological deficits and symptoms observed in these victims. A study that surveyed 99 women recruited from domestic-violence shelters, found that nearly 75 percent of them had sustained brain injury and a majority never sought medical attention.[41] In addition, research found that "even slight blows to the head, when repeated often enough, could result in long-term neurodegenerative disease."[42] In an autopsy of a 76-year-old woman who died after years of documented abuse from her husband—having sustained "rib fractures, bruises and abrasions to the head"—it was found that:

> Her brain was similar to what [medical professionals] saw in brains with Alzheimer's—tangles of tau and beta amyloid proteins associated with neurodegeneration. Her autopsy revealed a brain that had deteriorated to a degree comparable to boxers suffering from chronic traumatic encephalopathy, or C.T.E., once known as "punch-drunk syndrome." It was the first time the literature had connected abused women with neurodegenerative disease.[43]

---

39. Christa Hillstrom, *Why Can't I See Straight: Research Shows That Victims of Domestic Violence Can Sustain Head Trauma More Often than Football Players—Hinting at a Hidden Epidemic of Brain Injury in Women*, N.Y. Times Mag. 39–48, 41 (Mar. 6, 2022).

40. *Id.* at 42.

41. *Id.*

42. *Id.* at 41.

43. *Id.* at 42.

These victims of physical violence in domestic or intimate settings could have experienced traumatic brain injury, whose symptoms—the headaches, the shaking, the blankness—are indistinguishable from post-traumatic stress disorder, a common diagnosis for victims of IPV. A significant number of IPV victims complain of having been strangulated. Although strangulation has been well documented in medical literature, traumatic brain injury suffered by victims of domestic violence and IPV is only now being addressed.[44] The vast majority of domestic violence and IPV victims who show signs of traumatic brain injury never receive a formal diagnosis, in part because they may not have visible injuries. Given how physical violence affects a victim's neurocognitive functioning, family law practitioners and professionals dealing with victims of family violence must be vigilant for signs of such abuse. If not, the very symptoms that could be proof of physical neurotraumatic abuse—scrambled stories, nervous laughter, irritability, memory gaps—could end up casting doubt on victims' credibility. There are nationwide efforts to train domestic violence advocates, law enforcement, and legal and healthcare professionals in screening for signs of brain injuries, including concussions, displayed by victims of physical violence. This training teaches everyone, "from beat cops to detectives, that women displaying inconsistency, hostility and bewilderment aren't necessarily being uncooperative."[45] The professionals who work in the area of IPV have to realize that although the victims may not show a visible injury, the injury could be potentially inside their head: "You have to realize that potentially inside their head, they're trying to tell you a story, but it's just not coming out."[46]

Physical abuse or violence could overlap with sexual violence. The CDC's National Center for Injury Prevention and Control identified that 1.27 million women had been raped in 2010, and another 6.65 million women had been subjected to some other form of sexual violence.[47] For men, the Center reported no rapes but did report 6.03 million men had been the victim of another form of sexual violence.[48] Some states, for instance, Louisiana, define "family violence" and "domestic violence" as

44. Rachel Louise Snyder, No Visible Bruises: What We Don't Know About Domestic Violence Can Kill Us 68 (2019).

45. *Id.* at 47.

46. *Id.*

47. Kathleen C. Basile et al., *supra* note 7.

48. *Id.* at 19.

including sexual abuse.[49] Similarly, Oklahoma includes sexual abuse in its definition of domestic violence.[50] By overlapping family law statutes and criminal law, Arizona includes intentional, knowing or reckless causing or attempting to cause sexual assault.[51]

Sexual violence or abuse in an intimate or domestic relationship may affect the perpetrator and victim's custodial rights and access to the minor children. In the Alaska custody dispute *Angelica C. v. Jonathan C.*, the couple had a sexual relationship when the father was 19, and the mother was 13 years old. The mother became pregnant. The court held the father's statutory rape of the mother, for which he was convicted of sexual abuse, was domestic violence.[52] Likewise, in *Johnston v. Johnston,* a Kentucky stepfather appealed the entry of a domestic violence order (DVO) against him for his alleged attempt to kiss his 12-year-old stepdaughter with his tongue.[53] In affirming the DVO, the appellate court agreed that a 12-year-old would have sufficient fear that a sexual assault was imminent from such an act, and, accordingly, it comprised domestic violence.[54]

In the North Carolina appeal of an adjudication of abuse and neglect, the father had been found guilty of raping his 13-year-old child.[55] Among the findings made by the trial court and affirmed on appeal was that the "father's continual promise of a 'last time' he would perpetrate against his daughter also demonstrates the acute manipulation of a domestic violence perpetrator."[56]

Sexual violence could also encompass conduct that is known as "revenge porn." In fact, "domestic violence and revenge porn often go hand in hand."[57] "[R]evenge porn is used in tandem with other abusive tactics, such

---

49. La. Stat. Ann. § 9:364(A).

50. Okla. Stat. tit. 43, § 109(I)(2).

51. Ariz. Rev. Stat. § 25-403.03(D) (West). For other statutory definitions that include sexual assault, *see, e.g.* Del. Code Ann. 13 § 703A(a) (West); N.D. Cent. Code Ann. § 14-07.1-01(2) (West); Cal. Fam. Code § 6203(a)(1) (West); Mo. Stat. Ann. § 455.010(1)(f) (West); Wash. Rev. Code Ann. § 7.105.010(9) (West); 750 Ill. Comp. Stat. Ann. § 60/103(3), (14) (West); and N.J. Stat. Ann. § 2C:25-19(a)(7) (West).

52. Angelica C. v. Jonathan C., 459 P.3d 1148, 1160 (Alaska 2020).

53. Johnston v. Johnston, 639 S.W.3d 428, 429 (Ky. Ct. App. 2021).

54. *Id.* at 432.

55. *In re* K.W., 666 S.E.2d 490, 492 (N.C. Ct. App. 2008).

56. *Id.* at 496.

57. Sarah Beechay, *If I Go There Will Be Trouble, If I Stay There Will Be Double: Revenge Porn, Domestic Violence, and Family Offenses*, 57 Fam. Ct. Rev. (4) 539, 542 (Oct. 2019).

as physical violence, threats to take children away, financial deprivation, property destruction, and more."[58] For example, "the abusive partner coerces the victim into sharing digital sexually explicit images (or films/photographs the victim secretly) and then uses the images as leverage to convince the victim not to leave or file a police report."[59]

More than 20 states, as well as the District of Columbia, have legislation criminalizing the perpetration of revenge porn.[60] Such laws serve a substantial government interest and protect the health and safety of the citizens.[61] Courts have found that revenge porn not only "engender[s] domestic violence," but also "prevent[s] victims from ending relationships, reporting abuse, or obtaining custody of children."[62]

In the Colorado criminal matter, *People v. Pellegrin*, before the victim and perpetrator's breakup, the victim had allowed the perpetrator to "take private, intimate photos of her in various stages of undress."[63] When the perpetrator learned the victim was seeing someone else, he "repeatedly called and texted the victim . . . called the victim lewd names and sent nude photos he had taken of her"; then he "threatened to post the nude photos online and to send them to her twelve-year-old brother."[64] Even more, the perpetrator hacked the victims Facebook profile such that "her cover and profile photos had changed to nude photos of her on a bed."[65] He also apparently posted a Craigslist advertisement for her on its "casual encounters" board with other photos.[66] In convicting the perpetrator of stalking, posting private images on Craigslist, and harassment, the trial court also made a finding of domestic violence.[67]

In a California case the court found a father engaged in child abuse and sexual violence.[68] The father had sent a "sex video" of the mother to "her adult son, the children's caregiver, the father of one of [the] Mother's older

58. *Id.* at 542.
59. *Id.*
60. *Id.* at 540.
61. People v. Austin, 2019 IL 123910, ¶ 61.
62. *Id.* ¶ 66.
63. People v. Pellegrin, 2021 COA 118, ¶ 4.
64. *Id.* ¶ 6.
65. *Id.* ¶ 7.
66. *Id.* ¶ 8.
67. *Id.* ¶¶ 11, 12.
68. *In re* O.M.-P. (2d Dist. Jan. 31, 2022) No. B311185, 2022 WL 276277, at *1.

children . . . Mother's 15-year-old niece . . . [and] Mother's oldest minor son."[69] In addition to sending the child "sexually explicit videos," Father also sent explicit text messages, such as "You'll hear ur mom moaning so good."[70] In another case, the husband threatened to send the wife's nude photographs to her "potential employers" if she did not agree to reconcile with him.[71]

A study of IPV behaviors shows that stalking can be both physical and sexual violence. Victims of IPV speak of being stalked by their spouses or partners who follow them to their workplaces, schools, or public and private venues to "mak[e] sure she was going where she said she was going, doing what she said she was doing."[72] On many occasions, perpetrators make no attempt to hide the fact that they are following their victims. Seemingly, the perpetrator wants the victim to get the message that the perpetrator was always in control and the luxury of stepping outside the home could be taken away in an instant from the victim. Typically to qualify as stalking, something more than just unwanted attention must occur. The attention must be of a type that would cause a reasonable person to fear for their safety. Examples of conduct that rise to this level are "damage, attempted damage, or destruction of property . . . threatened, attempted, or completed attacks on the victim, someone close to them, or a pet."[73]

In general, there are two types of stalking: (1) traditional and (2) through the means of technology. Traditional stalking includes following; watching; showing up and/or driving/riding by; harassment; asking family and friends for information; waiting at known places such as work or school; leaving and sending unwanted items; and sneaking into the home or car.[74]

Stalking through the use of technology includes unwanted calls, voice messages, texts, emails and direct messages, monitoring social media activity, inappropriate and unwanted posts and threats to post, and spying and tracking via technology.[75] In 2019, the Bureau of Justice Statistics reported that

69. *Id.* at *1–2.

70. *Id.* at *2.

71. *In re* a Member of the State Bar of Arizona, David D. White, State Bar No. 14-0016, 2016 WL 7048470, at *2 (Az. Disp. Com. 2016).

72. Snyder, *supra* note 44, at 48.

73. Rachel E. Morgan et al., *Stalking Victimization*, Bureau of Justice Statistics, at 3 (Feb. 2022).

74. *Id.* at 2.

75. *Id.*

3.4 million people over the age of 16 were victims of stalking but less than one-third of these individuals reported stalking to the police.[76] That same report revealed women were stalked at double the rate of men, and victims were more likely to be stalked by an intimate partner.[77] Just over two-thirds of the victims knew their stalker, and an equal percentage were fearful of physical harm or even being killed.[78]

Victims of stalking report that most were stalked for less than one year, and most were stalked two to ten times; however, 26.8 percent reported being stalked for more than two years, and 24.8 percent reported between 11 and 50 incidents of stalking.[79] The reasons some victims gave for not reporting stalking were: (1) they didn't think it was important enough; (2) they dealt with it in another way; (3) police couldn't help; (4) police wouldn't help; and (5) fear of the offender.[80] Victims who dealt with being stalked "in another way" engaged in self-protective actions that included (1) blocking the perpetrator, (2) changing daily activities, (3) changing personal information, (4) taking self-defensive actions or enacting security measures, and (5) applying for a no-contact order or order of protection.[81]

Many states recognize stalking as a form of domestic violence[82] and define it as "the willful course of conduct by a person who repeatedly follows or harasses another person."[83] Evidence of stalking behaviors is highly relevant in divorce and post-divorce cases, and may have significant impact on child custody and parenting time decisions.

For instance, in the Alaska custody dispute of *Joy B. v. Everett B.*, the mother was found by the custody investigator to be guilty of IPV, through stalking and harassing behaviors that included accusatory, blaming,

---

76. *Id.* at 1.

77. *Id.*

78. *Id.*

79. *Id.* at 9.

80. *Id.* at 5.

81. *Id.* at 10.

82. Mich. Judicial Inst., Domestic Violence Benchbook A Guide to Civil & Criminal Proceedings 1–2 (2021).

83. 43 Okla. Stat. Ann. § 109(I)(2). For other states that include stalking in their definitions, *see, e.g.* N.J. Stat. Ann. § 2C:25-19(a)(14) (West); Mo. Stat. Ann. § 455.010(5) (West); Wash. Rev. Code Ann. § 7.105.010(9) (West); Ky. Rev. Stat. Ann. § 403.720(2)(a) (West); and W. Va. Code Ann. § 48-27-202(3) (West).

insulting, shaming, belittling, and threatening conduct.[84] The court, however, refused to find "psychological abuse alone amounts to a history of perpetrating domestic violence."[85]

Utah has held that an objective standard was required for finding emotional distress to the alleged victim, rather than a subjective one, to determine when to issue an injunction for stalking.[86] In *Baird v. Baird*, an adult disabled son who had self-care deficiencies moved from his mother's home. The mother called him frequently and even threatened him with a guardianship if he did not return home or move to a residence that, to her, was more suitable.[87] The son was granted a three-year civil stalking injunction, but this was reversed by the appellate court because the trial court failed to determine if the son's claimed emotional distress was reasonable under the circumstances.[88]

A South Carolina ruling for conviction of stalking was upheld even though the only overt act resulted in property damage.[89] In *State v. Prince*, the defendant slashed his estranged wife's tires and scratched an X into every surface of the car. The defendant argued that this conduct did not suffice for an "act of violence."[90] In holding it was, the Court noted the legislature had not limited the phrase to "bodily injury," and also that the defendant's interpretation would undermine the public policy of anti-stalking laws, which are to "provide help and intervention *before* a pattern of harassing conduct results in bodily injury or death."[91] It probably also did not help the defendant's position that prior to the vandalism, he had repeatedly violated a restraining order and told the victim, "If I can't have you, nobody else will."[92]

At times, courts wrestle with the tension between allegations of stalking and protections guaranteed under the First Amendment. For instance, a Florida trial court issued an injunction to enjoin stalking behavior, which

84. Joy B. v. Everett B., 451 P.3d 365, 369–70 (Alaska 2019).

85. *Id.* at 370.

86. Baird v. Baird, 2014 UT 08, 322 P.3d 728, ¶ 1.

87. *Id.* ¶ 4.

88. *Id.* ¶ 2.

89. State v. Prince, 517 S.E.2d 229, 231 (S.C. Ct. App. 1999).

90. *Id.*

91. *Id.* at 231.

92. *Id.*

was reversed by the appellate court.[93] The appellate court found some of the behavior that was characterized as stalking served "a legitimate purpose of reporting suspected criminal activity."[94] It also reversed the portion of the injunction that prohibited contact with "anyone connected with [the victim's] employment or school," because, it held, "a domestic violence injunction cannot act as a prior restraint on speech."[95]

In some instances, perpetrators accused or charged with stalking victims have claimed protection under the Double Jeopardy Clause. However, prosecutors in several states have successfully argued that strict application of the Double Jeopardy Clause to cases involving stalking behaviors would give stalkers "one free stalk" of their victim after an initial conviction.[96] In *State v. Lindell*, five days after Lindell received a deferred judgment for stalking his former paramour, Lindell sat in his vehicle outside of her office and made eye contact with her briefly.[97] He was arrested and charged. The State relied on "stalking incidents that had formed the factual basis for Lindell's prior conviction," which Lindell claimed violated double jeopardy.[98] In holding it did not, the trial court explained: "A mere overlap in proof between two prosecutions does not establish a double jeopardy violation."[99] A Pennsylvania court in *Commonwealth v. Roefaro* put it more bluntly: "This is a ludicrous argument ( ) that misstates and contorts the law of double jeopardy and . . . leads to absurd results."[100] Additionally, a Georgia court identified the flaw in the logic: "[The] interpretation of double jeopardy would eviscerate the purpose of the stalking statute, leaving would-be stalkers free to begin stalking their victim with a clean slate. . . . We cannot believe the legislature intended such a result."[101]

---

93. DiTanna v. Edwards, 323 So. 3d 194, 194 (Fla. 4th DCA 2021).

94. *Id.* at 202.

95. *Id.* at 203.

96. State v. Lindell, 828 N.W.2d 1, 4 (Iowa); Commonwealth v. Roefaro, 691 A.2d 472, 474–75 (Pa. Super. Ct. App. 1997); Daker v. State, 548 S.E.2d 354, 356 (Ga. App. 2001); Snow v. State, 216 P.3d 505, 511 (Wyo. 2009); Jones v. State, 915 So. 2d 78, 83 (Ala. Crim. App. 2005).

97. *Lindell*, 828 N.W.2d at 3.

98. *Id.* at 3–4.

99. *Id.* at 7.

100. Commonwealth v. Roefaro, 691 A.2d 472, 474–75 (Pa. Ct. Super. App. 1997).

101. Daker v. State, 548 S.E.2d 354, 356 (Ga. App. 2001).

Emotional, Psychological, and Other Non-Physical Forms of Violence

While physical and sexual violence forms a big component of the IPV phenomenon, it is by no means the exclusive form of violence. IPV includes other forms of abusive behavior and conduct, which result in cognitive, emotional, and psychological harm to the victim and are widely acknowledged as separate and distinct forms of abuse. For instance, family courts have increasingly recognized the abusive dynamic in relationships where coercion and control exist together, creating a condition of "unfreedom" for a victim, also known as "entrapment."[102] Coercion, a form of IPV, involves "use of abusive tactics to dominate and control one's partner's autonomy and independence . . . through demands and threats, sometimes reinforced by physical or sexual violence."[103] Such coercive tactics include isolation, degradation, and subordination, as well as "prior incidents of intimate partner violence to prime the victim, exerting control through coercive threats without needing to resort to physical and/or sexual violence every time."[104]

Some states recognize coercion, intimidation, isolation, and threats as forms of domestic violence,[105] while others include psychological and emotional abuse in its definition of domestic violence.[106] In domestic relations, child welfare, and juvenile matters, courts have acknowledged emotional or psychological abuse to be as serious as physical abuse. For instance, in a New York case involving allegations of child neglect, authorities sought to charge a father with neglect due to his abuse of the mother, which did not comprise of physical abuse, but rather through "a pattern of behavior [that included] not allowing [the mother] to leave the home, making accusations against her saying she sleeps with everybody, not allowing her to see her friends or family, taking her financial benefits, throwing away her belongings . . . speak[ing] to [the mother] in a demeaning manner which their

---

102. *In re* Aisha R., 190 N.Y.S.3d 657, 661 (N.Y. Fam. Ct. 2023).

103. Avieli, *supra* note 26, at 1392.

104. *Id.*

105. Mich. Judicial Inst., *supra* note 82, at 1–2.

106. N.J. Stat. Ann. § 2C:25-19(a)(13), (15) (harassment & coercion) (West); Ill. Comp. Stat. Ann. 750 § 60/103(7) (harassment) (West); Mo. Stat. Ann. § 455.010(1)(d), (e) (coercion & harassment) (West); Wash. Rev. Code Ann. § 7.105.010(9) (coercion) (West); Ky. Rev. Stat. Ann. § 403.720(2)(b) (coercion) (West); W. Va. Code Ann. § 48-27-202(3) (harassment & psychological abuse) (West).

two-year-old repeats [which] has threatened to take the children away."[107] Describing this abuse as "serious domestic violence," that caused "actual or imminent impairment of the children," the court compared "the circumstances of victims of coercive control to that of prisoners-of-war, hostages, and other 'capture crimes.'"[108]

Courts have found that children who were not direct victims of violence but were exposed to family violence may have suffered emotional abuse from such exposure. For instance, in a case out of Kansas, a toddler and an infant too young to "witness" domestic violence were both determined to be "a child in need of care," by the court due to the older child being exposed to domestic violence between their parents.[109] The toddler who witnessed the violence also "exhibit[ed] violent behavior," to the point that "during a supervised visit [the case manager] saw him [the toddler] punch Mother extremely hard in the face two times in a row," and concluded he had "learned that from watching Father punch [mother]."[110] The Kansas court determined that both children "suffered emotional abuse," due to the "chaotic and abusive–emotionally abuse situation," because they had "been exposed to domestic violence in the home."[111]

Emotional abuse or violence as a form of IPV has been acknowledged as conduct that destroys the mental or emotional calm of a victim. Importantly, in some jurisdictions, such an act of violence is not assessed from an objective standard of a reasonable person, but that of the subjective victim.[112] For instance, in the California case, *Parris J. v. Christopher U.*, the court found that the non-physical abuse under state's domestic violence protection act is not subject to a heightened standard of "conduct that would destroy the mental or emotional calm of a reasonable person," but instead covers conduct that destroyed the mental or emotional calm of the victim.[113] The abusive conduct at issue was coercive control, through which the former husband "manipulated [Wife] into becoming financially dependent on him [such that] whenever [Wife] did something [Husband] disliked, he aggressively berated, insulted, and demeaned her. . . accused her

107. *Aisha R.*, 190 N.Y.S.3d at 661.

108. *Id.*

109. *In re* A.H., 334 P.3d 339, 340–41 (Kan. Ct. App. 2014).

110. *Id.* at 341.

111. *Id.* at 342–43.

112. Parris J. v. Christopher U. (2d Dist. 2023) 314 Cal. Rptr. 3d 225, 225.

113. *Id.* at 234–36.

of cheating on him with her male roommate . . . demanded she give him the text messages."[114] The court found that this abuse continued after the parties separated and the husband even threatened to sue former wife's father and ruin the wife's career.[115]

Evidence of emotional and psychological abuse and violence in an intimate relationship may also be used as a mitigating factor by a victim who is charged with criminal conduct. In a Colorado criminal case, *People v. Johnson*, the court approved the use of generalized expert testimony "about emotional abuse, male privilege, pet abuse, intimidation, coercion and threats, and using family members and children against victims." The "recording of phone conversations between [perpetrator] and the victim reflect emotional abuse, intimidation, and the male privilege power dynamic."[116] This included "belittling the victim, mocking her . . . swearing at her . . . berating the victim . . . for not saying what he had told her to say, and telling the victim to do things that placed his well-being above hers . . . [and he] threw her personal property over the apartment's balcony."[117]

One subset of emotional abuse related to the IPV dynamic is litigation abuse, through which "batterers use courts to continue the abuse" by threatening to seize custody of the children and to "bleed the other parent dry."[118] Those most successful with litigation abuse "have the persona and social skills to present themselves positively in court and convince assessors and judges to award them custody."[119] Others choose to take advantage of the opportunity to gain access toward their victims and intimidate or berate a former partner in cross-examination, unless an astute judge intervenes.[120]

In the Arizona case, *Kempton v. Chappell*,[121] a father received an attorney fee award, despite having "greater financial resources" than the mother, due

114. *Id.* at 236–37.

115. *Id.* at 241

116. People v. Johnson, 2022 COA 118, ¶¶ 38, 40, 523 P.3d 992, *rev'd*, 2024 CO 35, 549 P.3d 985.

117. *Id.* ¶¶ 41, 42.

118. Toby Kleinman, *Accountability & Oversight: Domestic Violence, Child Abuse and Custody Cases*, N.Y. L.J. unnumbered p. 4 (July 11, 2023).

119. Peter G. Jaffe et al., *Custody Disputes Involving Allegations of Domestic Violence: Toward a Differentiated Approach to Parenting Plans*, 46 Fam. Ct. Rev. (3) 500, 503 (July 2008).

120. *Id.* at 503.

121. Kempton v. Chappell, No. 1 CA-CV 18-0205 FC, 2019 WL 2480204 (Ariz. Ct. App. June 13, 2019).

to her "pattern of litigation abuse," including that she "twice removed Child from the state in violation of . . . orders, sent nearly 7,000 emails and texts to Father or his counsel during a six-month period . . . refused to provide an accurate address to Father or the court, launched unfounded full scale attacks on the [Court appointed professional] and Father's counsel, [and] failed to comply with discovery and disclosure obligations as a strategic maneuver."[122] The court characterized this as "gamesmanship" and "destructive behavior designed to frustrate Father's relationship with the child."[123]

Similarly, in a California domestic relations case, the wife was found guilty of being a vexatious litigant and was ordered to pay husband's significant attorneys' fees and costs.[124] The matter began with the wife seeking a domestic violence relations order (DVRO) and receiving a temporary restraining order. Approximately one year later, litigation to determine the DVRO began, during which the wife was being "obstructionist" and refused "to answer questions in her deposition," even "after a court order issued compelling her testimony."[125] She also refused to serve filings on former husband's counsel and filed frivolous requests, and after the DVRO was denied as "her allegations [were] completely without any credibility whatsoever," she continued to pursue the action.[126] Even after sanctions were awarded against her, she pursued a meritless motion for reconsideration, and then a meritless challenge of the trial judge "based upon a declaration with . . . 95 . . . pages of haphazardly labeled, nonsequential exhibits."[127] The appellate court affirmed the trial court's award of sanctions and designation of the wife as a "vexatious litigant" under California law because such laws "are designed to curb misuse of the court system by those persistent and obsessive litigants who . . . through groundless actions, waste the time and resources of the court system and other litigants."[128]

Another kind of emotional or psychological abuse is conduct that may be defined as economic or financial abuse.[129] Economic or financial

---

122. *Id.* ¶ 24.

123. *Id.*

124. *In re* Marriage of Javanbakhsh Dahms, No. H046034, 2022 WL 1447550, at *1 (Cal. Ct. App. May 9, 2022).

125. *Id.* at *2.

126. *Id.*

127. *Id.*

128. *Id.*

129. Okla. Stat. Ann. 43 § 109(I)(2) (West).

abuse has been defined as "causing or attempting to cause the other parent to be financially dependent," but it also includes financial conduct that approaches, and sometimes achieves, fraud.[130] Such conduct is illustrative of efforts made by a spouse or a partner in "sabotaging efforts to gain financial independence," "withholding or interfering with access to money," causing damage to the victim's credit ratings, acquiring debt that is unfairly imposed on the partner, "using credit or property without authorization," and fraudulently misusing tax refunds and government assistance of the partner.[131] Among the laundry list of behaviors included in this category are "preventing someone from attending school . . . forcing an intimate partner to write bad checks," and "default on payments related to household needs," and even "forcing an intimate partner into bankruptcy."[132]

A particularly harmful type of economic abuse is conduct that is known as coerced debt.[133] Coerced debt is defined as "all non-consensual, credit-related transactions that occur in a relationship where one person uses coercive control to dominate the other person."[134] Such coercive controlling behavior includes forcing a victim to incur debt by taking out loans, using credit cards, or putting household bills in the victim's name.

The recently reauthorized Violence Against Women Act (VAWA) recognizes the links between violence and economic insecurity, noting that victims of "severe intimate partner violence [collectively] lose nearly 8,000,000 days of paid work . . . and almost 5,600,000 days of household productivity each year."[135] "Studies indicate that one of the best predictors of whether a survivor will be able to stay away from his or her abuser is the degree of his or her economic independence."[136] "In relationships in which there

---

130. National Council of Juvenile and Family Court Judges, *Revised Chapter Four: Families and Children, in* MODEL CODE ON DOMESTIC AND FAMILY VIOLENCE 32 (2022).

131. *Id. See also* Schechter v. Schechter, 37 N.E.3d 632, 636 n.5 (Mass. App. 2015) ("Economic abuse has also been defined as making or attempting to make a person financially dependent, e.g., maintaining total control over financial resources, withholding access to money, forbidding attendance at school or employment.").

132. *Findings Relating to Pub. L. 117-103* [VAMS Reauthorization] 34 U.S.C. § 12501, Statutory Notes (15).

133. Rebecca Shiemke et al., *Coerced Debt: How Abusers Used It and What Can Be Done to Address It*, MICH. FAM. L.J., 8–12 (Feb. 2023).

134. *Id.* (internal citations omitted).

135. *Findings Relating to Pub. L. No. 117-103* [VAMS Reauthorization] 34 U.S.C. § 12501, Statutory Notes (5).

136. *Id.*, Statutory Notes (13).

is domestic violence, the victim is often economically dependent on the perpetrator."[137]

Economic or financial abusive behavior may not only deter a victim from fleeing the abusive environment but also compel him or her to "reconcile" with the abuser. In an egregious case of attorney disciplinary proceeding in Arizona, a client, who experienced "the worst case of domestic violence [the attorney] had ever encountered," reported severe financial abuse by the husband. The client's husband had "removed substantially all of the funds and assets of the marriage and attempted to close her access to all funds. . . . He had cleaned out their properties and destroyed other assets to preclude their utilization by her. He obtained an Order of Protection against her and closed her access to their two businesses."[138] Due to the husband's "widespread and complete" control over the wife and her finances, she was forced to fire her attorney and be "reconciled" with her husband.[139] The complaint by the husband against the attorney was dismissed.[140]

Situational and Systemic Family Violence

Professional literature has attempted to differentiate situational couple violence, which could be considered as low-level IPV, from systematic violence, which demonstrates high-level, clinically significant IPV. Historically, IPV has been classified into two categories: (1) patriarchal terrorism and (2) common couple violence. The gendered term "patriarchal terrorism" was characterized as "behaviors engaged in typically by men against women, and men did so because of a belief that they had a right to control women."[141] Perpetrators of such violence used threats, systematic violence, and coercive power tactics to control their partners. "Common couple violence," on the other hand, arose from escalated conflicts, poor impulse control, and "referred to lower levels of IPV like pushing, slapping, and shoving and such

---

137. Schechter v. Schechter, 37 N.E.3d 632, 636 n. 5 (Mass. App. 2015) ("Experts in the field of domestic violence describe economic or financial abuse as an element of the perpetrator's coercive control of the victim.").

138. *In re* a Member of the State Bar of Arizona, David D. White, State Bar No. 14-0016, 2016 WL 7048470, at *2 (Ariz. Disp. Com. 2016).

139. *Id.* at *5.

140. *Id.* at *1.

141. K. Daniel O'Leary, *Implications of Intimate Partner Physical Violence and Substance Misuse for Parenting*, 62 Fam. Ct. Rev. 31–44 (2024).

aggression was often engaged in by both partners."[142] Over a period, social scientists revised their characterization of patriarchal terrorism to coercive controlling violence, and common couple violence was re-labeled as situational violence. This does not mean that common couple violence or situational violence is benign or somehow "normal." Rather it was an attempt to separate high-level IPV that demonstrated a systematic pattern of violent behavior from a low-level IPV, which consisted of isolated incidents of aggression found between couples or partners. Both could result in injury, stress, and possibly trauma. "[T]he extent to which the violence is part of a pattern of coercive control and domination (rather than a relatively isolated incident) is a crucial indicator of the extent of stress and trauma suffered by the child and family and the potential for future violence."[143] While there can be an overlap between the two categories of violence, family dynamics are inherently complex and it may be difficult to classify a dynamic between a couple in a simplistic category.

Whether incidents constituting IPV are systematic or situational is highly relevant in family court disputes. The findings could result in a court awarding or denying child custody to an alleged perpetrator. In the Alaska custody dispute *Joy B. v. Everett B.*, the court asserted "We have repeatedly recognized that trial courts may consider the 'situational' nature of domestic violence when deciding whether the presumption [against custody for the perpetrator] applies and whether it has been overcome."[144] In upholding the award of custody to the husband who had a "history," the court reiterated the distinction between "situational violence as a result of high conflict," compared with "a pattern of intimate partner violence . . . [sometimes] defined as a pattern of control, or intimidation, often solidified through some type of violence."[145]

Likewise, in the Ohio custody dispute, *Jones v. Jones*, the court affirmed the appointment of the father as residential parent and legal custodian, despite his history of domestic violence, because none had occurred since the parties separated three years before.[146] Similarly, in *Martin v. Martin*, where all acts of domestic violence occurred prior to the parties' marriage

142. *Id.*

143. Jaffe et al., *supra* note 119, at 504.

144. *Joy B.*, 451 P.3d at 370–71.

145. *Id.* at 371.

146. Jones v. Jones, No. L-10-1044, 2012 WL 180957, at *6 (Ohio Ct. App. May 18, 2012).

and children, and it "was a one-time incident that did not result in serious bodily injury," Louisiana's presumption against custody did not apply.[147]

In *In re Marriage of Richards*, a Missouri court's determination that a single incident in which "Father once raised his hand as if to strike her" was not a "pattern of domestic violence" to be factored into a custody determination and was upheld on appeal.[148]

Lethality of IPV and Safeguards for Victims and Children

In 2021, the Bureau of Justice Statistics reported that 34 percent of the 4,970 female victims of murder and non-negligent manslaughter were killed by an intimate partner; whereas 6 percent of the 17,970 male victims of murder and non-negligent manslaughter were killed by an intimate partner.[149] The risk factors for intimate partner homicide include prior IPV, the age difference between the abuser (older) and victim (usually between 15 and 44 years), unmarried but cohabitating, "estrangement, and a child in the home that is not the biological child of the abuser."[150] Other risk factors include the abuser's "mental illness, illicit drug use, prior criminal involvement, and the presence of firearms in the home."[151] And the danger continues post-separation: "In extreme cases, domestic violence following separation is lethal . . . women are three to four times more likely than men to be the victims in intimate partner homicides."[152]

Statistics show that "one in five homicides is a result of [IPV]."[153] But IPV does not have to be fatal to be lethal. More than one in three women

---

147. Martin v. Martin, 833 So. 2d 1216, 1221 (La. Ct. App. 2002).

148. *In re* Marriage of Richards, 188 S.W.3d 478, 482 (Mo. Ct. App. 2006).

149. Erica L. Smith, *Female Murder Victims and Victim-Offender Relationship, 2021*, Bureau of Justice Statistics (Dec. 2022), https://bjs.ojp.gov/female-murder-victims-and-victim-offender-relationship-2021.

150. Jacquelyn C. Campbell et al., *The Danger Assessment: Validation of a Lethality Risk Assessment Instrument for Intimate Partner Femicide*, 24(4) J. Interpersonal Violence 653, 656 (2009). However, see the critique of *The Danger Assessment* by John Hamel, PhD, in several of his writings, including *Gender-Inclusive Treatment of Intimate Partner Abuse*, 2d ed.: Evidence-Based Approaches (Springer, 2014).

151. *Id.* at 656.

152. Jaffe et al., *supra* note 119, at 502.

153. Katy Reed, *Beyond the Abuse: The Long-Term Health Effects and Economic Consequences for Survivors of Domestic Violence*, Mich. Fam. L.J. 8–9 (May 2022).

(35.6 percent) and one in four men (28.5 percent) report that they have experienced physical violence, rape, or stalking in their intimate partner relationship.[154] Non-fatal physical violence—"being slapped, pushed, or shoved in their relationship"—and psychological, emotional, verbal, sexual, technological, or financial violence result in long-term consequences.

Victims of IPV often fail to disclose the violence or minimize it when this occurs for a number of factors, including (1) fear of retaliation; (2) the violent partner will harm the children; (3) loss of child custody; (4) reticence to discuss sexual coercion and assault; (5) fear of not being believed; (6) internally minimizing or disbelieving they are subject to IPV; (7) financial, social, or other isolation; (8) fear of repercussions due to immigration or criminal justice status; (9) prior experience not being believed; (10) fear of being stigmatized by friends, family, employers, or community; (11) cultural norms; (12) fear of being seen as manipulative; and (13) fear of escalation of conflict, litigation, and costs.[155] Much of failure to report IPV is a result of deep cultural biases and misunderstanding of how family violence, including IPV, works. "We assume that victims incite abuse, or that if the situation at home was truly threatening they would leave."[156]

The costs of IPV are significant. According to surveys of IPV victims, "73% of women and 36% of the men report at least one measured negative impact," and among women, "62% reported feeling fearful, 57% reported being concerned for their safety, 25% missed at least one day of school or work . . . 19% reported needing medical care, and 8% needed housing services."[157] Among men, "18% reported feeling fearful, 17% reported being concerned for their safety, 14% missed at least one day of school or work . . . 5% reported needing medical care, and 2% needed housing services."[158]

In family court disputes where IPV is present, it could have a significant impact on the court's decision on the matters related to child custody and parenting time. Even in cases of non-physical IPV, courts have found "stalking behaviors . . . ongoing harassment behaviors . . . accusatory, blaming, insulting, shaming, belittling, and threatening" to be harmful.[159] When confronted with evidence of such acts of IPV, courts could put in safety

---

154. *Id.*

155. Ass'n of Family & Conciliation Cts., *supra* note 6, at 9–10.

156. Rachel Louise Snyder, *A Raised Hand*, The New Yorker, July 15, 2013.

157. Niolon et al., *supra* note 5, at 10.

158. *Id.* at 10.

159. *Joy B.*, 451 P.3d at 369–70.

measures, such as ordering supervised visitation between the perpetrator of IPV (the abusive parent) and the children, or allowing unsupervised visitation on the condition that the abusive parent engage in cognitive behavioral therapy (CBT) to stop the use of manipulative, controlling, or threatening behavior. In these situations, it is important that the perpetrator of IPV is ordered to engage in therapeutic intervention with a therapist who is "well versed in CBT and [possesses] an in-depth knowledge of personality disorders, high conflict divorce, and coercive control battering within intimate partner relationships."[160]

Presence of IPV is a red flag for child custody evaluators who assist family courts in making custody and parenting time decisions. Evidence of IPV between the couple—physical, sexual, emotional, or psychological—should alert the evaluator to prioritize the safety of not only the victim but also the minor children. The Model Guidelines for assessing IPV in the context of child custody evaluations caution the family court professionals to make the safety of the child the highest priority in the evaluation process. The Guidelines counsel the professionals to be "on the lookout for" a variety of variables and risk factors, including high levels of violence, injury, and increases in violent acts; threats, willingness, and means for lethal violence; excessive control, jealousy, or obsession; unwillingness to accept responsibility and/or willingness to evade the law; psychological and substance problems; and recent separation, unemployment, and/or the presence of children in the home who are not biologically related to the violent partner.[161] Some jurisdictions, such as Texas, preclude an IPV perpetrator's access to children if the perpetrator has demonstrated a "history or pattern of committing family violence during the two years preceding the date of filing of the suit," unless the court finds such access "would not endanger the child," and the order of possession protects the child and any other victim of the violence.[162]

The timing of implementing safety mechanisms to protect a victim of IPV (and the minor children) is important. Research demonstrates that in some cases of IPV, "especially abusive battering relationships," "the intensity and lethality of domestic violence escalates after the victim leaves the relationship."[163] In these situations, it is not only important to ensure that

160. *Id.* at 374.

161. Ass'n of Fam. & Conciliation Cts., *supra* note 6, at 4.

162. Tex. Fam. Code Ann. § 153.004(d)(2) (West).

163. Jaffe et al., *supra* note 119, at 501–02.

the victim is able to exit the abusive environment in a safe and timely manner, but it is also critical to ensure that the perpetrator does not get opportunities to subject the victim to additional abuse. Court-ordered parenting time may allow some abusers an opportunity to continue the coercive controlling behavior. In such violent relationships, "parent-child contact . . . may create opportunities for renewed domestic violence over visitation issues and exchanges of children."[164]

It is important to have clear, unambiguous language in child custody and parenting time court orders where the case involves IPV. Vague, flexible terms that may be common in parenting plans where no IPV is present could be highly problematic in IPV cases. "Batterers can take advantage of vague terms . . . [s]o parenting plans should clearly state the places, dates and times that the children will be exchanged."[165] It is also recommended that child exchanges occur in public places with security cameras or guards.[166] Some jurisdictions have statutory authority that requires or allows a family court to order that "the exchange of possession of the child occur in a protective setting," for those families with a "history or pattern of committing family violence during the two years preceding the date of filing of the suit."[167] In some cases of severe IPV, practitioners should consider asking the court to limit contact between the child and the IPV perpetrator-parent to non-video remote means, for instance, through voice calls, as video calls can allow a batterer to see into the home.[168] Depending on the severity and type of IPV present in the case, communications between the perpetrator-parent and the victim-parent regarding the minor children could be limited to text-only or an app-based communication, such as My Family Wizard, Talking Parents, AppClose, Divvito Messenger, or CoParenter[169] to keep contact transparent, and to a minimum. Also, while a "right of first refusal" (given to each parent when the other cannot care for the children) is common in matrimonial / divorce cases, it would not be advisable in cases involving IPV. Also not advisable are the terms that call for notifying the other parent

---

164. *Id.* at 502.

165. Melissa Mangiaracina, *10 Things to Know About Parenting Plans in Cases Involving Domestic Violence*, Nat'l Council of Juvenile & Fam. Ct. Judges 3 (undated).

166. *Id.* at 7.

167. Tex. Fam. Code Ann. § 153.004(d)(2) (West).

168. Mangiaracina, *supra* note 165, at 4.

169. *Id.* at 8.

when and where travel is to occur.[170] Depending on the type and frequency of the IPV behavior, practitioners may have to consider asking a court to order a personal protection order (PPO). For example, Michigan has one for domestic relationships, one for nondomestic stalking, and nondomestic sexual assault.[171]

However, PPOs or restraining orders are fact-specific and may not be appropriate in every situation. For instance, in the California case of *Jennifer K. v. Shane K.*, the mother's request for a restraining order was denied, despite allegations that the parties' child was conceived by rape, the father punched a refrigerator while trying to punch the mother, and the father being accused of having slammed the mother into a door jamb.[172] The trial court found the mother and her evidence to be less credible than the father's for a variety of reasons: her conduct of pushing through the door as the father was attempting to shut it during a shouting match with the father, her statements in the eight years before the allegations (no other allegations were made previously), and the fact that the allegations arose only after the father informed the mother he intended to have a child with his new partner, and that they established boundaries with the mother, such that, she could no longer enter the father's home.[173]

Family courts are encouraging collaborative approaches and alternatives to litigation, which, if not managed in a timely manner, could turn into high conflict. This search for alternatives to litigation and mediation have led to "some states and provinces adopt[ing] the role of a parenting coordinator."[174] Parenting Coordinators (PCs) "work with families . . . to help parties implement their parenting plan and resolve child-related parenting disputes. . . . Additional goals of parenting coordination are to reduce conflict between coparents and improve their communication and problem-solving skills."[175] However, PCs are not necessarily appropriate in all situations. While having a PC involved in a case may be helpful to determine issues related to "existing parenting plans, relevant custody orders, and child custody or other

---

170. *Id.*

171. Mich. Judicial Inst., *supra* note 82, at 5 (MCL 600.2950; MCL 600.2950a(1); MCL 600.2950a(2)).

172. Jennifer K. v. Shane K. (1st Dist. 2020) 47 Cal. App. 5th 558, 562, 574–75.

173. *Id.* at 560.

174. Leslie M. Drozd et al., *Parenting Coordination in Cases Involving Intimate Partner Violence*, 58(3) Fam. Ct. Rev. 774, 775 (July 2020).

175. *Id.* at 775.

evaluations," PCs may not be appropriate in cases involving IPV.[176] PCs are encouraged to conduct IPV screening,[177] as well as for "substance abuse, mental illness and treatment compliance, child maltreatment allegations and findings" prior to serving on these cases.[178]

Families that may benefit from parenting coordination share several factors, such as no history of violence, substance abuse, personality disorder, major mental disorder, or threats or stalking.[179]

> Cases that are generally inappropriate for the parenting coordination process include coercive controlling violence; incompetence due to severe untreated mental illness; severe personality difficulties or disorders including paranoid and antisocial in which the parent has difficulties forming trusting relationships and telling the truth; ongoing child maltreatment concerns; chronic violations of court orders or previous parenting coordination agreements; parent who is unwilling to engage in the process.[180]

Bidirectional IPV: Where Both Partners Engage in Violence

Cases involving IPV are complex, beyond a simplistic presentation where one party is a perpetrator and the other a victim. In some cases, one could find that both parties engaged in abusive or violent behavior. For instance, one partner could have engaged in emotional or psychological abusive behavior, while the other may have demonstrated physical violence. Where a case presents evidence of bidirectional IPV, where both partners appear to have demonstrated abusive or violent behaviors, family courts may attempt to identify the primary aggressor: the party who the court considers more at fault and who may carry a greater share of responsibility for the IPV present in the family dynamic. For instance, in determining the "primary physical aggressor" in child custody disputes where both parents or parties may have engaged in a pattern of abusive behavior, the State of Washington considers the following factors: (1) prior acts of IPV; (2) relative severity of injuries inflicted; (3) likelihood of future injury to the parties from IPV;

176. *Id.* at 778.
177. *Id.*
178. *Id.* at 781.
179. *Id.* at 785.
180. *Id.* at 781.

(4) whether self-defense was involved; and (5) any pattern of coercive or abusive behavior.[181]

Mississippi, on the other hand, considers the likelihood of future violent behavior and encourages its family courts to award custody to a parent less likely to repeat violent behavior: "If the court finds that both parents have a history of perpetrating family violence . . . custody may be awarded solely to the parent less likely to continue to perpetrate family violence." And the court could put in additional safeguards, such as ensuring "completion of a treatment program by the custodial parent."[182] Other states, such as Louisiana and Arkansas, have similar laws that prefer awarding custody to a parent who is less likely to repeat abusive or violent behavior in cases involving bidirectional IPV.[183,184]

In some jurisdictions, such as Arizona, the rebuttable presumption—that a parent who commits IPV cannot be awarded legal decision-making—is not triggered when both parents have engaged in abusive or violent behavior.[185] Other jurisdictions contain prohibition against appointing parents as joint conservators in cases involving IPV, including bidirectional IPV. For example, in *Watts v. Watts*, the Texas court clarified that the prohibition against appointing joint managing conservators applied in any situation involving a pattern of IPV: "where a history or pattern of abuse between two parents exists regardless of whether the abuse is inflicted by one parent against the other or by both parents against each other," they cannot be appointed as joint managing conservators.[186]

In cases involving bidirectional IPV allegations, it may be important for a family court to make findings regarding the primary aggressor as such findings could greatly impact the decisions regarding child custody and parenting time for the minor children. In *Queen v. Martel*, a North Dakota case, each party had credible evidence of having engaged in abusive or violent conduct: The mother was convicted with a deferred imposition of sentence for striking the father, and the father had a PPO entered after he "choked [the mother], struck her head on the floor several times causing loss of consciousness, a sprained wrist and multiple bruises on her

181. Wash. Rev. Stat. Ann. § 767.41(2)(3)(2) (West).

182. Miss. Code Ann. § 93-5-24(9)(b)(2) (West).

183. La. Stat. Ann. § 9:364(D) (West).

184. Ark. Stat. § 25.24.150(i) (West).

185. Ariz. Rev. Stat. § 25-403.03(D) (West).

186. Watts v. Watts, 396 S.W.3d 19, 22 (Tex. Ct. App. 2012).

body."[187] However, because the trial court failed to make required findings regarding the various instances of IPV in determining custody, the case was remanded.[188]

Aside from a finding of a party being the primary aggressor, the severity of the violent behavior is a factor that some courts take into consideration. In the Alaska custody dispute *Dennis Q. v. Monika M.*, while both parents were found to have committed IPV, and the children were found to "have been safe the last year in both parents' care," the court awarded sole legal and physical custody to the wife because "she was less likely to continue to perpetrate domestic violence."[189] The court supported this finding with the fact that "there was a great disparity in the severity of Monika's and Dennis's assaults [and] the severity of the assaults is a reasonable factor for making a difficult prediction about future behavior."[190]

IPV's Effect on the Victim's Parenting and the Children

IPV affects a victim's cognitive, emotional, and psychological functioning, and their day-to-day behavior, including their parenting. Victims of domestic abuse and violence "have unique experiences and reactions to [IPV] that have differing effects on the way they parent and their capacity to co-parent."[191] These victims may demonstrate a variety of behaviors including "monitoring and appeasing the other parent, shielding the child, intervening when the child is abused, regulating the child's behavior to avoid abuse [and] leaving with the child."[192] A victim's coping mechanism could include supplementing the other parent's inadequate care or neglect of the child or "navigating around the other parent's control" and "managing safety."[193] Gender-specific factors may play a role in how victims cope with incidents of IPV. In that regard, "[f]emale victims may have been brainwashed by the abuser into accepting their own and their children's abusive treatment,"

---

187. Queen v. Martel, 2022 ND 178, ¶ 6.

188. *Id.* ¶ 7.

189. Dennis Q. v. Monika M., No. S-15084, 2014 WL 1888270, at *7 (Alaska May 7, 2014).

190. *Id.*

191. Ass'n of Fam. & Conciliation Cts., *supra* note 6, at 3.

192. *Id.* at 13.

193. *Id.* at 14.

while "intimidated and embarrassed male victims tend not to protect the children from their abusive mother's rages."[194]

In a 2022 report, the CDC's National Center for Injury Prevention and Control reported a wide range of impacts demonstrated by the victims of IPV that could significantly affect their parenting style or behavior, including anxiety; depression; fear; safety concerns; PTSD symptoms; injuries; and a need for services such as medical care, housing, victim's advocate, legal, and crisis hotline.[195] Ten percent of these victims also identified that they had missed at least one day of school and/or work, and a small number (under two percent) reported they had contracted an STD or become pregnant from the IPV.[196] Male victims reported similar adverse effects, although they did not report contacting advocate services or crisis hotlines, contracting STDs, and, of course, pregnancy.[197] The report also examined the physical and mental health outcomes of IPV victims, who reported difficulty sleeping, limitations on activity, chronic pain, frequent headaches, high blood pressure, asthma, diabetes, irritable bowel syndrome, and poor physical and mental health.[198]

Experiencing such violence also negatively impacts a victim's ability to parent, as they may be "physically and emotionally exhausted, inconsistently available, overly dependent upon, or unable to protect their children from the abuser."[199] A parent-victim of IPV could be overwhelmed and consumed by a singular focus on one thing: *How do I avoid getting hit?*

> She spent whole days strategizing how to avoid his wrath: "How am I going to do all this stuff he wants me to do, so I don't get hit?" "How am I still going to go to work and maintain this job, so I don't get hit?" "How am I going to get to the grocery store and buy the things that he wants, so I don't get hit?"[200]

Ironically, female victims may develop an "inability to control their children especially their older sons," which "makes the female victim an obvious

194. Jaffe et al., *supra* note 119, at 503.

195. R.W. Leemis et al., *The National Intimate Partner and Sexual Violence Survey: 2016/2017 Report on Intimate Partner Violence*, Atlanta, GA: National Center for Injury Prevention and Control, Centers for Disease Control and Prevention (2022).

196. Kathleen C. Basile et al., *supra* note 7, at 54.

197. *Id.* at 55.

198. *Id.* at 62–63.

199. Jaffe et al., *supra* note 119, at 503.

200. Hillstrom, *supra* note 39, at 40.

target of blame by the abusive ex-spouse and may raise the suspicions of family court professionals as to her fitness to parent."[201] In addition, victims may be seen as "abandoning, neglectful, or irresponsible," when they "leave the family home without the children," even though this was in the victim's view, "the only way that . . . they appease their volatile partner."[202]

Children, too, are affected by IPV. Research demonstrates that children may be harmed by exposure to IPV, both physically and emotionally, even when they are not direct targets of such violence.[203] Social science has moved from describing a "child witness of violence" to a "child exposed to violence."[204] Such exposure to family violence could consist of prenatal exposure, victimization, participating, eyewitness observation, overhearing, observation of initial effects, experiencing the aftermath, and hearing about the violence.

Abusers could control the child's behavior by forcing the child to watch a parent being abused:

> Her boyfriend never touched her daughter, Nelly. But for years he controlled the child's behavior by hitting her mother in front of her. Nelly . . . wasn't allowed to sit on the couch or eat junk food. She never had friends over. If she didn't obey, he beat her mom.[205]

Witnessing violence between their parents or caregivers may place a heavy burden on children, and it is increasingly recognized as a form of child abuse to expose a child to IPV.[206] "Children have unique experiences of and reactions to [IPV], and it affects them in different ways."[207] Children subjected to IPV may have "developmental, behavioral, emotional, cognitive, and/or health-related reactions as well as issues in relationships, academic problems, and/or economic problems."[208] On the other hand, some children "show no obvious reactions," and others "may be minimally or not

---

201. Jaffe et al., *supra* note 119, at 503.

202. *Id.* at 504.

203. Barbara Fallon et al., Ontario Incidence Study of Reported Child Abuse and Neglect, 2013 (OIS-2013), http://cwrp.ca/sites/default/files/publications/en/ois-2013_final.pdf.

204. Saini et al., *supra* note 8.

205. Hillstrom, *supra* note 39, at 40.

206. Carlijn van Baak et al., *Children Exposed to Intimate Partner Violence: Type of Exposure, Coping Responses and Consequences*, J. Fam. Violence (Feb. 2025).

207. Ass'n of Fam. & Conciliation Cts., *supra* note 6, at 3.

208. *Id.* at 12.

affected by their exposures."[209] Moreover, some children "identify with and show affection toward the abusive parent."[210] Childhood exposure to IPV can result in both short- and long-term consequences, such as negative academic functioning, depression, lower social competence and emotional regulation skills, poor physical health, and lower physiological functioning.[211] More alarmingly, children who are exposed to IPV are more prone to continue the "cycle of violence as adults, either as victim or as perpetrator."[212]

IPV and Presumptions Affecting Child Custody

"In the United States, it is estimated that 25%–50% of child custody disputes involve allegations of domestic violence."[213] Such allegations, if found credible, could upend several presumptions in such cases, and often trigger others. Absent allegations of IPV, the usual presumption favors maintaining a healthy relationship with both parents.[214] Likewise, another presumption is that ample visitation or parenting time with the noncustodial parent is in the best interests of the child.[215] Under those presumptions, some states have a presumption that favors joint custody absent domestic violence or IPV allegations.[216]

However, these presumptions yield to a presumption against custody when a pattern of domestic violence or IPV is shown against a parent in those states with that presumption, which is about half.[217] In order to rebut the presumption, the National Council of Juvenile and Family Court Judges (NCJFCJ) recommends consideration of several factors that include: (1) the nature and context of the abuse, (2) its effects on the child's well-being, (3) current or future risk posed by the parent who is abusive, (4) whether the perpetrator will prioritize the child's well-being, (5) whether the perpetrator is able to make shared decisions about the child in a manner and place that

---

209. *Id.*

210. *Id.*

211. van Baak et al., *supra* note 206.

212. *Id.*

213. Avieli, *supra* note 26, at 1392.

214. *See* Angelica CC. v. Ronald DD., 197 N.Y.S.3d 743, 747 (N.Y. App. Div. 2023).

215. *See* Matter of Paternity of J.K., 184 N.E.3d 658, 663 (Ind. 2022) ("Indiana has a legislatively-expressed presumption in favor of parenting time with the noncustodial parent.").

216. *See* Granados v. Granados, 339 So. 3d 1281, 1285 (La. Ct. App. 2022).

217. National Council of Juvenile and Family Court Judges, *supra* note 130, at 19.

does not pose a risk to the child or other parent; (6) whether the perpetrator has adhered and is likely to adhere to court orders, and (7) whether the perpetrator has taken ownership and responsibility for his or her actions.[218]

California has a rebuttable presumption that awarding child custody to a person who has committed domestic violence or IPV within five years of a custody determination, "is detrimental to the best interest of the child," and this "may only be rebutted by a preponderance of the evidence."[219] This presumption "arises only when a party is seeking custody" and, therefore, cannot be used to change custody in a purely domestic violence restraining order proceeding.[220] The presumption does not apply to domestic violence or IPV that occurred more than five years before seeking custody.[221] To protect children, when domestic violence or IPV within the time frame is present and the perpetrator is seeking child custody, the court has no discretion in whether or not to apply the presumption.[222]

South Dakota also has "a rebuttable presumption that awarding custody to the abusive parent is not in the best interest of the minor," which may be rebutted "by greater convincing force of the evidence."[223] In a custody dispute, a trial court in that state refused to consider the presumption and awarded primary custody to the spouse with a history of violence (she had a conviction for biting the other spouse during a fight when both were intoxicated).[224] Affirming the award, the court reasoned the victim spouse's argument failed to "not correctly account for the fleeting nature of . . . presumption in instances where the evidence is sufficient to rebut it.[225] That evidence included the recommendation of a court-appointed custody evaluator.[226]

Some jurisdictions require evidence of a pattern of abusive or violent conduct and not just isolated instances of bad behavior to trigger the

---

218. *Id.* at 65.

219. Cal. Fam. Code Ann. § 3044(a) (West).

220. *In re* Marriage of Willis (4th Dist. 2023) 93 Cal. App. 5th 595, 602 (reversing the court's grant of sole legal custody during the DVRO proceedings).

221. *In re* Marriage of Destiny & Justin Co. (4th Dist. 2023) 87 Cal. App. 5th 763, 768.

222. City & Cnty. of San Francisco v. H.H. (1st Dist. 2022) 76 Cal. App. 5th 531, 541.

223. S.D. Comp. Laws Ann. § 25-4-45.5 (West).

224. Harwood v. Chamley, 2023 S.D. 35, ¶¶ 6, 16. Affirming the award, the Court found the victim spouse's argument "does not correctly account for the fleeting nature of SDCL 25-4-45.5's presumption in instances where the evidence is sufficient to rebut it."

225. Harwood v. Chamley, 2023 S.D. 35, ¶ 22.

226. *Id.* ¶¶ 5, 11.

presumption. For instance, Arkansas law triggers the rebuttable presumption after "a finding by a preponderance of the evidence that the parent has engaged in a pattern of abuse."[227] In *Pilcher v. McWilliams*, the appellate court in that state clarified that a pattern of IPV is required, and it cannot be satisfied by one incident of violent behavior against the other parent, and one incident with a former paramour.[228]

Similarly, if there is "credible evidence . . . [of] a pattern of domestic violence within a reasonable time proximate to the proceeding," in North Dakota, this "creates a rebuttable presumption that a parent who has perpetrated domestic violence may not be awarded residential responsibility for the child," which may only be overcome by "clear and convincing evidence that the best interests of the child require that parent have residential responsibility."[229] While slapping a child on two occasions could constitute domestic violence, it would not establish a pattern that would trigger the presumption.[230] In another North Dakota case, *Queen v. Martel*, the appellate court remanded the case to the trial court given credible evidence that both spouses had committed domestic violence, but the trial court failed to make the requisite findings under the statute to determine whether the rebuttable presumption existed and whether it could be overcome.[231] On the other hand, in *Kershaw v. Finnson*, the appellate court's refusal to find domestic violence despite upholding a protection order because the trial court's findings that the accuser's "statements about the incident were contradictory, and . . . her testimony . . . unpersuasive."[232]

In Louisiana, the presumption is raised by "a history of perpetrating family violence . . . or domestic abuse," and applies to both the abuser and a parent who "has willingly permitted another to abuse . . . children or stepchildren, despite having the ability to prevent the abuse."[233] Family violence and domestic abuse are defined to include (but are not limited to) physical or sexual abuse.[234] The Louisiana presumption may be overcome by three things under the preponderance of the evidence standard: completion of a

---

227. Ariz. Rev. Stat. Ann. § 9-13-101(c)(1) (West).
228. Pilcher v. McWilliams, 655 S.W.3d 868, 873–74 (Ark. Ct. App. 2022).
229. N.D. Cent. Comp. Ann. § 14-09-06.2(1)(j) (West).
230. Thomas v. Thomas, 2020 ND 18, ¶¶ 5, 6.
231. Queen v. Martel, 2022 ND 178, ¶ 7.
232. Kershaw v. Finnson, 2022 ND 165, ¶¶ 15–16.
233. La. Stat. Ann. § 9:364(A) (West).
234. *Id.* §§ 9:362(4), 2132(3) (West).

"court-monitored domestic abuse intervention program," proving the abuser is not abusing alcohol or illegal substances, and that "[t]he best interest of the child or children . . . requires" the abuser's "participation as a custodial parent because of the other parent's absence, mental illness, substance abuse, or other circumstance negatively affecting the child."[235] Moreover, the parent with the "history of perpetrating family violence" may only have supervised visitation, and one where the court finds "by clear and convincing evidence, that a parent has sexually abused his or her child," all visitation and contact is prohibited.[236]

The factors considered by the court in determining a "history of perpetrating family violence" are "the entire chronicle of the family . . . the number, frequency, and severity of incidents . . . whether the violence occurred in the presence of the children . . . [and] to what extent there existed provocation."[237] Notably, so long as family violence occurred, it "does not require that the events be frequent or continuous."[238]

Mississippi also has a rebuttable presumption for a "history of perpetrating violence," which is shown by a preponderance of the evidence whether there was just a single incident that "resulted in serious bodily injury" or by a "pattern of family violence."[239] To overcome the presumption, a court considers the following: (1) "[t]he best interest of the child" requires that abusive parent get custody "because of the other parent's absence, mental illness, substance abuse, or other circumstance negatively affecting the child"; (2) successful completion of a batterer's treatment program; (3) successful completion of alcohol and drug abuse counseling; (4) successful completion of a parenting class; (5) if "the perpetrator is on parole, whether he or she is restrained by a protective order granted after a hearing, and whether he or she has complied with its terms and conditions"; and (6) whether there have been any "further acts of domestic violence."[240]

In *Lambes v. Lambes*, although there were allegations of domestic abuse against the father and he admitted to having committed "cruel and inhuman treatment," the appellate court affirmed the trial court's award of custody to

---

235. *Id.* § 9:364(B) (West).

236. *Id.* § 9:364(E), (F) (West).

237. Durand v. Rose, 366 So. 3d 484, 490 (La. App. 4 Cir. 2022) *quoting* Simmons v. Simmons, 649 So. 2d 799, 802 (La. App. 2 Cir. 1995).

238. Durand v. Rose, 366 So. 3d 484, 490 (La. App. 4 Cir. 2022).

239. Miss. Code Ann. § 93-5-24(9)(a)(i) (West).

240. *Id.* § 93-5-24(9)(a)(iii) (West).

the father because "the record demonstrates that any statutory presumption was rebutted by a preponderance of the evidence."[241] That evidence included a guardian ad litem's report that recommended custody to the father, an expert's conclusion that the mother had a personality disorder, the father's completion of a parenting class and sessions with a court-ordered counselor, his compliance with all court orders, and, equally important, the lack of any violence subsequently.[242]

Arizona's similar rebuttable presumption that a parent who commits domestic violence cannot be awarded legal decision-making is not triggered "if both parents have committed an act of domestic violence."[243] The factors considered in rebutting the presumption are similar to those of Mississippi's.[244] Washington's rebuttable presumption is triggered when "the court finds by a preponderance of the evidence that a party has engaged in a pattern or serious incident of interspousal battery . . . or domestic abuse."[245] In order to rebut the presumption, the perpetrator must establish three things: (1) he or she has successfully completed a certified treatment for batterers; (2) he or she is not abusing drugs or alcohol; and (3) that joint or sole custody with the perpetrator is in the best interest of the child.[246] Proof of completing a domestic violence treatment program requires more than just the bare testimony of the perpetrator; rather, there must be sufficient proof that the program was certified and completed.[247]

Similarly, Delaware's rebuttable presumption statute precludes awards of custody and primary residence to the perpetrator of domestic violence, and its factors to rebut the presumption are like other states.[248] Iowa also recognizes a rebuttable presumption, against an award of joint custody.[249] An incarcerated father who had overcome the substance abuse problems that he claimed caused his domestic abuse was held to have not shown sufficient

---

241. Lambes v. Lambes, 345 So. 3d 592, 606–08 (Miss. Ct. App. 2022).
242. *Id.* at 608
243. Ariz. Rev. Stat. Ann. § 25-403.03(D) (West).
244. *Id.*
245. Wash. Rev. Code Ann. § 767.41(2)(d)(1) (West).
246. *Id.*
247. Valdez v. Valdez, 2022 WI App. 2, ¶ 17.
248. Del. Code Ann. 13 § 705A (West).
249. Iowa Code Ann. § 598.41(1)(b) (West).

evidence to rebut the presumption: "Clearly the abuse did occur and he is incarcerated. [Mother] continues to have concerns about his behavior."[250]

In Maryland, although the child custody statutes do not specifically mention presumption, the state's laws regarding child abuse and welfare effectively create one.[251] The statute states: If "the court has reasonable grounds to believe that a child has been abused or neglected," it must "determine whether [it] . . . is likely to occur if custody or visitation rights are awarded."[252] Moreover, "[u]nless the court specifically finds that there is no likelihood of further . . . abuse or neglect . . . the court shall deny custody," to the parent who has engaged in abusive or violent conduct, except that it may approve supervised visitation.[253] This statute is to be read together with another statute that directs the court to consider domestic violence of any kind in the home when determining custody.[254]

Alaska's statutory presumption against "a parent who has a history of perpetrating domestic violence against the other parent, a child or a domestic partner"[255] could also be triggered by one incident that caused serious injury. The presumption may be overcome by a preponderance of the evidence showing (1) that the perpetrator has successful completed a batterers' intervention program; (2) that they do not engage in substance abuse; and (3) that custody with the batterer is in the best interests of the child.[256] However, in one case, the father successfully rebutted the presumption without completing a batterers' intervention program; because he was examined by an expert as part of the intake process, but "not recommended for the program because he posed no risk of committing domestic violence in the future."[257] As the appellate court identified, "[w]e do not read the first condition for overcoming the presumption—successful completion of an intervention program for batterers—as intending to require an empty exercise."[258]

---

250. *In re* Marriage of Cloyed, 765 N.W.2d 607, at *2 (Iowa Ct. App. Feb. 19, 2009).

251. Gizzo v. Gerstman, 226 A.3d 372, 387 (Md. Spec. Ct. App. 2020) ("Section 9-101 embodies a presumption that a child's best interest is not served by placing the child in the custody of someone with a history of child abuse or neglect.").

252. Md. Code Ann., Fam. Law § 9-101(a) (West).

253. *Id.*

254. *Id.*

255. Alaska Rev. Stat. § 25.24.150(g) (West).

256. *Id.* § 25.24.150(h) (West).

257. *Joy B.*, 451 P.3d at 369.

258. *Id.* at 370.

Alabama recognizes "a rebuttable presumption . . . that it is detrimental to the child and not in the best interest of the child" to be placed in sole or joint legal or physical custody of "the perpetrator of domestic of family violence."[259] The failure to raise this during the custody determination could waive it.[260] The presumption applies both to initial custody determinations as well as modifications.[261]

Massachusetts' statute is similar. Under that statute, "by a preponderance of the evidence, that a pattern or serious incident of abuse has occurred," a court-finding creates a rebuttable presumption against awarding sole or shared legal or physical custody.[262] In *K.A. v. T.R.*, a father with a history of domestic violence was awarded primary physical custody after he rebutted the presumption solely on the best interest of the children standard, by demonstrating that the children had a toxic relationship with the mother.[263]

Texas's rebuttable presumption arises "if credible evidence is presented of a history or pattern of past or present child neglect, or physical or sexual abuse by that parent directed against the other parent, a spouse, or a child."[264] In addition, a rebuttable presumption against unsupervised visitation exists for those parents with "a history or pattern of past or present child neglect or abuse or family violence."[265]

Oklahoma's rebuttable presumption arises for "domestic violence, stalking or harassment,"[266] and encompasses a wide array of misconduct from being a "nuisance" to the other parent to "harassing or obscene telephone calls or conduct that would cause a reasonable person to have a fear of death or bodily injury."[267]

New York has rebuttable presumptions against a custody award to a person convicted of committing violence against a close family member.[268] To rebut it, the perpetrator must show he or she was a victim of abuse or

259. Ala. Code Ann. 1975 § 30-3-131 (West).
260. Griggs v. Griggs, 304 So. 3d 741, 745 (Ala. Civ. App. 2020).
261. John E. v. Andrea E., 445 P.3d 649, 655–56 (Alaska 2019).
262. Mass. Gen. Laws. Ann. ch. 208, § 31A.
263. K.A. v. T.R., 18 N.E.3d 1107, 1114 (Mass. App. Ct. 2014).
264. Tex. Fam. Code Ann. § 153.004(b) (West).
265. *Id.* § 153.004(d).
266. Okla. Stat. Ann. tit. 43, § 109(I)(1) (West).
267. *Id.* tit. 43, § 109(I)(2).
268. N.Y. Dom. Rel. Law § 240 (1-c) (McKinney 2025).

violence by the victim, such abuse or violence "was causally related to the commission" of the violent act by the perpetrator, and granting the perpetrator the visitation or custody is in the best interests of the child.[269]

In Texas, presence of IPV when not part of a pattern, is characterized as more of a factor than a presumption, despite the statutory presumption. In *Maples v. Maples*, the court described it as "a parent has engaged in abusive or neglectful conduct in the past permits an inference that the parent will continue this behavior in the future."[270] However, the presumption remains in place against a person with "a history or pattern of past or present child neglect, or physical or sexual abuse by one parent against the other parent, a spouse, or a child."[271] Additionally, "[t]he court may not allow a parent to have access to a child for whom it is shown by a preponderance of the evidence that . . . there is a history or pattern of committing family violence during the two years preceding the date of filing of the suit," unless it finds such access "would not endanger the child," and the order of possession protects the child and any other victim of the violence.[272]

Credibility Issues for IPV Victims: "Why Didn't S/he Just Leave?"

When confronted with horrific tales of IPV, practitioners often wonder aloud: *Why did he or she hang in there? Why didn't he or she just leave?* There are many reasons why a victim of IPV may remain with his or her abuser. "These may include financial constraints created by the abuser prohibiting the survivor from working or by creating debt in her name; being convinced that if she leaves he will kill her . . . when a survivor also has children, leaving can become more complicated. . . . They often face the seemingly no-win dilemma of leaving to protect the child or staying to protect the

269. *Id.* § 240 (1-c)(c).

270. Maples v. Maples, 601 S.W.3d 23, 28 (Tex. App. Tyler 2020). *See also* Tex. Fam. Code § 153.004(a) ("In determining whether to appoint a party as a sole or joint managing conservator, the court shall consider evidence of the intentional use of abusive physical force, or evidence of sexual abuse . . . directed against the party's spouse, a parent . . . or any person younger than 18 years of age . . . within a two-year period.").

271. Tex. Fam. Code Ann. § 153.004(b) (West).

272. *Id.* § 153.004(d).

child."[273] Sometimes there's nowhere to go. And it may not really matter how educated or successful or "strong" the victim is. Here is how one survivor, who happened to be a family law attorney herself, described the dilemma:

> In my experience, being in a relationship with an abuser, particularly one with personality disorders, is akin to being an addict. You know the substance is bad for you and might even kill you. You might even quit it for a while, but you go back. The love bombing was always intense. I think survivors become used to the intensity of emotion, good and bad, in an abusive relationship. Other relationships look humdrum, boring in comparison.[274]

For a victim caught in the tangles of not just physical IPV but also emotional and psychological violence, it may seem impossible to leave the relationship or the environment. Take, for example, a victim of "gaslighting," who has been manipulated by the abuser into believing a false narrative, leading the victim to believe they are the problem (and not the abuser), even to the extent of questioning their own sanity.[275] For these victims who have been gaslighted, robbed of their agency, and whose day-to-day activities have been strictly scrutinized and controlled, leaving is seemingly not an option:

> Becky hadn't been to a primary-care doctor in 20 years because her boyfriend would not allow it. When she finally ventured to medical clinics after she fled, her symptoms were dismissed. She was told to take ibuprofen for her migraines—her history with Percocet made doctors wary of prescribing anything stronger. Many looked skeptical when she told them how many years her boyfriend had hit her. They didn't understand how hard it had been for her to leave, that the fog she lived through felt like day-to-day survival. "When you've got somebody second-guessing you, it almost makes you feel like, God, am I crazy?"[276]

---

273. Pamela Wall, *Between a Rock and a Hard Place—The Domestic Violence Survivor's Conundrum*, Mich. Fam. L.J. (Dec. 2021).

274. Lisa McNiff, *Diary of a Domestic Violence Survivor / Lawyer*, Mich. Fam. L.J. (Oct. 2023).

275. DV Committee of the Family Law Section, *Why Does She Stay?* Mich. Fam. L.J. (Feb. 2022).

276. Hillstrom, *supra* note 39, at 43.

Victims of IPV may also face liability if they are accused of making a false report of abuse. False statements to police, which is a crime in multiple jurisdictions, have been defined "as an allegation of a crime filed by a complainant . . . while, in reality, no crime has occurred."[277] Falsely accusing a genuine victim of IPV of making false allegations may have serious consequences. Yet such abusive litigation tactics have been found to be "highly effective ways for abusers to exert control over survivors [of IPV] for years after a relationship had ended."[278] The corrosive effect of false allegations burn in both directions, leading to investigation, abuse reports, arrest, and registration of the accused, and undermining law enforcement and other's belief in reports made by victims of IPV.[279] At the same time, it is undeniable that false allegations of IPV do exist and they "have irreparable effects on individuals' employment and financial situations, psychological and physical health, and family member's health and wellbeing."[280] If arrested, individuals accused of IPV "are almost immediately labeled 'batterers' regardless of whether they are guilty or not and [the] negative psychological consequences remain even after exoneration or overturned convictions."[281]

While substantiation of claims of domestic abuse and IPV can be difficult, some studies indicate that such allegations can be substantiated 50 to 75 percent of the time, and child abuse allegations 22 to 52 percent of the time.[282] One relevant factor that may affect substantiation of IPV allegations is "the timing of the disclosure and stage of the legal proceedings," where allegations made for the first time in the context of family litigation could appear self-serving in order to buttress a claim for custody.[283] However, it must be remembered that "victims may hesitate to report violence . . . to reduce conflict," or they "may not initially recognize what they have experienced as abuse until they have some distance and counseling."[284] On the other hand, experts have found that a significant number of allegations that have been unsubstantiated were not a result of "deliberate or malicious

277. Avieli, *supra* note 26, at 1391.

278. *Id.* at 1393.

279. *Id.* at 1392.

280. Teresa C. Silva, *Assessment of Credibility of Testimony in Alleged Intimate Partner Violence: A Case Report*, J. Forensic Psychol. Res. & Prac. 1, 4 (2021).

281. *Id.* at 4.

282. Jaffe et al., *supra* note 119, at 506.

283. *Id.* at 507.

284. *Id.*

fabrication"; rather they arose "from distressed behavior of the child . . . or relatively benign incidents that are misreported to parents."[285] Some parents may feel "inordinately humiliated by the divorce," and then "defend themselves by vigorously deflecting the blame onto the former partner, becoming convinced that the other parent is . . . dangerous, in contrast to themselves."[286] The risk of false allegations of abuse is exacerbated where "parents harbor fear, distrust, and negative convictions about one another," and these "distortions are too often reaffirmed by family, friends, and even professionals."[287]

Conclusion

IPV has a huge impact on family law and domestic relations cases. The nuances of IPV create challenges in categorizing its type and effect on different aspects of law, particularly family law that relates to child custody and parenting time. Given the short- and long-term harm associated with IPV, we have seen an increase in the number of legal and mental health interventions for IPV victims and for children who have been exposed to such violence. As seen in this chapter, IPV is perpetuated by men and women. It is found in domestic settings and in intimate relationships spanning across race, gender, ethnicity, marital status, sexuality, educational background, and socioeconomic status.

285. *Id.* at 508.

286. *Id.*

287. *Id.*

Chapter 2

Coercive Control: A Slow but Steady Stripping Away One's Sense of Self

Intimate partner violence, commonly understood as domestic violence, for the most part has been recognized as physical abuse—the realm of blood, bruises, and black eyes. While physical violence is deeply troubling, an equally problematic aspect of domestic violence, coercive control, often goes unnoticed under that rigid approach. Many abusers stop short of physical violence but maintain the same or greater level of power and control over their victims. These abusers engage in violence of a different kind. They engage in a distinct pattern of behavior: They attack, commandeer, and usurp their victims' agency, their sense of self, their mental and emotional calm, and, ultimately, their identity, free will, and personal liberty.

Although domestic violence can impact everyone, it is a bigger threat to women and children in our society. "Described as a 'pattern of abusive and controlling behavior injurious to its victims,'[1] domestic violence 'persists as a grave threat to the family, particularly to women and children.'"[2] Overall, it is becoming clear that the effects of domestic violence are disproportionately experienced by minorities and marginalized people. For instance, "Black and American Indian/Alaskan Native women experience [intimate partner violence] at significantly increased rates compared to other racial groups."[3]

1. Cesare v. Cesare, 154 N.J. 394, 398, 713 A.2d 390, 391 (1998) (citing Peranio v. Peranio, 280 N.J. Super. 47, 52, 654 A.2d 495 (App. Div. 1995); Corrente v. Corrente, 281 N.J. Super. 243, 246, 657 A.2d 440 (App. Div. 1995)).

2. *Cesare*, 154 N.J. at 398 (citing State v. Chenique–Puey, 145 N.J. 334, 340, 678 A.2d 694 (1996)).

3. Family Violence Law Center Policy Dep't, *A Series on Economic Abuse* (Mar. 2021).

Additionally, "[a]n inverse relationship exists between class and experienced intimate partner violence, meaning as one's socioeconomic status increases there is an accompanying decrease in experienced violence."[4] "[P]eople identifying as LGBTQ+ also experience intimate partner violence at alarmingly higher rates than the general population."[5] Coercive control, similar to domestic violence, impacts individuals from all walks of life, although women and children throughout the world are more vulnerable to it, and most jurisdictions' laws are ill-equipped to counter this problem. In fact, in the United States, studies have shown that "between three and four million women each year, from all socio-economic classes, races, and religions, are battered by husbands, partners, and boyfriends."[6]

Identifying Coercive Control

The very definition of coercive control gives prima facie reasons for all legislatures to quickly address it. Coercive control is "a pattern of behavior which seeks to take away the victim's liberty or freedom, to strip away their sense of self."[7] Put another way, as a Massachusetts family court defined by citing the Centers for Disease Control and Prevention's (CDC) definition, the phenomenon of coercive control is "a form of psychological aggression that includes 'behaviors that are intended to monitor, control, or threaten an intimate partner.'"[8] In short, "[a] victim of coercive control is a prisoner in his or her own life, terrified by the implied 'or else' warnings if he or she does not comply with the wants and demands of the abuser."[9] There are many forms of coercive control in intimate partner relationships. For

4. *Id.*

5. *Id.*

6. *Cesare*, 154 N.J. at 391 (citing Brennan v. Orban, Jr., 145 N.J. 282, 299, 678 A.2d 667 (1996) (citations omitted)); William G. Bassler, *The Federalization of Domestic Violence: An Exercise in Cooperative Federalism or a Misallocation of Federal Judicial Resources?*, 48 Rutgers L. Rev. 1139, 1140 (1996) ("No class, religion or race is immune.").

7. *What Is Coercive Control?*, *CedarNetwork.org*, https://cedarnetwork.org.uk/about/what-is-domestic-abuse/coercive-control/?highlight=coercive%20control (last visited November 6, 2023) (discussing Evan Stark's theory of coercive control).

8. Schechter v. Schechter, 88 Mass. App. Ct. 239, 242, 37 N.E.3d 632, 637, n.5 (2015) (citing Kim, *Credit Cards: Weapons for Domestic Violence*, 22 Duke J. Gender L. & Policy 281, 285 (2015)).

9. Kristy Candela, *Protecting the Invisible Victim: Incorporating Coercive Control in Domestic Violence Statutes* 54(1) Fam. Ct. Rev. 112 (2016). https://doi.org/10.1111/fcre.12208.

instance, the CDC has defined "economic abuse," or "behaviors that control a woman's ability to acquire, use, and maintain economic resources" as a form of domestic violence.[10] While coercive control "manifests itself in many shapes and sizes, [] the intention and effect remain the same: to control and manipulate another person, entrapping the victim in their personal life."[11]

Moreover, "[t]he legal definition of coercion is 'the intimidation of a victim to compel the individual to do some act against his or her will by the use of psychological pressure, physical force, or threats.'"[12] Therefore, the fact that this form of abuse is more nuanced and is likely to be overlooked because it deals with the psyche rather than the physical is reason enough for all legislatures to deal with coercive control with a sense of urgency.

As a psychological theory, the term *coercive control* was coined by Dr. Evan Stark, who based his work on the research of Dr. David Adams, a leading expert on domestic violence.[13] Dr. Stark defines coercive control as "an ongoing strategy of isolation of the victim from friends, family and children; control of access to resources such as transportation, money and food; and control of access to employment and education."[14] Grounded in concepts derived from the Power and Control Wheel,[15] the major forms of coercive control are "intimidation; emotional abuse; isolation; minimizing, denying, and blaming; using children and male privilege; economic abuse; and coercion and threats."[16] While physical abuse can manifest in a singular incident, coercive control is evident through a "pattern and repetition of tactics" used by the abuser against the victim.[17] Because of the pervasive pattern and repetition of abuse, victims of coercive control often struggle with fear and anxiety; loss of self-esteem; depression; post-traumatic stress disorder; substance abuse; isolation from the world; loss of jobs, friends, family;

---

10. *Id.*

11. *Id.*

12. Ashish Joshi, *Coercive Control: What Family Practitioners Should Know About This Insidious Form of Mental Abuse*, MICH. FAM. L.J. 17 (2021) (citing Coercive. (n.d.) West's Encyclopedia of American Law, edition 2 (2008), https://legal-dictionary.thefreedictionary.com/coercive).

13. *See supra* note 7.

14. *Id. See also* EVAN STARK, COERCIVE CONTROL: HOW MEN ENTRAP WOMEN IN PERSONAL LIFE (2007).

15. Power and Control Wheel, Domestic Abuse Intervention Programs, http://www.theduluthmodel.org/pdf/PowerandControl.pdf (last visited Nov. 23, 2020).

16. *See supra* note 7.

17. *Id.*

and loss of a sense of self.[18] What's more, "[w]omen who had experienced coercive control were also at greater risk of revictimization."[19] Additionally, coercive control "harms children whether it is directed toward them or their victim parent, and therefore it is not in the best interests of the child."[20] This has important implications because a majority of states require judges to consider domestic violence as a factor in custody determinations.[21]

Coercive control is achieved by "(1) setting the stage or grooming; (2) coercive behavior; and (3) victim response."[22] Grooming often looks like a honeymoon or "love-bombing" phase where abusers "sweep the victim off their feet using passionate communications, notes, gifts, and demonstrations of devotion that feel flattering, thoughtful, attentive, and genuine."[23] Grooming draws the victim into an ever-entangling web. Once the web is spun, it is difficult for the victim to get out. This is when the abuser begins using coercive control behaviors. The Association of Family and Conciliation Courts (AFCC) defines these behaviors as "harmful conduct that subordinates the will of another through violence, intimidation, intrusiveness, isolation, and/or control."[24] These behaviors are both explicit and implicit and may appear innocuous when examined singularly. But when they are examined as a whole, the insidious nature of coercive control emerges. Social scientists often look at coercive control from a typology paradigm, rather than a "single broad phenomenon."[25] In this way, "'coercive controlling violence,' used to establish and maintain power and control over the partner, stands in contrast to the more commonly reported 'situational couple

18. *Id.*

19. Melissa E. Dichter et al., *Coercive Control in Intimate Partner Violence: Relationship with Women's Experience of Violence, Use of Violence, and Danger* 8(5) Psychology of Violence 596-604 (2018), doi:10.1037/vio0000158.

20. Glenda M. Lux & Sandy Gill, *Identifying Coercive Control in Canadian Family Law: A Required Analysis in Determining the Best Interests of the Child,* Fam. Ct. Rev. (2021).

21. Lisa A. Tucker, *Domestic Violence as a Factor in Child Custody Determinations: Considering Coercive Control,* 90 Fordham L. Rev. 2673, 2679 (2022).

22. Lux & Gill, *supra* note 20.

23. *Id.*

24. Association of Family and Conciliation Courts, Guidelines for Examining Intimate Partner Violence: A Supplement to the AFCC Model Standards of Practice for Child Custody Evaluation (2016), (https://www.afccnet.org/Portals/0/PDF/Guidelines%20for%20Examining%20Intimate%20Partner%20Violence%20(1).pdf?ver=7EXH-_wzs2YkbfqOls60LA%3D%3D.

25. *See supra* note 19 at 2.

violence,' referring to that which is used within the context of a specific conflict and without the motivation of power and control."[26] Explicit behaviors could include tangible incidents, such as blocking financial accounts. However, the implicit behaviors are "psychological tactics employed, especially gaslighting, which is a method of undermining the abused person's sense of reality. Its insidious nature aligns well with phrases such as 'walking on eggshells' and 'death by 1,000 cuts.'"[27] The implicit behaviors may be much more difficult to prove, requiring careful documentation and explanation in court.

Types of Coercive Control

Coercive controlling behaviors rob the victim of his or her sense of reality, credibility, and mental and emotional calm. Unlike brute physical domestic violence, coercive control may involve beguiling but superficial charm and subtle, complex layers of patterns of behavior that may appear on the surface to be anything but abusive. In fact, it may appear as loving or caring, if a bit too intense. "Perpetrators of coercive control can be particularly adept at manipulating professionals, agencies, and systems, and may use a range of tactics to achieve this objective."[28] These abusers may make false allegations to "therapists, assessors, teachers, medical doctors, counsellors, police, counsel, and other authority figures who might be useful to reinforce their control of the victim."[29] They are master manipulators, easily able to persuade skilled professionals to "adopt their preferred course of action."[30] For instance, a parent-litigant's efforts of maintaining coercive control might involve numerous filings of requests to show cause for parenting time—even outside of the scope of the order—which may be misunderstood by professionals as devotion to the child.[31] On the other hand, a seemingly "protective" parent-litigant's steadfast refusal to allow the child to visit or spend time with the other parent on the grounds that the latter parent is abusive may also be a deliberate pattern of alienating the child and portraying the rejected parent in a false light. Cases involving allegations of coercive control

---

26. *Id.*
27. *See supra* note 20 at 815.
28. *Id.* at 823.
29. *Id.*
30. *Id.*
31. *Id.*

require a thorough examination of facts, including a careful review of the historical relationship between the alleged perpetrator and the alleged victim, their interactions, and the surrounding family dynamics.

Litigation Abuse

The term *litigation abuse* has also been called by other names, such as, paper abuse, systems abuse, judicial terrorism, legal system abuse, vexatious litigation, custody or procedural stalking, or family court corruption and abuse.

Litigation abuse is a pattern of conduct where the perpetrator misuses or abuses the legal system to force the victim into submission. Such pattern of conduct is typically motivated by a perpetrator's desire to continue his or her efforts at controlling the victim and forcing the victim to continue engaging with the perpetrator at a great financial, emotional, and mental cost. This pattern of conduct could include acts such as filing unnecessary or frivolous motions or court filings to stonewall, delay, and stretch out litigation; refusal to follow court orders; refusal to provide disclosures when served with proper discovery requests; repeatedly seeking adjournments of court hearings; taking unreasonable positions in negotiations; making unfounded claims of misconduct by judges or professionals involved in the case; making unfounded claims of "child abuse," "parental alienation," or even "domestic violence"; making unfounded reports of abuse or neglect to the child protection agencies or law enforcement; and undertaking repeated and frivolous appeals of trial courts' decisions.

Legal interventions that presume an "equality of bargaining power" between parties are at risk of being manipulated by a coercive controlling party.[32] In fact, "legal proceedings can serve as platforms for post-separation coercive control as they enable abusive partners to have direct contact with their victims, often over an extended period of time."[33] Tactics used by abusers in the courtroom include prolonging legal cases; seeking child custody or parental visitation for the purpose of exerting power and control over survivors during separation; defaming the victim in court by making them appear unstable or unfit to parent; and using financial abuse in the courtroom; such as failure to pay child support.[34] Some abusers have

---

32. *Id.*

33. Ellen R. Gutowski & Lisa A Goodman, *Coercive Control in the Courtroom: the Legal Abuse Scale (LAS)* 38(3) J. Fam. Violence 527 (2023), doi:10.1007/s10896-022-00408-3.

34. *Id.*

sought contempt against victims for issues in custody, "which can lead to extensive investigations."[35] Finally, unnecessarily prolonging litigation can cause financial strain and undue stress on a victim. Further documentation of tactics used by abusers in the courtroom shows the use of "legal abuse including by forcing survivors into distressing face-to-face contact through court proceedings, attacking the survivor's parental rights or visitation time, threatening the children's safety, publicly denigrating the survivor's capabilities as a parent, and exerting financial abuse against the survivor through the process."[36]

Law professor Nicholas Bala and his colleagues undertook an empirical research project based on an analysis of Ontario Family Court decisions over a three-year period exploring litigation abuse.[37] The key findings of this research project were:

1. Family courts and professionals often fail to recognize litigation abuse;
2. Litigation abuse often causes victims of intimate partner violence to give up claims or agree to outcomes that impoverish them or expose them and their children to risk;
3. Both men and women engage in litigation abuse, although men are somewhat more likely to engage in this pattern of conduct than women.

Economic Control

Most victims who have experienced coercive control have experienced economic control.[38] Economic control occurs when "a person's ability to acquire, use, and maintain economic resources" is controlled.[39] Economic control strips a victim of "the material and economic means to access safety and security."[40] This often occurs in combination with other coercive control

35. *Id.*

36. *Id.*

37. Nicholas Bala et al., *Exploring Litigation Abuse in Ontario: An Analysis of Costs Decisions*, Fam. Ct. Rev. (2024), DOI: 10.1111/fcre.12819.

38. The Maine Coalition to End Domestic Violence, *A Report on the Impact of Economic Abuse on Survivors of Domestic Violence in Maine,* Feb. 7, 2019, https://www.mcedv.org/wp-content/uploads/2019/02/Economic-Abuse-Report_FINAL.pdf.

39. *Id.*

40. *Id.*

tactics.[41] Economic control can look like "depriving the victim of their own money or authority over accounts; taking the victim's earnings; requiring an accounting for monies spent; controlling household spending; putting debt in the victim's name; making the victim work multiple jobs; not allowing the victim to have gainful employment; and discrediting the victim to their employer."[42] The costs of economic control "can include the financial and emotional costs of finding a new apartment, securing gainful employment, taking care of children, and recovering from an abusive relationship."[43] The perpetrator of such tactics limits the freedom of their partner, and often their children, through financial control by direct or indirect means. Additional factors, such as an inability to speak fluent English or tenuous immigration status may exacerbate vulnerabilities of victims and create more opportunities for exploitation.

Intimidation

Direct intimidation can include physical acts such as punching, kicking, slapping, pinching, biting, or choking the victim. It can also include symbolic interaction, such as "using threatening gestures; breaking things, throwing objects, or punching walls; driving dangerously to intimidate the victim; picking up weapons whilst talking to the victim; threatening to engage in self-harm or commit suicide; threatening to harm or kill the victim or their children; locking the victim in a room; and holding the victim down for someone else to assault."[44] Intimidation can also include stalking behaviors such as "remote spying; logging into accounts; monitoring emails, phone calls, and social media accounts; tracking the victim's use of time; watching or following the victim, or using others to do so; bugging the victim's smartphone or using GPS devices to track the victim; and appearing unexpectedly when the victim goes out."[45] The CDC reports that "the vast majority of stalking victims know the offender."[46] However, stalking, similar to sexual coercion, is linked to its adjudicative context and the "definitions

---

41. *Id.*
42. *See supra* note 20 at 816.
43. *See supra* note 3.
44. Lux & Gill, *supra* note 20.
45. *Id.*
46. Stalking, Prevention, Awareness, and Resource Center, Judicial Officer Guide: Responding to Stalking (July 5, 2022).

of stalking continue to vary widely from state to state."[47] For instance, as held by the United States Supreme Court, "states often place the definitional onus on the restraining order as the jurisdictional apparatus by which the behavior is defined and identified."[48]

Stalking behavior is a form of intimidation and a distinct pattern of coercively controlling pattern of conduct. A main defense to stalking is that the action was performed for a legitimate business purpose.[49] This defense fails if the complainant is able to show the stalker's "behavior is a pattern that shows the intent to survey, invade, intimidate, or interfere with/sabotage the victim."[50] These four tactics used by stalkers may include various forms of coercive control. The documentation of the duration, intensity, and frequency of these tactics by the stalker will enable the victim to demonstrate to the court the need for protection.[51]

Additionally, in most jurisdictions, a victim must show that the stalker's tactics have caused the victim unreasonable fear. To determine the reasonableness of a victim's fear, a practitioner should assess "[t]he specific implicit or explicit threats; [t]he context of those threats; and [v]ictim fear or concern for safety."[52] The victim's experience of fear will be contextual.[53]

Emotional Abuse

Emotional abuse is the most commonly known form of coercive control and includes "denying that behavior is controlling; rejecting the victim's lived experience and evidence; projecting one's own behavior onto the victim; denying responsibility and blaming others for one's own choices; denying the impact of coercive controlling behavior; engaging in circular arguments and manipulative behavior; responding to the victim's concerns using 'whataboutism'; intentionally failing to provide the complete context when arguing with the victim; and outright lying."[54] These types of behaviors cause

47. Michelle Mohr Carney & John R. Barner, *Prevalence of Partner Abuse: Rates of Emotional Abuse and Control,* 3 Partner Abuse 286 (2012).

48. *Id.*; *also see generally* Castle Rock v. Gonzales, 545 U.S. 748 (2005).

49. Stalking, Prevention, Awareness, and Resource Center, Judicial Officer Guide: Responding to Stalking (July 5, 2022).

50. *Id.*

51. *Id.*

52. *Id.*

53. *Id.*

54. *See* Lux & Gill, *supra* note 20.

the victim to question their own sense of reality and strip the victim of their sense of self. Science research points out that emotional abuse "can be categorized as either expressive aggression such as 'their partner acted angry in a way that seemed dangerous, told them they were a loser or a failure, insulted or humiliated them' or coercive control, 'which includes behaviors that are intended to monitor and control or threaten an intimate partner.'"[55]

From a practice standpoint, identifying and understanding a victim's perspective in contrast to the victim's case file, which may be filled with sterile facts, is paramount to showing how the emotional abuse has unfolded and has distorted the victim's sense of identity. The identification of patterns of emotional abuse can be used to show the court and evaluators the imbalance of power between the parties that may affect the proceedings, particularly the division of property and child custody. While little research has examined coercive control on parenting, perpetrators who are highly controlling of their former partners often interact in similar ways that constrain and engender fear in their children.

Threats

Threats are a form of coercively controlling behavior that manipulates a victim to do what the abuser wants. These tactics may include "threatening those whom the victim cares about most, including friends, family, children, and pets; bombarding the victim with text messages, emails, phone calls, or legal correspondence; relentlessly criticizing everyday matters, including how the victim cooks and cleans, dresses, or styles their hair; threatening to publish information about the victim to friends, family, the public, the police, or other authorities; criticizing the victim as a human being; engaging in humiliations, put downs, intimidation, and name-calling; accusing or undermining the victim; destroying or "misplacing" the victim's personal property and keepsakes; damaging or threatening to damage property or household items; interfering with the victim's sleep; using information shared in trust against the victim; not listening or responding to the victim; breaking promises or agreements; exerting control over the victim's behavior; making false reports of abuse to authorities; and pressuring the victim to sign documents."[56]

---

55. *Id.*
56. *Id.*

Isolation

Isolating and controlling a person's social interactions is an insidious pattern of conduct that is often found in cases involving coercive control. Abusers use isolation tactics to strive to maintain control over their victims. For instance, an abuser may try "controlling who the victim speaks to, both online and in person; constantly checking up on the victim; monopolizing the victim's time; creating drama when going out to discourage or prevent the victim from going; exhibiting jealousy; limiting the victim's time with others, including friends, family, and coworkers; isolating the victim from family and social supports; speaking on behalf of the victim; interrupting the victim's conversations; instructing others not to speak with the victim; inserting themselves into and taking over the victim's relationships; disrespecting or embarrassing the victim in front of others; sharing the victim's intimate secrets; and edging the victim out of relationships."[57]

Weaponizing Children

Children may not just be victims of intimate partner violence, but may also be deployed as weapons to create and maintain control over a victim-parent. Counterintuitive as it may seem, in some cases children appear to be bonded with the abuser and are enlisted in waging war by proxy on the victim. In such scenarios, a perpetrator uses the victim's children to accomplish his or her goals that involve maintaining power and control over the victim.

The tactics involved when children are weaponized and used against a victim of such a pattern of behavior include communicating hurtful or abusive messages to the victim via the children; attempting to alienate or turn the children against the victim; ignoring the children's medical conditions in order to punish or torment the victim; withholding child support; refusing to return the children's possessions; refusing to agree to parenting plans, or constantly demanding accommodations to parenting plans; refusing to communicate or share information as a means of control; denying the victim contact with the children while in the abuser's care; creating stress and conflict during the children's transitions; failing to ensure proper supervision; threatening to harm the pets that the children love and are attached to, and overall triangulating the children in the conflict.[58]

57. *Id.*
58. *Id.*

When demonstrating to the court the debilitating effects of coercive control on the children in a case, it is critical to document the duration, frequency, and intensity of the abuse. Research demonstrates that "perpetrators who are highly controlling of their former partners often interact in similar ways that constrain and engender fear in their children."[59] In fact, "[c]oercive control during the relationship may place women at risk of future violence following separation, including post-separation sexual assault, escalating physical violence, or threats to their lives or lives of their children."[60]

Sexual Coercion

Sexual coercion could include unwanted sexual contact, including vaginal, oral, or anal sex, after being pressured in ways that include being worn down by someone who repeatedly asks for sex or shows they are unhappy; feeling pressured by being lied to, being told promises that were untrue, having someone threaten to end a relationship or spread rumors; and sexual pressure due to someone using their influence or authority.[61]

Sexual coercion is used to pressure, persuade, insist, or manipulate an unwilling partner to have sexual contact.[62] Sexual abuse of power is broader than "sexual coercion," which is typically narrowly construed to include only cases in which explicit threats to harm a complainant are demonstrated. Sexual abuse of power aims to cover abusive conduct above and beyond threats to harm to include additional forms of placing complainants in fear of economic or professional harm.[63] Sexual coercion is typically defined in state criminal statutes. For instance, "Michigan law establishes that term 'force or coercion' in the criminal sexual conduct statute carries its ordinary meaning, and refers to touching achieved by power or compulsion, or accompanied

---

59. Kathryn J. Spearman et al., *Post Separation Abuse: A Literature Review Connecting Tactics to Harm* 21(2) J. Fam. Trauma, Child Custody & Child Dev. 145 (2024).

60. *Id.*

61. University of Washington, *Child Abuse Increases Risk For Later Sexually Coercive Behavior in Some Men,* ScienceDaily (Oct. 24, 2008). www.sciencedaily.com/releases/2008/10/081021185103.htm. *See also Child Abuse Increases Risk for Sexually Coercive Behavior in Men*, 27 Child. L. Prac. 190 (2009).

62. *See* University of Washington, *supra* note 61.

63. Michal Buchhandler-Raphael, *The Failure of Consent: Re-Conceptualizing Rape as Sexual Abuse of Power*, 18 Mich. J. Gender & L. 147, 228 (2011).

by circumstances sufficient to create a reasonable fear of dangerous consequences, and does not encompass any and all physical contact."[64]

As such, in Michigan, criminal sexual conduct encompasses not only incidents in which a perpetrator overcomes the victim through physical force, but also when the perpetrator coerces the victim to submit by threatening to use force or violence on the victim, and the victim believes that the actor has the present ability to execute these threats.[65] Courts have found that "[f]orce or coercion exists, for purposes of offense of criminal sexual conduct involving force or coercion, whenever a defendant's conduct induces a victim to reasonably believe that the victim has no practical choice because of a history of child sexual abuse or for some other similarly valid reason.[66]

Sexual coercive behavior may include not just unwanted or nonconsensual sex, but could also include forcing the viewing of pornography; posting explicit or embarrassing images and recordings of the victim on social media without consent, or engaging in revenge pornography; recording the victim engaged in sexual activities without consent; taking or distributing explicit or embarrassing images of the victim without consent; engaging in sexual activities that demean the victim; in some instances, being unfaithful to gain an unfair advantage; controlling the victim's reproductive choices or engaging in sexual activities without contraception; and controlling the victim's sexual health, such as by refusing to take steps to prevent the transmission of sexually transmitted disease.

However, in the family law context, there are several obstacles to legal interventions for victims of sexual coercion. Sexual coercion has a "monolithic definition" that is outside the scope of intimate partner violence.[67] For instance, rape is defined and adjudicated in a criminal context. Secondly, sexual violence is grossly underreported.[68] Lastly, sexual coercion is viewed with a gender bias, with the perspective that only women are sexually abused by men.[69] Research shows that sexual violence is multidirectional and the

---

64. *See* Alman v. Reed, C.A.6 (Mich.) 2013, 703 F.3d 887, rehearing and rehearing en banc denied.

65. Mich. Comp. Laws Ann. § 750.520e (West).

66. People v. Green, 884 N.W.2d 838, 313 Mich. App. 526 (2015).

67. Stalking, Prevention, Awareness, and Resource Center, Judicial Officer Guide: Responding to Stalking (July 5, 2022).

68. *Id.*

69. *Id.*

conception of bidirectional sexual coercion in interpersonal relationships remains a minority subset of the overall intimate partner violence literature.

Legislative Attempts to Define Coercive Control

While a few jurisdictions have legislated laws on coercive control, these laws are not without their fair share of criticism. The most poignant criticism is that "[n]o law is self-enforcing."[70] The criticism is directed more toward the lack of understanding and training of professionals who swore to protect the public and uphold the law than the laws themselves. The worry is "[i]f police fail to arrest abusers who physically assault their victims, prosecutors fail to bring charges in court, and judges fail to sentence them seriously, there is no reason to believe they will take the more nuanced crime of coercive control any more seriously."[71] This concern is not unfounded—if bruises and black eyes fail to elicit an immediate and proper response from law enforcement, what can one say about claims of coercive control? Internationally, in the jurisdictions with laws against coercive control, the number of cases addressing the issue is meager. For instance, in a study in Tasmania, an island state in Australia that has criminalized coercive control, it was found that this behavior or conduct was not only "rarely prosecuted in either criminal or civil courts," but to make matters worse, such laws were "used against victims for yelling at their abusers."[72] In other parts of the world, for instance, in Scotland, "[t]he law has been better enforced [because] police received extensive training."[73]

Statutory Definitions of Coercive Control

Some states have passed laws that have defined coercive control and have broadened the definition of "abuse" by acknowledging that abuse is not limited to the actual infliction of physical injury or assault. For instance,

---

70. State of Victoria, Royal Commission into Family Violence: Report and Recommendations, Vol I, Parl Paper No 132 (2014–16), at 19.

71. *Id.*

72. *Id.*

73. Michele Burman, Oona Brooks-Hay & Ruth Friskney, *Operationalizing Coercive Control: Early Insights on the Policing of the Domestic Abuse (Scotland) Act 2018, in* The Criminalization of Violence Against Women: Comparative Perspectives (Heather Douglas et al. eds., 2023), https://doi.org/10.1093/oso/9780197651841.003.0011.

California Family Code section 6320 subdivision (a) allows a court to issue an ex parte order enjoining a party from engaging in a pattern of conduct that could result in "disturbing the peace of the other party." The Code envisages a court from enjoining a party from "molesting, attacking, striking, stalking, threatening, sexually assaulting, battering, credibly impersonating . . . falsely personating . . . harassing, telephoning, including but not limited to, making annoying telephone calls . . . destroying personal property, contacting . . . by mail or otherwise, coming within a specified distance of, or disturbing the peace of the other party . . . [or] of other named family or household members."[74]

California law has codified certain patterns of behavior or conduct, which, if engaged in, could result in "disturbing the peace of the other party," and therefore could be enjoined. Upon the discretion of the court, such conduct could also be enjoined if it could result in disturbing the peace of named family or household members, such as the children or other dependents. Classifying such behavior as "coercive control," California law defines it as "a pattern of behavior that in purpose or effect unreasonably interferes with a person's free will and personal liberty."[75] Examples of coercive control, under California law, include, but are not limited to, unreasonably engaging in any of the following:

"1. Isolating the other party from friends, relatives, or other sources of support.
2. Depriving the other party of basic necessities.
3. Controlling, regulating, or monitoring the other party's movements, communications, daily behavior, finances, economic resources, or access to services.
4. Compelling the other party by force, threat of force, or intimidation, including threats based on actual or suspected immigration status, to engage in conduct from which the other party has a right to abstain or to abstain from conduct in which the other party has a right to engage.
5. Engaging in reproductive coercion, which consists of control over the reproductive autonomy of another through force, threat of force, or intimidation, and may include, but is not limited to, unreasonably pressuring the other party to become pregnant, deliberately

74. Cal. Fam. Code § 6320(a) (West).

75. *Id.* § 6320(c).

interfering with contraception use or access to reproductive health information, or using coercive tactics to control, or attempt to control, pregnancy outcomes."[76]

Hawaii has a similar statute that bans coercive control. In it, the legislature defines coercive control as "a pattern of threatening, humiliating, or intimidating actions, which may include assaults, or other abuse that is used to harm, punish, or frighten an individual."[77]

Other states, while not explicitly defining and enjoining coercive control conduct, have passed laws to interpret coercive control as illegal. For instance, Alabama's domestic violence laws includes criminal coercion within the meaning of abuse.[78] And the State defines criminal coercion as when a person, without legal authority, "threatens to confine, restrain or to cause physical injury to the threatened person . . . damage the property or reputation of the threatened person or another with intent thereby to induce the threatened person or another against his will to do an unlawful act or refrain from doing a lawful act."[79] Although the State used the term *criminal control,* it is clear that it intended to curtail the same undue influence on another person against that person's will that California and Hawaii have enjoined.

Similarly, Arkansas, Michigan, and Illinois have statutes that can be interpreted by the judiciary as a bulwark against coercive control. Part of Arkansas' definition of domestic abuse is "[m]ental harm caused by the infliction of fear of imminent physical harm, bodily injury, or assault against an individual in a dating relationship by the other individual in the dating relationship or against a member of a family or household by another member of the family or household."[80] Michigan laws prevent behaviors that place, attempt to cause, or cause physical or mental harm to a family or household member.[81] Illinois includes "physical abuse, harassment, intimidation of a dependent, interference with personal liberty or willful deprivation . . ." in its definition of abuse.[82] Other states, such as Colorado and

76. *Id.*
77. Haw. Rev. Stat. Ann. § 586-1 (West).
78. Ala. Code § 30-5-2.
79. Ala. Code § 13A-6-25.
80. Ark. Code Ann. § 9-6-102 (West).
81. Mi. Stat. 400.1501(d).
82. 750 Ill. Comp. Stat. Ann. 60/103.

Delaware, provide victims with some recourse where they have been victims of nonphysical but still abusive conduct.[83]

However, there are still jurisdictions, such as Florida and Arizona, that require physical violence for a finding of domestic violence.[84] Under Florida law, domestic violence means "any assault, aggravated assault, battery, aggravated battery, sexual assault, sexual battery, stalking, aggravated stalking, kidnapping, false imprisonment, or any criminal offense resulting in physical injury or death of one family or household member by another family or household member."[85] The courts have adhered to this strict meaning of domestic violence, which makes it extremely difficult for victims to seek justice. In these jurisdictions, a claim of domestic violence "requires some showing of [physical] violence or a threat of violence."[86] Florida courts have also explained that "general harassment, general relationship problems, and uncivil behavior are not enough."[87] The problem is that visceral reality of coercive control does not always match with these outdated unmalleable and inelastic rules.

Worldwide, domestic violence advocates have argued in favor of changing laws to "ensure that victims of coercive control can receive legal remedies[.]"[88] They have argued in favor of legislation that explicitly mentions the term *coercive control* and defines it for the professionals and jurists to have a clear understanding of the issues.[89] In cases where coercive controlling behavior or conduct is present, it is important to assess such behavior from an objective standpoint, and not to look for subjective intent of the perpetrator. For instance, one model currently used in the United Kingdom proposes:

1. A person (A) commits an offense if –

83. *See also* Colo. Rev. Stat. Ann. § 18-6-800.3 (West); 10 Del. Code § 1041(d) (West).

84. *See* Engstrom v. McCarthy, 243 Ariz. 469, 473, 411 P.3d 653, 657 (Ct. App. 2018) ("It is the Legislature's job to define what conduct constitutes 'domestic violence.'" "And the Legislature has defined domestic violence in Title 13 and Title 25 [to require physical violence].") (citing A.R.S. § 25–403.03(A); A.R.S. § 13–3601; A.R.S. § 25–403.03(D)).

85. Fla. Stat. Ann. § 741.28 (West).

86. Young v. Smith, 901 So. 2d 372, 373 (Fla. 2d DCA 2005).

87. Leal v. Rodriguez, 220 So. 3d 543, 545 (Fla. Dist. Ct. App. 2017).

88. Candela, *supra* note 9.

89. *Id.*

a. A repeatedly or continuously engages in behavior towards another person (B) that is controlling or coercive,
b. at the time of the behavior, A and B are personally connected,
c. the behavior has a serious effect on B, and
d. A knows or ought to know that the behavior will have a serious effect on B.

The law in the United Kingdom defines coercive controlling behavior as:

> a range of acts designed to make a person subordinate and/or dependent by isolating them from sources of support, exploiting their resources and capacities for personal gain, depriving them of the means needed for independence, resistance and escape and regulating their everyday behavior. Coercive behavior is defined as: an act or pattern of acts of assault, threats, humiliation and intimidation or other abuse that is used to harm, punish or frighten their victim. This can encompass, but is not limited to, the following types of abuse: psychological; physical; sexual; financial; and emotional.[90]

This model provides a gender-neutral statutory definition that clearly outlines the elements of coercive control.[91] What is clear is the statutory language "must be crafted so that it is not overbroad, thereby harming the individuals the language is intended to protect and aid."[92] More importantly, the law should enumerate specific conduct or behavior, which has been found to have been so harmful to the victims of coercive control.

Domestic Relations Cases on Coercive Control

Family courts deal with allegations of coercive control with an increasing frequency, particularly in cases that have been termed as "high conflict." But, as discussed later in this chapter, there is a difference between a "high conflict" situation wherein the parties are fanning the flames of toxic litigation because of their inherent failure or refusal to cooperate at any level and a "chronic conflict" situation wherein one party has demonstrated a pattern

---

90. *Id.*

91. *Id.*

92. Battered Women's Justice Project, *Coercive Control Codification A Brief Guide for Advocates and Coalitions* (2021), https://bwjp.org/assets/documents/pdfs/cc-codificationbrief.pdf.

of abusive, coercive controlling behavior while the other party has been desperately trying to protect itself (and other vulnerable family members) from such conduct.

Courts have long expressed concerns regarding coercive control. For instance, in *Kent v. Green*, an Alabama court expressed its fear of the effect of domestic violence and coercive control on both the mother and the child as early as 1996. This is because if "the judiciary is [not] carefully informed about the impact of domestic violence on children and the abused parent, it will inadvertently issue custody and visitation awards that further endanger the abused parent and the children . . . who are at risk of both abuse and severe emotional repercussions."[93] This fear is based on the belief that custody cases that involve domestic violence happen at times when "battered women and children may be most acutely vulnerable to the coercive controls and violent manipulations of battering men."[94] Additionally, "[r]esearch . . . reveals that more than half of men who batter their female partners also abuse their children. . . . The more severe the abuse of the mother, the worse the child abuse."[95] In that case, the court was particularly worried about the effect of coercive control not only on the mothers, but also on the children who were exposed to it as well.

Sometimes a case involving coercive control and allegations of domestic violence requires a careful and deliberate analysis for it that requires an outcome that may appear counterintuitive. For instance, in the Alaskan case of *Joy B. v. Everett B.*, coercive control was enough to overcome the presumption that Everett, the father, could not be awarded custody. The court found in this case that

> husband rebutted the statutory presumption that a parent with a history of perpetrating domestic violence should not be awarded sole legal or sole physical custody of a child; before trial the court found husband had a history of perpetrating domestic violence, husband applied for a batterers' intervention program, during an examination by an expert as part of the intake process for the program it was determined that husband was not recommended for the program as he was the victim of domestic violence, and a custody investigator reported the same conclusion that husband was

93. Kent v. Green, 701 So. 2d 4, 7 (Ala. Civ. App. 1996).
94. *Id.*
95. *Id.*

the victim and that wife engaged in "intimate partner stalking behaviors" and "ongoing harassment behaviors."[96]

In *Joy B.*, the wife claimed that the husband was unfaithful and physically abused her, but the husband alleged that the wife was physically and emotionally abusive toward him.[97] He declared that the wife once hired a hit man to kill him.[98] An investigator and a licensed clinical worker found that the "[husband] was 'passive and avoidant,' whereas [wife] was 'aggressive and domineering' and 'engaged in long-standing patterns of battering through coercion, control, manipulation and domination over [husband] physically and psychologically.'"[99] The investigator also found that the "[wife] engaged in 'intimate partner stalking behaviors which are a form of domestic violence' as well as 'ongoing harassment behaviors' that were 'accusatory, blaming, insulting, shaming, belittling, and threat[en]ing.'"[100] Based on the record, the husband rebutted the presumption that he could not be awarded custody.[101]

Colorado has taken a broader view of domestic violence and included coercive control conduct within the definitional framework. Colorado courts have found that a crime of domestic violence occurs "when it is used as a method of coercion, control, punishment, intimidation, or revenge directed against a person with whom the actor is or has been involved in an intimate relationship."[102] Under that definition, any action that is used to coerce, control, punish, intimidate, or exact revenge within the context of an intimate relationship could be classified as domestic violence. Colorado courts have also understood that when addressing claims of domestic violence, physical violence is only one component of it and that there may be other components that could be equally if not more harmful to the victims of domestic violence. Case in point, a Colorado court found that "while people have historically thought of domestic violence as purely physical violence," the Power and Control Wheel illustrates that "physical

96. Joy B. v. Everett B., 451 P.3d 365 (Alaska 2019).

97. *Id.* at 367.

98. *Id.*

99. *Id.*

100. *Id.*

101. *Id.* at 370.

102. People v. Disher, 224 P.3d 254, 258 (Colo. 2010) (citing Colo. Rev. Stat. Ann. § 18-6-800.3 (West)).

violence is only one component of a domestic violence situation."[103] Thus, "although physical violence may occur in an abusive intimate relationship, 'what makes an abusive relationship abusive' is the 'power and control' that a person exerts over his or her intimate partner."[104] The Power and Control Wheel illustrates the types of nonphysical control a person might exert over another (see Figure 2.1). Based on both cases, it is a safe assumption that coercive control is accepted as a type of domestic violence in Colorado.

Figure 2.1 Power and Control Wheel[105]

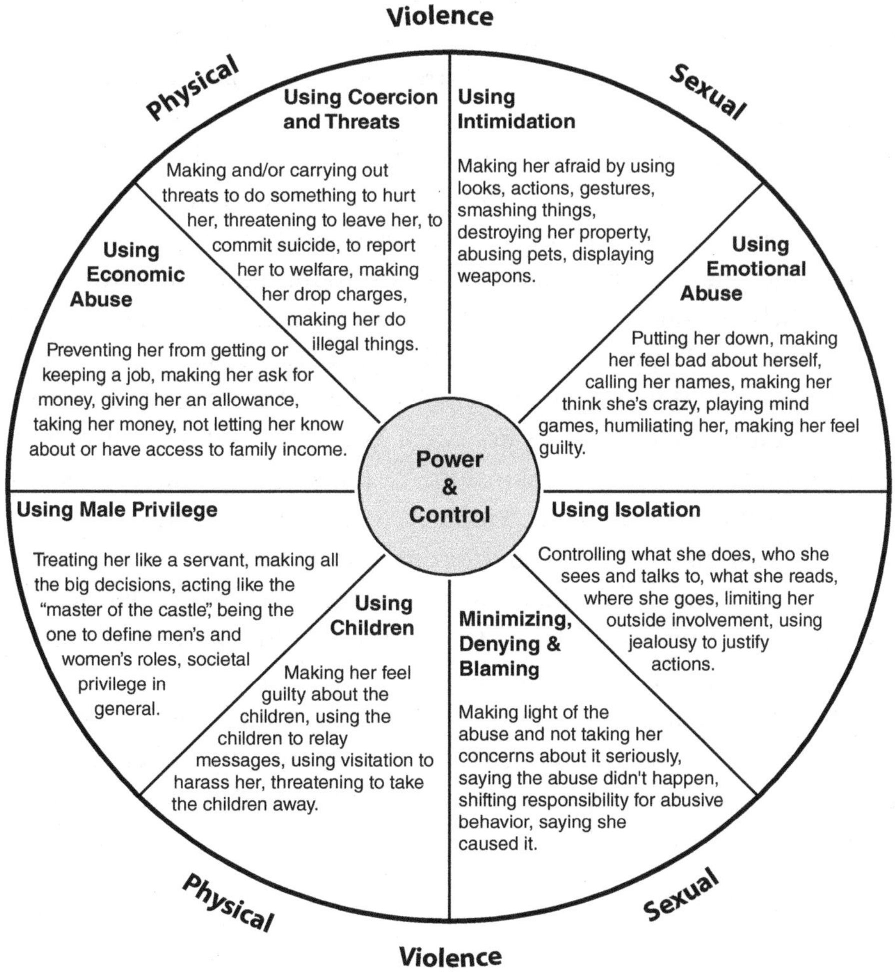

103. People v. Coons, 2021 CO 70, ¶ 35, 495 P.3d 961, 967–68.

104. *Id.*

105. Power and Control Wheel, Domestic Abuse Intervention Programs, http://www.theduluthmodel.org/pdf/PowerandControl.pdf (last visited Nov. 23, 2020).

Delaware has also interpreted coercive controlling behavior as a form of domestic violence under the "alarming and destressing behavior" section of the state's domestic violence laws. In *G.I. v. J.S.*, the victim reported to the therapist that her partner was abusive and controlling.[106] According to her, he controlled when she worked, what she wore, removed her and the children from the house, and threatened to shoot her.[107] The court-ordered therapist described the coercive control dynamic present in the case as "domestic violence [which] isn't necessarily physical but may be more dangerous because it's emotional and much harder to detect," and it "describes the action meant to be addressed by the statutory definition of abuse, 'engaging in a course of alarming or distressing conduct in a manner which is likely to cause fear or emotional distress or to provoke a violent or disorderly response.'"[108]

In *G.I.*, since coercive control had not been addressed in Delaware case law, the court looked to other jurisdictions. It found that the U.S. Court of Appeals for the Ninth Circuit assessed a relationship that involved coercive control under the "extreme cruelty" standard to immigration status applications.[109] The Delaware court also looked at the relevant literature in the field and found that it "emphasizes that, although a relationship may appear to be predominantly tranquil and punctuated only infrequently by episodes of violence, 'abusive behavior does not occur as a series of discrete events,' but rather pervades the entire relationship."[110] The court considered the other courts' definitions of domestic violence, which defined the term as "the physical, sexual, psychological, and/or emotional abuse of a victim . . . with the goal of asserting and maintaining power and control over the victim."[111] Relying on these authorities, the Delaware court ultimately concluded that the evidence supported a holding that the father had abused the mother.[112]

Similarly, in another Delaware case, a court found the father to have exercised coercive control over the mother based on similar behaviors. The therapist concluded that the mother was "presented as someone who is

---

106. G.I. v. J.S., No. CK16-03072, 2017 WL 4792366, at *4 (Del. Fam. Ct. May 18, 2017).

107. *Id.* at *5.

108. *Id.* at *4.

109. *Id.* at *5.

110. *Id.*

111. *Id.*

112. *Id.*

typical for a victim of domestic violence . . . [because] she was a victim of coercive control, which means that it has happened over a fairly long period of time. And she's afraid of the individual, the perpetrator."[113] The father admitted that he threw hot coffee on the mother and that he threatened to confuse the mother for a burglar and shoot her.[114] In both cases, Delaware courts found the father's actions were tantamount to domestic violence.

Sometimes, abusive behaviors do not end even when the victim decides to get help; the abuser may continue to indulge in abusive behaviors whenever possible. For example, in a Connecticut case, *In re Omar I*, the father was controlling the mother financially by "refusing to let her work outside of the home, limit[ing] the use of her motor vehicle, and [taking] her cell phone."[115] He threatened to take the children out of the country and never let the mother see them again.[116] He also "took the family out for a 'last supper' . . . at which time he confronted the mother about her affair, all in the presence of her children."[117] He also began swearing and degrading the mother in front of the children while driving the car erratically and speeding through red lights.[118] The father texted the mother that "he would be waiting in the garage with a gun to shoot her lover, that he had a knife and would kill her lover."[119] The mother told him to leave, which led to a physical struggle "at which time [father] struck her in the face with a glass oil diffuser."[120] Unfortunately, the mother could not bring criminal charges against the father because she would be "without any financial support if he were incarcerated."[121] Even more distressing than her inability to seek justice is that the father attempted to maintain control over her while the case was pending. The father told the evaluator that the mother was suicidal, had a substance abuse issue, and had a mental disorder in an effort to prevent the

113. Irwin v. Shelby, 210 A.3d 705, 708 (Del. 2019).

114. *Id.* at *721.

115. *In re* Omar I., 197 Conn. App. 499, 513, 231 A.3d 1196, 1209, *cert. denied*, 335 Conn. 924 (2020), *and cert. denied sub nom.* Ammar I. v. Connecticut, 141 S. Ct. 956, 208 L. Ed. 2d 494 (2020).

116. *Id.*

117. *Id.*

118. *Id.* at 513-14, 1209.

119. *Id.* at 514.

120. *Id.*

121. *Id.*

mother from receiving proper help.[122] The evaluator did not find any evidence to support any of those claims.[123]

As discussed earlier, Florida's definition of domestic violence places an overwhelming focus on physical violence, while minimizing claims of other forms of violence, such as emotional or psychological. That focus on physical violence has led some courts to downplay claims of coercive control and related conduct. For instance, in *Young* and *Leal*, Florida's courts insisted that domestic violence "requires some showing of violence or a threat of violence."[124] In *Leal*, the court held that "[g]eneral harassment, general relationship problems, and uncivil behavior are not enough" to be considered domestic violence.[125] The type of behaviors that the court found to be "general harassment or general relationship problems," in this case however, are deeply concerning. For example, father would not allow the mother to have friends, go to work, or interact with her family.[126] If she were five minutes late to a pre-planned meeting, father would accuse her of being somewhere else that she was not allowed to be. Also, the father would take her immigration papers whenever he was upset with her. He would also threaten to prevent her access to a car or money. One time, while exchanging custody of their minor child, "the [father] ran up to the [mother] and said 'f**kin' A, I'm going to destroy your life, you don't know who I am. . . . Your mother and your father are going to cry. And you are safe because you are the mother of my son, if not I will destroy your life."[127] The court considered [Father] taking the Mother's immigration information and his threat to "destroy [her] life" to be acts of domestic violence.[128] However, the court did not consider the other controlling behavior, such as preventing her from working or interacting with her family and isolating her, to be domestic violence because there was no physical or threat of physical violence.

Like Florida, Arizona too appears to take a strict and antiquated approach to defining and addressing claims of domestic violence. In *Engstrom v. McCarthy*, the trial court found that the case involved significant domestic violence coercive control.[129] The record showed that the father

122. *Id.* at 515, 210.

123. *Id.*

124. *Young*, 901 So.2d at 373; *Leal*, 220 So. 3d at 545.

125. *Leal*, 220 So. 3d at 545.

126. *Id.*

127. *Id.*

128. *Id.* at *546.

129. Engstrom v. McCarthy, 243 Ariz. 469, 473, 411 P.3d 653, 657 (Ct. App. 2018).

"us[ed] the parties' children to further traumatize Mother."[130] The father "exerted control over Mother by encouraging Mother to participate in online sexual activity, have sex with prostitutes, threatening to have affairs or leave Mother if Mother failed to gratify Father, and convincing Mother that she was the one who tried to 'control' [him]."[131] The father's actions became progressively worse. He drove by "Mother's workplace with the children in the car to ensure Mother was at work," and bought clothes "for the children with the same-sounding name as Mother's online porn name[.]"[132] The trial court held that the father "manipulate[d] the children in order to further control Mother" and that such behavior "is untenable and intolerable."[133] But the Court of Appeals disagreed. It ruled that "[e]ncouraging Mother to participate in certain activities, threatening to be unfaithful if Mother did not perform in the way Father wanted, and acting in a controlling manner might be distasteful, but those actions do not necessarily support the legal conclusion that [Father] is a perpetrator of domestic violence."[134] The court did state that it is possible that some of the father's behavior might be domestic violence, but it nonetheless found the acts just mentioned did not to amount to the State of Arizona's legal definition of domestic violence.[135]

Indiana has also dealt with claims of coercive control. In *Matter of E.M.*, the trial court made a finding of domestic violence based on a pattern of coercive controlling behavior demonstrated by the father, which included physical violence, but also other kinds of abusive conduct:

> (1) Father "hit [K.S.] regularly" during their marriage; (2) Mother requested to speak with "the domestic violence people" because "in her past, she has experienced ... domestic violence"; (3) Father "[did not] like that another male [was] talking to [Mother]"; (4) Mother is controlled by Father and depends on him "for everything"; (5) Mother could not take the children to the doctor because Father controls when the children can get medical attention and refused to let his children be seen; (6) S.M., E.M., and P.M. have all been referred to cognitive behavioral therapy because of trauma related to domestic violence.[136]

130. *Id.*
131. *Id.*
132. *Id.*
133. *Id.*
134. *Id.*
135. *Id.* at *474, *658.
136. Matter of E.M., 112 N.E.3d 237 (Ind. Ct. App. 2018).

Although this Indiana case involved instances of physical violence, most of the trial court's findings focused on the pattern of the father's coercive control of the mother and the children. Additionally, in this case, a domestic violence counselor conducted two domestic violence assessments on the father and concluded that the father "used power control tactics such as intimidation and isolation to control Mother."[137] This case, and many others, underscore the importance of family practitioners using mental health experts to educate the courts on coercive control behaviors and the harms associated with such behaviors.

It is important to not limit oneself to family court cases when trying to find judicial decisions on coercive control and other psychologically and emotionally abusive behaviors. Sometimes, cases emanating from probate, juvenile, and criminal courts shed light on how the courts assessed claims of coercive control and protected the victims therein. Even in states without statutory laws to guide the family courts' interpretation of coercive control as a form of domestic violence, coercive control continues to appear in cases that are litigated in other areas of law, such as probate, juvenile, and criminal.

For instance, one could analyze a Michigan case involving termination of parental rights addressing a pattern of behavior that clearly demonstrates a high degree of criminal, pathological, and coercively controlling behavior. In that case, according to the mother, the father, after physically abusing the mother for several hours in front of the children, "obtained his gun from the kitchen, held it to his head, and threatened to kill himself while holding one child's hand. He then put on a television show for the children and raped mother in a nearby bedroom."[138] He then held the entire family captive for four to five hours while trying to evade the police.[139] During the trial, the father asked "why [the mother] did not leave or try to escape the violence that [the father] inflicted on her."[140] The mother attributed her decision to stay to the level of coercive control that abusive partners have over the person being abused in the relationship.[141] Given the father's behavior, his termination of parental rights were affirmed.[142]

---

137. Matter of M.E., 152 N.E.3d 1095 (Ind. Ct. App. 2020).

138. *In re* Cage, No. 353851, 2020 WL 7640287, at *4 (Mich. Ct. App. Dec. 22, 2020).

139. *Id.*

140. *Id.*

141. *Id.* at *3.

142. *Id.* at 9.

In a Minnesota case, the fear was that the father would "use joint legal custody as a weapon" against the mother because he had engaged in coercive control and manipulation of her throughout their entire relationship.[143] Father's coercive control and manipulation of the mother included "secretly photographed pages from [the mother's] private diary and gathered information about her foster care background and the criminal history of her family members."[144] The father then used the information from the diary to threaten to take custody of the child.[145] "[The father] also secretly dumped out [the mother's] breastmilk on his unfounded suspicion that she was abusing alcohol."[146] Even though the referee concluded that the father's behavior did not amount to the statutory definition of domestic abuse, the referee found that the behavior was "offensive and demeaning and contribute[d] to an unhealthy dynamic which is central to [the] case."[147]

In a non-family law setting, coercive control and other mental stresses were seen as "extraordinary mitigating factors" in deciding whether to suspend an attorney in Nebraska for ethical breaches.[148] The attorney's husband used intimidation, emotional abuse, isolation, blame, economic abuse, coercion, and threats to maintain control over the wife.[149] The therapist found that the husband "became increasingly abusive, and the escalating demands began to overwhelm the respondent 'to the point of being actually immobilized at some point and not able to use . . . the intellectual and emotional capacity that she actually ha[d].'"[150] Although coercive control had not previously been considered as a mitigating factor for ethical breaches, based on her medical records, the court determined that her mental and emotional state contributed to her misconduct.[151] This is because she "was affected by numerous mental and emotional traumas related to sexual assault and domestic partner violence."[152]

143. Thornton v. Bosquez, 933 N.W.2d 781, 788 (Minn. 2019).

144. *Id.* at *787.

145. *Id.*

146. *Id.*

147. *Id.*

148. State ex rel. Couns. for Discipline of Nebraska Supreme Ct. v. Castrejon, 311 Neb. 560, 565–66, 973 N.W.2d 701, 706 (2022).

149. *Id.* at *565, *706.

150. *Id.*

151. *Id.* at *572, *709.

152. *Id.* *571, *709.

In the New Jersey case of *C.C. v. I.C.*, the case of coercive control was not as graphic, but nonetheless demonstrated how traumatic coercively controlling behaviors could be. In that case, the abuser threatened to call the police, called and texted the abused when he was prohibited from doing so, and emailed her to inform her that he would not allow the court-appointed parenting time.[153] He also entered her home in violation of court orders and improperly called the police once inside the house on multiple other occasions.[154] The court found that the accused asserted coercive control over the victim by "remaining in the church parking lot while she was working."[155] Although this example of coercive behavior is not as life threatening or as violent as the others, it nevertheless illustrates the magnitude of control an abuser can possess over another person's life by creating an environment in which the person being abused feels trapped. In *C.C.*, although the abuser was trespassing on the abused property, he called the police as if he had a reason to do so. Such behavior could have created a belief in the victim that the perpetrator was above the law and that the police would not help her since her abuser felt no qualms in contacting them himself. As expressed by the victim in *In re Cage*, it is difficult for an abused women to escape her abuser because of behaviors like this that make the abuser seem invincible.

New York courts have adopted "a 'zero tolerance' zone for domestic violence of any sort."[156] In *L.M.L v. H.T.N.*, the court removed a parent from the home as a "drastic remedy."[157] In the court's view, the drastic action was necessary to protect the best interests of these children.[158] Based on previous cases and the definition of coercive control by the New York Office for Prevention of Domestic Violence,[159] the court ruled coercive control is a form

153. C.C. v. I.C., No. A-0771-19, 2021 WL 978521, at *6 (N.J. Super. Ct. App. Div. Mar. 16, 2021).

154. *Id.*

155. *C.C.*, No. A-0771-19, 2021 WL 978521, at *6: (citing State v. J.T., 294 N.J. Super. 540, 545, 683 A.2d 1166, 1168 (App. Div. 1996)).

156. L.M.L. v. H.T.N., 57 Misc. 3d 1207(A), 68 N.Y.S.3d 379, at *11 (N.Y. Sup. Ct. 2017).

157. *Id.*

158. *Id.*

159. "The New York Office for Prevention of Domestic Violence describes 'coercive control' as including restricting daily activities, manipulating or destroying family relationships, stifling a parties' independence, controlling access to information and services, extreme jealousy, excessive punishments for violations of rules, and other inter-personal conduct." L.M.L. v. H.T.N., 57 Misc. 3d 1207(A), 68 N.Y.S.3d 379 (N.Y. Sup. Ct. 2017).

of domestic violence.[160] This form of abuse includes "the monitoring and/or regulation of commonplace activities of daily living, particularly those associated with women's default roles as mothers, homemakers and sexual partners and run the gamut from their access to money, food and transport to how they dress, clean, cook or perform sexually."[161]

Another New York case, *People v. Byrd*, exemplifies how abusers maintain control over their victims, and what the person subject to such abusive control is willing to do to protect the abuser. In *Byrd*, the defendant smashed his partner's "head against the tile floor of their kitchen and, wearing hard plastic sandals, repeatedly stomped on her abdomen, breaking her ribs and causing her pancreas to split in half."[162] The defendant then refused to take her to the hospital. He told her that "he had not hurt her as much as he could have."[163] She was not able to go to the hospital "until six days after the attack, when defendant took their daughter out."[164] The surgeon who operated on her testified "had she waited longer, she would have died."[165]

The defendant then went to the hospital where his partner had finished receiving life-saving surgery and apologized, begged for forgiveness, told her he loved her, and begged her not to break up the family.[166] According to the expert who testified in the case, this type of behavior is known as the "honeymoon phase."[167] Although those behaviors appear remorseful, or even romantic, their purpose is to solidify the abuser's control over the victim. The defendant's partner subsequently testified that she was not afraid of him. She also lied under oath to protect the defendant. She testified that the defendant only contacted her "two or three" times, when he made "400 calls" to her since his incarceration.[168] Over 400 phone calls and the hospital visits begging her "not to break up the family" demonstrate how much pressure the defendant placed on his partner. The fact that she lied under oath

---

160. *Id.* at 6.
161. *Id.*
162. People v. Byrd, 51 A.D.3d 267, 269, 855 N.Y.S.2d 505 (2008).
163. *Id.*
164. *Id.*
165. *Id.*
166. *Id.* at *271.
167. *Id.*
168. *Id.*

for him demonstrated that he still maintained control over her even after he almost caused her death.[169]

In Texas, a court construed the threat of committing suicide or self-harm as a coercive controlling tactic. In a footnote in an unreported opinion, the court mentioned that a threat of suicide can be a form of domestic violence. Specifically, the court mentioned that "[s]uicide threats sometimes occur as part of a course of violent conduct and a person's using threats of suicide to manipulate a romantic partner is a common coercive control tactic and, in a domestic violence or stalking situation, can sometimes be an indicator of a higher risk of violence."[170]

In Washington, a court found a pattern of behavior as troubling and controlling.[171] Two years into a marriage, "[the wife] disclosed to [the husband] that she had another relationship shortly before the wedding."[172] After learning of the previous relationship, [the husband] demanded to know when she was going out with anyone outside of a work-related event.[173] In 2015, the husband began monitoring the wife's location through an application on her phone.[174] On one occasion, the wife visited her grandmother's home. "Convinced she was with someone else, [the husband] demanded that [she] put her grandmother on the phone in the middle of the night to confirm [the wife] was with her grandmother."[175] When she returned to the marital home, "[the husband] went through her travel garments, looking for evidence of an affair."[176] Eventually, the couple separated, but while [the wife] was distracted, "[the husband] looked through her phone and read text messages confirming that [the wife] was having a relationship with her law partner."[177] Although the relationship started after the separation, the

---

169. *Id.*

170. Scott v. Wooley, No. 02-19-00318-CV, 2020 WL 7063292, at *5, n.9 (Tex. App. Dec. 3, 2020) (citing Isabell Scott & Nancy McKenna, Domestic Violence Practice and Procedure §§ 1:13, 1:18 (2020); Power and Control Wheel, Domestic Abuse Intervention Programs, http://www.theduluthmodel.org/pdf/PowerandControl.pdf (last visited Nov. 23, 2020)).

171. Clare v. Clare, 20 Wash. App. 2d 1039, at *1 (2021).

172. *Id.*

173. *Id.*

174. *Id.*

175. *Id.*

176. *Id.*

177. *Id.* at 2.

husband became angry, stating that he could "Pop [the wife's new partner]" and "Pop You [the wife]."[178]

In Wisconsin, the court, describing a coercive control dynamic domestic relationship, refused to give the father the same sentence as the mother of the child because he refused to show remorse or accept responsibility (other than pleading guilty).[179] He also blamed the mother for the child being neglected.[180] The father received a more severe sentence because "[p]art of the underlying issue in [the] case ha[d] to do with the manipulation of the child's mother, the ongoing domestic violence, and the concern that the Court ha[d] that so much of [which] could have been prevented if there wasn't the coercive control in the household."[181]

Victims of coercive control could end up being re-victimized after the end of the controlling relationship. At times, the victim ends up in another abusive relationship, which further complicates that person's ability to seek help. In a Connecticut case, *In re Greneo P.*, the mother accused the father of being abusive. She alleged his patterns of coercive control included "[s]talking her; Physical Violence—strangling her, punching her, hitting her, kicking; Using their children as a weapon; Threatening to kill her; Threatening to kidnap the children; Intimidation and abuse in front of family members."[182] She also reported that "he smashed her head into a table in front of her grandmother."[183] While she was able to report the father as an abuser, the child protective services investigator worker became concerned that her new partner was abusive as well. Unfortunately, the mother was afraid to report the new partner for his abusive behavior. As the protective services investigator explained the dynamic at a court hearing, "[i]t is suggested that Mother's reluctance be contextualized as Mother may be reluctant to share specific information regarding [the boyfriend] for fear of escalating the risks, she may also

178. *Id.*

179. State v. Mack, No. 2015AP1538-CRNM, 2016 WL 8604949, at *6 (Wis. Ct. App. Mar. 4, 2016).

180. *Id.*

181. *Id.*

182. *In re* Geneo P., No. :H12CP11013897A, 2011 WL 4582596, at *4 (Conn. Super. Ct. Sep. 9, 2011).

183. *Id.*

be economically dependent on him to pay for the motel room . . . or she may fear that sharing information will impact the . . . case."[184]

As a result of her fears, the mother created hollow excuses for her partner's behavior. She denied her boyfriend's abusive or controlling behavior, claiming that she sustained her black eyes and other injuries when he "accidentally elbowed her and the children accidentally kicked her while they were sleeping."[185] Many victims find themselves in other abusive relationships because abusers tend to target individuals who are vulnerable. As the protective services investigator explained, "[the mother was] likely more vulnerable as a result of her trauma."

At times, cases involving coercive control claims challenge the gender stereotypes. For instance, in the Connecticut case *Cohen v. Cohen*, the wife claimed to be a victim of coercive control and other abusive behavior by the husband.[186] She testified that she had been through counseling for years due to the husband's abusive behavior. However, the court found that "there have been no incidents of physical violence in the parties' present marriage."[187] Along with her claims of domestic violence, the wife alleged that the husband was financially coercive.[188] She stated that the husband became "enraged about her purchase of orthopedic shoes for one of the children for $50."[189] She testified that the husband was furious with purchases "he interpreted as for her boyfriend."[190] The court however found that in reality, "[the wife] had access to funds without interference throughout the course of the marriage, her own credit cards as well as her own considerable separate funds."[191] She spent hundreds of thousands of dollars on luxury handbags, antiques, and upscale home furnishing items.[192] Husband testified that "she had unfettered access to their joint funds," and "her own

184. *Id.*

185. *Id.*

186. Cohen v. Cohen, No. FSTFA144026825S, 2018 WL 4955695, at *10 (Conn. Super. Ct. Sep. 19, 2018), *aff'd*, 342 Conn. 354, 270 A.3d 89 (2022).

187. *Id.*

188. *Id.*

189. *Id.*

190. *Id.*

191. *Id.*

192. *Id.*

considerable separate assets."[193] The court found that "[t]hese are hardly facts which support a claim of coercive financial control."[194]

The wife next alleged that the husband was withholding sex during the marriage as a form of control over her.[195] The wife argued that the couple had separate bedrooms after a few years into their marriage and used this fact to support her claim of the husband withholding sex. But the court found this "need for separate bedrooms . . . a further example of [the wife's] inability to adjust her conduct to the expectations of others."[196] The husband had to wake up early for work, and the wife enjoyed staying up late to watch the television in the bedroom, which caused the husband to be unable to sleep.[197] When he complained, the wife responded "too bad, the TV is in here, go sleep somewhere else."[198] Moreover, when the couple used to sleep in the same bedroom, the wife would wake up the husband anytime during the night to discuss anything that she wanted.[199] The court concluded that "[t]here was no credible evidence as to the absence of an intimate relationship between the parties. . . . In fact, [the wife] herself often confirmed that this was so."[200] The court, upon considering the totality of evidence, refused to find that the husband had engaged in coercive control.

Coercive Control, "High Conflict," and Parental Alienation

Even though American courts follow the bedrock principle of adversarial system of justice, family courts put a premium on parent-litigants resolving conflicts out of court. The cases and controversies that stay in court and proceed toward litigation not only involve some level of conflict but are often categorized as "high-conflict cases." This pejorative label carries an implication that *both* parties are at fault for being involved in a conflict-laden litigation and unable to resolve the situation out of court. The fact

193. *Id.*
194. *Id.*
195. *Id.*
196. *Id.*
197. *Id.*
198. *Id.*
199. *Id.*
200. *Id.*

that the court, whose *raison d'etre* is to make findings of fact to adjudicate controversies, is being asked to do its job is somehow seen as a failure on the part of both litigants and a refusal on their part to be reasonable.

Unfortunately, for victims of coercive control and other forms of intimate partner violence, this assumption of mutuality and classification of their claims under the label "high conflict," may be tantamount to re-victimization at the hands of an abusive spouse or partner. A victim of coercive control who has been subjected to the power dynamics, manipulation, and usurpation of his or her agency and free will now risks being seen by the court as a litigant with a willingness to engage in toxic, unwarranted, and unnecessary litigation unless she or he forgoes all claims of being a victim of domestic abuse. Domestic violence advocates have taken issue with the validity and appropriateness of the term "high conflict" for a failure to distinguish high-conflict cases from those involving coercive control or other forms of intimate partner violence.[201] According to guidance provided by the National Council of Juvenile and Family Court Judges (NCJFCJ), the high-conflict label is often incorrectly assigned to cases involving intimate partner violence.[202] Guidance provided by the NCJFCJ clarifies that cases involving coercive control and abuse may have "high-conflict characteristics," but they require a different set of considerations, including but not limited to litigation and adjudication of facts, in order to promote safety for the at-risk parent and child.[203]

Coercive control cases may also pose a challenge to the family dynamics involving or appearing to involve parental alienation. The phenomenon of parental alienation could be a reason behind the contact resistance, contact refusal, or parental rejection demonstrated by a child in the post-separation context where there does not appear a legitimate or justifiable cause for the child's resistance toward or rejection of a parent. It would not be appropriate however to classify a family dynamic as a pure alienation dynamic where there is evidence of intimate partner violence on the part of the rejected parent, as the child's resistance to and rejection of the parent could be tied to having been exposed to family violence or being a victim of it, or both.

---

201. Lundy Bancroft, et al., The Batterer as Parent: Addressing the Impact of Domestic Violence on Family Dynamics 165 (2d ed. 2012).

202. A Judicial Guide to Child Safety in Custody Cases (NCJFCJ, 2008). https://www.ncjfcj.org/wp-content/uploads/2012/02/judicial-guide_0_0.pdf.

203. *Id.*

However, there is an overlap between what is understood in the field as parental alienating behavior and coercive control: Both include a tactic that weaponizes a child to create and maintain power and control in a family dynamic.

Parental alienating behaviors, commonly understood as 17 alienating strategies, include tactics such as denigrating, badmouthing, or undermining a parent; using a child to spy or inform on the other parent, putting the child in a loyalty bind; withdrawal of love if the child expresses positive thoughts about the target parent; confiding in the child; creating an impression that the other parent is unsafe, unfit, dangerous; creating an illusion that the other parent is incapable or undeserving of receiving love and affection. These same tactics are also found in abusive partners who engage in coercive control and weaponize children to achieve their nefarious goals. It is common for perpetrators of coercive controlling behaviors to accuse the victim of having engaged in "parental alienation" or restrictive gatekeeping. In such cases, it is important to consider two eventualities: (1) The alienating behavior may be occurring at the hands of the abusive party who has engaged in coercive control or similar controlling behavior; and (2) the parent who is the victim of such coercive controlling behavior may be engaging in protective gatekeeping, that is, trying to protect the child from the abusive parent's weaponization, even though it may appear on a superficial level as if the parent is interfering with the abusive parent's access to the child.[204]

Harms and Myths Associated with Coercive Control: Even Fierce Women Get Abused

Some professionals have pointed out that coercive control in families can be so harmful and overpowering that at times the victim does not even want to attempt to escape the situation.[205] Some victims do not come forward in fear of retribution. This is especially true in cases involving children where a harmful pattern of coercive influence occurs on children and their emotional attachments, typically after separation of the parents. Children from

---

204. *See generally* Ashish Joshi, Litigating Parental Alienation: Evaluating and Presenting an Effective Case in Court (ABA, 2021).

205. Nick Child, *Liberating 'Coercive Control' for Everyone to Use,* LinkedIn (Mar. 21, 2021). (https://www.linkedin.com/pulse/liberating-coercive-control-everyone-use-nick-child/.

abusive households can be easily influenced and often replicate behaviors of abuse, whether mental or physical.[206]

This is also true when men are victims. It is often thought that only women are victims of coercive control and domestic violence, but women too have been found to have engaged in coercive controlling behaviors and domestic violence. Their motives are similar to men—anger and the need to control.[207] Data from nationally representative surveys suggest that men and women are equally violent in intimate relationships, a conclusion borne out by meta-analysis of 82 couple-conflict studies that found that women were more likely to use physical aggression than men and to resort to violence more often than men.[208] Male victims also face the shame, humiliation, dismissal, and ignorance that women face.[209] Additionally, male victims of intimate partner violence have reported that "they were turned away from DV agencies in their quest to seek help for themselves and their children."[210] Unfortunately, because of gender bias, men are three times less likely to report domestic abuse than women. Ultimately, both female and male victims of domestic violence deserve the support of our justice system.[211]

It is also a myth that strong women are immune to coercive control: Neither power nor social status offers a shield against coercive control. As an example, the successful film producer and activist Tanya Selvaratnam found herself in an abusive relationship with former New York attorney general, Eric Schneiderman. Ms. Selvaratnam highlighted how alarmingly

---

206. *Id* at 3.

207. J. W. White & R. M. Kowalski, *Deconstructing the Myth of the Nonaggressive Woman: A Feminist Analysis*, 18 Psych. of Women Q. 487–508 (1994), https://journals.sagepub.com/doi/10.1111/j.1471-6402.1994.tb01045.x

208. Michelle Carney, Fred Buttell & Don Dutton, *Women Who Perpetrate Intimate Partner Violence: A Review of the Literature with Recommendations for Treatment* 12 Aggression & Violent Behavior 108-115 (2007). *See also* J. Archer, *Sex differences in aggression between heterosexual partners: A meta-analytic review* 126 Psych. Bull. 651 (2000) and J. Archer, *Sex Differences in Physically Aggressive Acts Between Heterosexual Partners: A Meta-Analytic Review* 7 Aggression and Violent Behavior 313 (2002).

209. Jan James, *Male Victims of Domestic Abuse Getting Re-victimized in Corporate Training Sessions Designed to "help" Them,* LinkedIn (2020), https://www.linkedin.com/pulse/male-victims-domestic-ab, use-getting-re-victimised-corporate-jan-james/.

210. Denise Hines & Emily Douglas, *The Reported Availability of U.S. Domestic Violence Services to Victims Who Vary by Age, Sexual Orientation, and Gender*, 2 Partner Abuse 1 (2011).

211. *Id.*

effortless it is to lose power, even for someone who is strong and independent. She wrote how "even fierce women get abused."[212] Cori Bush, a Congresswoman, told her story about her experience with domestic violence and how she hoped to help reshape laws regarding domestic violence in the future.[213] Law enforcement and court officials frequently fail to treat victims of mental abuse and coercive control as victims of domestic abuse given the difficulty proving coercive control or mental abuse in court. Fortunately, the process of understanding coercive control and mental abuse has begun with decision makers, who have acknowledged that coercive controlling behaviors not only can lead to physical abuse but are criminal acts themselves.[214]

In addition to the common myths associated with coercive control, professionals who work in this area should understand the research on how coercive control and intimate partner violence affect victims. Research demonstrates that victims of domestic violence commonly present with undiagnosed trauma symptoms that could cause an untrained or unskilled professional to perceive them as less credible. They engage in nervous laughter; are unable to maintain eye contact; have faulty memory; second guess themselves and their recollection; and minimize abuse. In addition, protective measures taken by the victims could be mistaken for "vexatiousness, alienation, gatekeeping, and high-conflict behavior in a litigation and dispute resolution context."[215]

What holds true is that professionals need more education and victims need better and more protection from their abusers. Without clear language and a thorough understanding of the coercive control dynamics, it is almost impossible to help victims obtain the legal remedies that would help them live a safe and autonomous life. Legal interventions must be geared toward identifying coercive control as a pattern of violence, because "[w]hen interventions are guided by laws or policies that target discrete incidents, the typical pattern of physical abuse is trivialized."[216]

---

212. Katie Roiphe, *Survivor Network: Two Memoirists Write About Their Experiences with Powerful, Manipulative Men,* N.Y. Times Book Review Newspaper (Mar. 7, 2021).

213. *Id.*

214. Melena Ryzik & Katie Benner, *Unmasking Domestic Abuse That Begins Long Before Assault.* N.Y. Times (Jan. 24, 2021).

215. Gillian Chadwick & Stef Sloan, *Coercive Control in High-Conflict Custody Litigation*, 57(1) Fam. Law Q. 52 (2023).

216. Evan Stark, *Representing Battered Women: Coercive Control and the Defense of Liberty* 58 Alb. L. Rev. 973 (1994-1995).

Family law practitioners are in a unique position to identify and aid victims of coercive control. Separation and divorce are "unique risk factors for family violence and the intensification of coercive controlling behaviors. A family breakdown can be a critical point in both the discovery and the trajectory of such abuse."[217] Additionally, research indicated that "women who experience coercive control report that their parenting after separation is marked by fear, powerlessness, constant intrusion by the abuser, harassment, and ongoing threats to both themselves and their children."[218] As a family law practitioner, "when dealing with a high-conflict file, it is a serious error to fail to thoroughly consider coercive control."[219] Additionally, "if family law lawyers screen for and identify the presence of family violence, this information permits better consideration of the impact on the family and any children."[220] When assessing clients as victims of coercive control, understanding that coercive control is an antecedent to post-separation abuse is critical to case planning.[221]

In protecting a victim of coercive control, it is imperative for the family law practitioners to understand that coercive control has been found to be "the 'golden thread' running through risk identification and assessment for domestic violence."[222] Research has shown that risk assessment tools structured around coercive control can help professionals move beyond an 'incident-by-incident' response and toward identifying the dangerous patterns of behavior that precede domestic homicide.[223] Such is the case in the context of child custody cases, where childhood violence is often thought of in terms of physical violence.[224] However, this physical violence framework does not account for the harms from coercive control that children experience when, for example, their father calls their mother stupid in

---

217. Lux & Gil, *supra* note 20.

218. *Id.*

219. *Id.*

220. *Id.*

221. Kathryn J. Spearman et al., *Post Separation Abuse: A Concept Analysis* 79(4) Intimate Partner Violence 1225 (2023).

222. A. Myhill & K. Hohl, *The "Golden Thread": Coercive Control and Risk Assessment for Domestic Violence,* 34(21-22) J. Interpersonal Violence 4477 (2019).

223. *Id.*

224. Emma Katz, *Beyond the Physical Incident Model: How Children Living with Domestic Violence are Harmed By and Resist Regimes of Coercive Control,* 25(1) Child Abuse Rev. 46 (2016). Published online 24 November 2015 in Wiley Online Library (wileyonlinelibrary.com) DOI: 10.1002/car.2422.

front of them, prevents their mother from taking them to other children's houses, or forbids contact with their grandparents.[225] So when children experience coercive control, those experiences become invisible to experts and the courts intended to protect them.[226] The AFCC has suggested that evaluators seek "information on multiple forms of intimate partner violence including physical, sexual, economic, psychological, and coercive controlling behaviors of adults and children as well as threats and actions based on immigration status."[227]

To detect and address coercive control and related forms of family violence, the first step is to locate it in an existing controversy, which typically focuses on child custody disputes. On a corollary path, there could also be an interplay with the criminal justice system, in which such behaviors are seen as criminal and therefore, prosecuted. There is much speculation surrounding the criminalization of coercive control and whether that would be effective in helping victims. Arguments exist that restorative justice is the better route and criminalizing coercive control could make incarceration rates increase. Moreover, prosecutors may additionally have difficulty proving something like coercive control in court, because it is not as visible as physical abuse. Despite all this, domestic violence is much more refined than many states' laws initially regarded.[228]

Coercive control is a problem of dire proportions where no age, class, race, religion, gender, or sexual orientation is immune. Recognizing coercive control as a form of domestic violence is long overdue. Fortunately, we are seeing a legislative movement by which many states begin to incorporate coercive control provisions into their statutory and legal guidelines. Bringing coercive control out of the shadows and into our laws is a critical step to protect victims from abusers who perpetrate their abusive behaviors.

---

225. *Id.*

226. *Id.*

227. Association of Family and Conciliation Courts, *supra* note 24.

228. Evan Stark & Marianne Hester, *Violence Against Women* 25(1) Coercive Control: Update and Review 81, https://journals.sagepub.com/doi/pdf/10.1177/1077801218816191.

Chapter 3

Child Psychological Maltreatment: An Attack on a Child's Basic Need Fulfillment

Psychological maltreatment (PM) of children is a silent epidemic. Researchers have found that PM has a "negative developmental impact of great breadth, magnitude, and longevity," and "may be the cause of the majority of human suffering which has occurred throughout history."[1] Although PM is widespread, harmful, and has both short-term and long-lasting consequences, it lacks a clear definition and is often misunderstood by family-court professionals and child protective services investigators. PM is under-recognized and under-addressed by professionals that interact with children, whether such interactions play out in child-custody litigation, juvenile and dependency proceedings, child protective services investigation, treatment interventions, or child welfare. A key component of PM is the attack by a caregiver or parent on a child's fundamental need for security, love, affection, and attachment. Viewed from this vantage point, "PM can be understood to derive its power from being an attack on basic need fulfillment."[2]

Definitions of PM

In the United States, "there is a lack of [a] single definition that is both comprehensive and sufficiently operationalized to allow for its consistent

1. Stuart N. Hart, Marla R. Brassard, Amy J.L. Baker & Zoe A. Chiel, *Psychological Maltreatment of Children*, *in* APSAC Handbook on Child Maltreatment 146 (J. Bart Klika & Jon R. Conte eds., 4th ed., 2017).

2. *Id.* at 155.

recognition and application."[3] Federal law defines "child abuse and neglect" to require "at a minimum, any recent act or failure to act on the part of a parent or caretaker, which results in death, serious physical or emotional harm, sexual abuse or exploitation, or an act or failure to act which presents an imminent risk of serious harm."[4] The states define child abuse and neglect but do not use a consistent legal definition of each type of child abuse, including PM. Without an agreed upon and comprehensive definition, it is difficult for child welfare professionals, child protective investigators, law enforcement agents, and family court professionals to fairly and consistently assess for and make determinations about PM. Without a clear understanding of what constitutes PM, parents and caregivers also cannot be clear about what conduct, behavior, actions, or omissions "cross the line" and could be classified as PM, in contrast to what could be seen as sub-optimal or deficient parenting.

There is also an overlap between PM and a psychiatric or medical diagnosis of child psychological abuse. The Diagnostic and Statistical Manual of Mental Disorders (DSM-5) defines Child Psychological Abuse as:

> Child psychological abuse is nonaccidental verbal or symbolic acts by a child's parent or caregiver that result, or have reasonable potential to result, in significant psychological harm to the child. (Physical and sexual abusive acts are not included in this category.) Examples of psychological abuse of a child include berating, disparaging, or humiliating the child; threatening the child; harming / abandoning—or indicating that the alleged offender will harm / abandon—people or things that the child cares about; confining the child (as by tying a child's arms or legs together or binding a child to furniture or another object, or confining a child to a small enclosed area [e.g., a closet]; egregious scapegoating of the child; coercing the child to inflict pain on himself or herself; and disciplining the child excessively (i.e., at an extremely high frequency or duration, even if not at a level of physical abuse) through physical or nonphysical means.[5]

---

3. Amy M. Smith Slep, Danya Glaser & Jody Todd Manly, *Psychological Maltreatment: An Operationalized Definition and Path Toward Application*, Child Abuse & Neglect 134 (2022) Article 105882 (citing Amy J. Baker et al., *Psychological Maltreatment: Definition and Reporting Barriers Among American Professionals in the Field of Child Abuse*, Child Abuse & Neglect, 114, (2021) Article 104941).

4. 42 U.S.C. §§ 5116 *et seq.* (CAPTA, 2010); *see also* 45 C.F.R. § 1340.

5. Diagnostic and Statistical Manual of Mental Disorders (DSM-5) 719 (5th ed. 2013).

In searching for a clear and comprehensive definition of PM, the work done by the American Professional Society on the Abuse of Children (APSAC) appears to be foundational. While others have attempted to build upon the work done by APSAC, the organization's definition of PM remains a critical foundational tool. APSAC defines PM as:

> A repeated pattern or extreme incident(s) of caregiver behavior that thwart[s] the child's basic psychological needs (e.g., safety, socialization, emotional and social support, cognitive stimulation, and respect) and convey[s] a child is worthless, defective, damaged goods, unloved, unwanted, endangered, primarily useful in meeting another's needs, and/or expendable.[6]

APSAC's definition of PM appears to focus on the specific types of caregiver behavior that are likely to harm or have harmed a child.[7] Common examples of such impact or harm include "emotional harm," "serious harm," "emotional abuse," "mental injury," and "severe anxiety, depression, withdrawal."[8]

However, the APSAC researchers point out that "impaired child functioning can result from factors other than maltreatment."[9] Accordingly, they prefer to define PM according to "specific types of caregiver behavior."[10] Also, mental health professionals "prefer the term *psychological* to *emotional*, because it is more comprehensive, incorporating the cognitive, affective, volitional, and interpersonal aspects of perpetration and outcomes."[11] And they are careful to note that "PM includes acts of commission (e.g., threats by a parent or caregiver toward a child) and acts of omission (e.g., repeatedly ignoring a child's bids for attention)."[12]

Recently, some researchers have attempted to build on the APSAC's definition of PM. They have noted the APSAC-endorsed definition of PM as a critical foundational tool, but have sought to provide a different and overarching definition of PM. In their definition, PM "refers to caregiver behaviors towards or involving a child (excluding physical / sexual abuse and physical neglect) which cause or have a strong potential to cause serious

---

6. Hart et al., *supra* note 1, at 147.
7. *Id.* at 146.
8. *Id.*
9. *Id.*
10. *Id.* at 146–47.
11. *Id.* at 147 (emphasis in original).
12. *Id.*

harm to a child's emotional, cognitive, social, interpersonal, or physical well-being or development."[13] In their approach, these researchers determined that PM could reflect a single caregiver act or omission or could reflect repeated caregiver behaviors.[14] In differentiating their overarching definition of PM from the APSAC-endorsed model, these researchers chose to list examples of caregiver behaviors that might constitute PM, but specify that behaviors not listed therein might also meet the definition. Why? For two reasons: "First, humans are creative. We cannot be certain that any list of actual or potential examples sensitively captures every single way in which a caregiver might psychologically maltreat a child." Second, the definition "is written and formatted to aid consistent decision making in real-world settings. In those settings, it is neither necessary, expedient, nor desirable to note every act a caregiver engaged in that is a distinct act of PM."[15]

In contrast to the APSAC-endorsed model of PM, these researchers have also differentiated their definition of PM by not requiring a pattern of behavior. "If one requires a pattern in the definition, then the definition excludes rare but extreme examples of isolated incidents."[16] For example, researchers provide an example where an absent parent appears one night to force a young child to watch a beloved pet be hurt or killed while being told it is what they deserve for ruining the parent's life. Even if that is the only contact with that parent, it would be wrong to say that such isolated incident did not constitute PM because it happened once.[17] This definition of PM would include isolated incidents of a caregiver's actions or omissions if such behavior resulted in a demonstrable impact to the child.

In common practice, PM is understood to reflect a repeated pattern of behavior, and most professionals try to look for a pattern of behavior rather than isolated instances of acts or omissions. As one team of expert-researchers who collected narratives of horrific incidents of emotional childhood abuse and neglect for their qualitative research, opined: "What differentiates poor parenting from emotional abuse is the frequency and severity of the behaviors and the overall quality of the relationship."[18]

---

13. Smith Slep et al., *supra* note 3, at 3.
14. *Id.*
15. *Id.* at 6.
16. *Id.*
17. *Id.*
18. Amy J.L. Baker & Mel Schneiderman, Bonded to the Abuser—How Victims Make Sense of Childhood Abuse 71 (2015).

Characteristics of Perpetrators of PM

Caregivers or parents who have engaged in PM could possibly have undiagnosed personality disorders or could have been victims of childhood exposure to intimate partner violence or other forms of abuse. "The common thread appears to be the parent's inability or unwillingness to factor in the needs and experiences of the child."[19] These caregivers appear to lack empathy, are highly self-absorbed, and fail to be responsive to the basic needs of a child who is dependent on them for survival. "There was usually something more important to the emotionally abusive parent than accommodating the unique needs and experiences of the child."[20] It is important to note it is not necessary that these caregivers or parents are *always* inattentive or unloving; rather, what is pertinent for determination of PM is that "they are unable to consistently take into account that their children are separate individuals with legitimate, independent experiences of their own, and then modify their behavior accordingly."[21]

Underlying that unwillingness or inability of such a caregiver could be any number of factors "such as mental illness, cultural beliefs, religious beliefs, unrealistic expectations of children's capabilities, stress, lack of parenting knowledge, and addictions."[22] Some caregivers whose acts or omissions could be determined to constitute PM fit within the category of a "traumatizing narcissist."[23] Such caregivers will go to great lengths to preserve their dominance by suppressing the validity of the subjective experience of the child. "These parents only feel wholly alive and loved when their point of view is accepted as the only valid experience and perception."[24] As such, the child, rather than seen as an individual, a person in his or her own regard, is viewed "as a gratifying object."[25]

Traumatizing narcissist caregivers may have these common characteristics: (1) Having being subjected to such treatment as children themselves, (2) they are "obsessed with maintaining a rigid sense of omnipotent superiority and perfection"; (3) they avoid feelings of "self-loathing that

19. *Id.* at 78.
20. *Id.* at 83.
21. *Id.* at 78–83.
22. *Id.* at 83.
23. *Id.* at 95.
24. *Id.*
25. *Id.*

accompanies" their condition and (4) instead they project "unwanted and disavowed aspects" of themselves, "especially the shameful sense of neediness and inferiority" onto their children; and (5) they suppress "any expression of neediness on the part of the child," which they see as "selfish and unacceptable."[26]

Various Forms of PM

Enmeshment

In a healthy parent-child relationship, the parent encourages, enables, and facilitates the child toward adulthood and autonomy. While the parent-child relationship is close and nurturing, there is a distinct sense of boundaries and separate identities. In this normative, healthy relationship, the parent and the child go about building, adapting, and recreating relational and psychological boundaries. An emotionally secure parent's job "is to gradually launch his or her child toward autonomy," and in a normative age-appropriate course of development, the child's sense of a bounded and separate identity grows from infancy toward adolescent rebellion, and thereafter into "the faux autonomy of young adulthood" to, finally, "marriage and parenting."[27] In this process, as the child ages and matures, the boundaries between the parent and the child are created, constantly tested, challenged, and redefined. The child's age-appropriate limit testing and the parent's gradually eroding rules and restrictions create a fluid dynamic where psychological and physical boundaries "are breached and then recreated a million times over."[28]

But the same pressures on the parent-child dyad that encourages a child's normative and healthy transition toward autonomy could end up impeding it. The pressures, which could lead to a healthy transition in one parent-child relationship could also result in a different outcome in another parent-child relationship. This could occur "when a parent turns to a child for need fulfillment."[29] In this scenario, a child's transition toward a secure

26. *Id.* at 96–97.

27. Benjamin D. Garber, *The Dynamics of the Enmeshed Family System Ten Years Later: Family Court and Contemporary Understanding of Adultification, Parentification, and Infantilization*, 34 J. Am. Acad. Matrimonial L. 97, 99–100 (2021).

28. *Id.* at 100–01.

29. *Id.*

and separate identity and eventual autonomy is impeded by an unhealthy dynamic, which is termed *enmeshment*, or by some, *pathological enmeshment*.

Enmeshment, therefore, occurs when a parent and a child form an unhealthy coalition, in an unnatural way that breaches "the separation between generations," and crosses the psychological boundaries that are so integral to a child's healthy development.[30] The result of such enmeshment is "role reversal" or "role corruption," where the child's role is detrimentally changed due to "a distressed parent [who] looks to the child to meet unmet needs for comfort, intimacy, or companionship."[31] This could result into a situation where the child, crossing the psychological and generational boundary, begins to provide for a parent's unhealthy emotional needs. According to Salvador Minuchin, whose work on Family Systems has been foundational in this field of psychology and social science, this kind of "highly enmeshed subsystem" between a parent and child directly undermines the child's independence by requiring the child to yield autonomy, leading to the development of pathological symptoms and an inhibition of the child's cognitive-affective skills.[32]

Enmeshed parent-child relationships are frequently observed in the presence of "distorted systemic pressures," for instance, amongst poverty; within immigrant families; with physically or mentally ill, addicted, and/or incarcerated parents; and in the context of family dynamics that include intimate partner violence and high-conflict divorce.[33]

Effective treatment interventions for enmeshment must involve both parents as well as the child, and the enmeshed parent must establish "alternate, healthier resources so as to free the child of his or her instrumental and/or emotional burden."[34] At the same time, the non-enmeshed parent will need education and support as he or she "may have acted to or around the child in a manner that adds to estrangement to the resist/refuse recipe."[35]

Enmeshment dynamics typically present itself in three forms: parentification, adultification, and infantilization.[36]

30. Salvador Minuchin, Families and Family Therapy 54 (1974).
31. Garber, *supra* note 27, at 101.
32. Minuchin, *supra* note 30, at 55.
33. Garber, *supra* note 27, at 101.
34. *Id.* at 116.
35. *Id.* at 118.
36. *Id.* at 102.

Parentification

Parentification has been variously defined in social sciences literature. This unhealthy enmeshed family dynamic has been described as "a child's premature promotion to serve as his or her siblings' caregiver."[37] It has also been defined as "a genuine role reversal," where children offer comfort and support to a parent because of a parent's reliance on their children.[38] Parentification could vary depending on a child's age, with older children sometimes taking on parenting roles, comforting younger siblings (or a parent) or listening to adult problems and attempting to resolve them. This dynamic could present itself during post-separation or post-divorce situation where one or both parents vent negatively about the other parent and burden the child with adult problems, which could lead to a child being parentified and caught in a loyalty bind.

Parentification of a child poses a risk to the child's cognitive, emotional, and mental well-being. Because "parentified children minimize their own need to be nurtured," they "may develop significant relationship problems as adults," including co-dependency and overly self-sacrificing.[39] Other harmful impacts of this dynamic on a child include anxiety, loss of sleep, obsessive thoughts, obsession toward perfectionism, over-extension, and depression.[40]

Parentification has been classified into two kinds: instrumental and emotional. Instrumental parentification describes a more benign dynamic at work when a child serves the practical, mechanical, or ministerial needs of the parent. For instance, a child taking care of a disabled parent, or a bilingual child assisting a monolingual parent with communicating in a language that the parent lacks fluency in. Instrumental parentification is generally seen as not being harmful to the child, the reason being that the child who is "instrumental" does not lose the emotional support of their parent. The child continues to feel emotionally secure, and the appropriate psychological and generational boundaries continue to be in place in the parent-child relationship. Instrumental parentification can actually "build resilience, enhance problem solving abilities, and diminish the risk of substance abuse."[41] Such

37. *Id.* at 105.
38. *Id.* at 106.
39. *Id.*
40. *Id.*
41. *Id.* at 109.

family dynamic is often observed in children of recent immigrants, who serve as "culture brokers" for their parents.[42] Instrumental parentification is also commonly seen with impoverished families, working parents, parents with diagnosed pathology, parents who have substance dependency, and homeless families.[43]

In contrast, emotional parentification refers to a situation where a parent relies on a child for emotional support and nurturance.[44] Emotional parentification can have a significant negative impact on a child's well-being. Examples of emotional parentification include: a child who adopts the role of her father's caregiver, making certain that he takes his medications and checking on him throughout the night; a child who is forced to take care of a parent or a younger siblings due to the parent's drug addiction or substance abuse; a child who is compelled to run and manage the household, fend for herself and her younger siblings due to the intermittent presence of a parent or parents in her life, either due to the parent(s)' incarceration or hospitalizations due to drug overdoses or other reasons.[45]

Emotional parentification could also be observed in children who may have been caught in a loyalty conflict, aligning with one parent and against the other in a post-separation or post-divorce scenario. A parent who may have engaged in boundary violations may have "developed and fostered a pathological enmeshment" with the child in such manner that the child has been encouraged to emotionally align with one parent and reject the other parent.[46] Examples of emotionally parentifying parents engaged in needy behaviors are found in children's statements such as, "she phoned from airports, dinner parties, and the lobbies of movie theaters in which she stood weeping over a love story. She needed me, she said, to calm her down."[47] Treatment interventions for emotionally parentified children must include attention to the anxiety the child may feel when they are divested of their parenting role.[48]

42. *Id.*

43. *Id.* at 107.

44. *Id.* at 108–09.

45. *Id.* at 109.

46. *Id.* at 115, n.78.

47. Baker & Schneiderman, *supra* note 18, at 88.

48. Garber, *supra* note 27, at 117.

Adultification

Adultification involves a parent or caregiver sharing inappropriate information with a child and burdening a child with practical or emotional knowledge or responsibilities, which the child is not prepared, cognitively, emotionally, or mentally, to bear.[49] Whether such adultifying behavior arises out of practical necessity, as when a military parent is deployed, or as a result of social, ethnic, or religious isolation or as a "by-product of a psychologically disturbed adult's inappropriate emotional investment in her child," the impact is the same: It "deprives a child of the opportunity to remain a child, undermining his security."[50]

Like the parentification dynamic, some adultification could be relatively healthy, particularly if it is temporary, and the child is "given adequate support and acknowledged for their helpfulness."[51]

To determine whether adultification exists as a family dynamic, an evaluator would have to consider several factors, which could include age of the child, onset of behavior that demonstrates adultification, birth order of siblings, how the sibling group functions, cultural issues present within the nuclear and extended family, history and nature of co-parental conflict, and the child's exposure to such conflict.[52]

Adultification dynamic, where the parent and the child appear to be bonded in a very close, "friendly" relationship, could be challenging to assess, particularly from a superficial level. An adultified child may come across as highly intelligent, mature, and confident, and "may bask in the enmeshed parent's special attention and may even develop precocious social skills."[53] As one adultified child recalled hearing from their mother: "The other girls in your dorm can't stand you because you're so gorgeous. You should see the way they look at you. They want to kill you. But you're lucky. You have me. Mummy will always be your friend. I'm your best friend."[54] But this comes at a cost of "increased risks of social and emotional dysfunction," and a long-term risk of drug and alcohol abuse and addiction.[55]

---

49. *Id.* at 103.
50. *Id.*
51. *Id.* at 103–04.
52. *Id.* at 104.
53. *Id.*
54. Baker & Schneiderman, *supra* note 18, at 90.
55. Garber, *supra* note 27, at 105.

Treatment interventions for adultified children must include attention to the anxiety a child may feel when they are demoted and divested of their adult role.[56]

Infantilization

Infantilization occurs when a parent acts to inhibit a child's otherwise age-appropriate and culturally appropriate movement toward autonomy, and is associated with commonly used terms such as "helicopter parent" and "overparenting."[57] A child who has been infantilized "never learns how to tolerate frustration, delay gratification, or manage adversity. He is the ruler of his own private kingdom at home [but] out of place, rejected, and bullied in any environment that expects age-appropriate prosocial behavior."[58]

"Infantilizing parents are often described as inclined to anxiety and perfectionism."[59] Research has found that children of infantilizing fathers have greater difficulty with emotional functioning by young adulthood, whereas the children of infantilizing mothers tend to have more difficulty with social functioning.[60] Overall, infantilized children have been found to be academic and occupational underachievers, anxious or depressed, with a sense of entitlement, demonstrating weaker empathy, lower perceived self-efficacy in young adulthood, and a higher risk of substance abuse.[61]

Infantilization is classified in four types: adaptive, permissive, opportunistic, and as a factitious disorder imposed on another (FDIA).[62] Adaptive infantilization is transitory, and is described as a "child who may otherwise appear to be developmentally appropriate falls back into a regressed and needy state in the care of a parent who needs to be needed and recovers his or her more appropriate functioning in other caregiving environments."[63]

Permissive infantilization involves "a parent who cannot or will not set behavioral limits and follow through with associated consequences."[64] Opportunistic infantilization occurs "when a parent tacitly enjoys the social,

---

56. *Id.* at 117.
57. *Id.* at 110.
58. *Id.* at 110–11.
59. *Id.* at 111.
60. *Id.*
61. *Id.* at 111–12.
62. *Id.* at 113.
63. *Id.*
64. *Id.*

emotional, and practical benefits accrued as a result of her child's genuine illness, injury, and/or developmental difference."[65]

The last, infantilization, FDIA, arises when "a parent induces an illness, injury, or developmental difference in a child so as to benefit from the resulting professional attention."[66]

Treatment of infantilization depends on the sub-type, and ranges from coaching and scripting (adaptive infantilization) to psychotherapy, medication, or rehabilitation (permissive infantilization) to continuing oversight and intervention in severe cases, including cases involving FDIA.

Enmeshment Dynamics and Child Custody Litigation

High-conflict child custody litigation, where a child has been exposed to the family violence dynamics, including intimate partner violence and severe parental alienating behaviors, may present evidence of an enmeshed parent-child relationship. A child could be caught in a loyalty bind as a coping mechanism where the child has attempted to align with the parent that he or she perceives to be the victim of family violence. On the other hand, enmeshment dynamics could also be present where one parent has engaged in parentification or adultification of the child, to get the child to align with himself or herself and turn the child against the other parent. When enmeshment dynamics are present together with evidence of parental alienating behaviors, it can seriously interfere with a child's relationship with the non-alienating, target parent.[67] In such scenarios, the alienating parent creates and maintains a "perverse triangle," by "exploiting/corrupting," "isolating," and "terrorizing" the child.[68]

A parent who attempts to entice a child into aligning against the other parent often sends direct or indirect messages such as "(1) I am the only parent who loves you and you need me to feel good about yourself, (2) the other parent is dangerous and unavailable, and (3) pursuing a relationship with that parent jeopardizes your relationship with me."[69]

---

65. *Id.*

66. *Id.*

67. MINUCHIN, *supra* note 30, at 30.

68. Edward Kruk, *Parental Alienation as a Form of Emotional Child Abuse: Current State of Knowledge and Future Directions for Research*, 22(4) FAM. SCI. REV. 141–64 (2018).

69. Amy J.L. Baker & Paul R. Fine, *Educating Divorcing Parents: Taking Them Beyond the High Road, in* WORKING WITH ALIENATED CHILDREN AND FAMILIES: A CLINICAL GUIDEBOOK 90–107 (Amy J.L. Baker & S. Richard Sauber eds., 2013).

The result of being exposed to such behavior is that the child will "join or be enlisted by one parent against the other,"[70] and develop both loyalty conflicts and become enmeshed.[71] For example, a parentified child may be "expected to satisfy the [alienating] parent's emotional needs," coinciding with a divorce or separation.[72] And this could begin at a young age. In a Michigan case, *Krieg v. Baleja*,[73] by the time a child of divorce turned five, he was parroting negative statements about the father, the father's new partner, and the child's half-sister.[74] "The child also reported falsehoods . . . such as that [the father] had smacked down the door . . . and . . . kicked [the mother] out of his home."[75] When asked where he learned of these things, the child reported his mother told him.[76] The mother also reportedly sought "evidence" that the father was not feeding the child properly and tried to use the father's social media history to "prove" the father "was neglecting the child or using the Internet while driving."[77] Psychological evaluations determined both the mother's "alienating conduct and that . . . she was dependent on the child for her own nurturing, referred to as enmeshment."[78]

In upholding the change of primary custody from the mother to the father, the Michigan Court of Appeals agreed that "enmeshment . . . was usually unhealthy,"[79] and approved the lower court's best interest factors analysis; this included that the mother displayed no "recognition [that] some of the statements that would have been made could be considered parental alienation and enmeshment," and that she "has a diminished ability to co-parent, has issues around paranoia, and is manipulative."[80]

Once enmeshed, the "child willingly cooperates in attempting to meet the [enmeshed] parent's needs" by taking that parent's "side" in the custody "war" with the target parent.[81] Consider a chilling description of an

---

70. Minuchin, *supra* note 30, at 30.

71. Ivan Boszormenyi-Nagy & Geraldine M. Spark, Invisible Loyalties 278–79 (1984).

72. *Id.* at 278.

73. Krieg v. Baleja, No. 359264, 2022 WL 12072124 (Mich. Ct. App. Oct. 20, 2022).

74. *Id.* at *2.

75. *Id.*

76. *Id.*

77. *Id.*

78. *Id.*

79. *Id.*

80. *Id.* at *5.

81. Boszormenyi-Nagy & Spark, *supra* note 71, at 279.

enmeshed mother-daughter relationship described by a team of researchers, where they describe an adult's recollection of her experience as a childhood victim of her mother's enmeshment:

> "I cannot wait to make my mother happy."
>
> Her mother, however, was not happy. In fact, after one such evening she entered the room with a shotgun in hand. "She looks at me with her tear-streaked, puffy face. She holds me with her eyes, terrified like an animal in a chute, and raises her hand to cock the trigger. . . ."
>
> "You kids want me to kill myself, don't you?". . . I'm crying for her, telling her no we don't hate you, no, Mommy, we love you and we don't want you to kill yourself. . . . She drops the gun to her lap, her chin collapses to her chest. I cling around her like a baby monkey.
>
> Appeased, [the] mother confided in [the child] about the horrors of her childhood gang rape and then asked, "Isn't your father a no-good son of a bitch for turning you kids against me?"[82]

In the Maryland custody dispute case *Reichert v. Hornbeck*,[83] the court affirmed granting sole legal and physical custody of a ten-year-old child to the mother who had previously had her custody seriously curtailed due to substance abuse because of the father's alienation and adultification of the child.[84] The father refused to produce the child for visitation, to the point that he was jailed for contempt.[85] The child reported his father "shared some of the things that were going on in court with his mother," and the child "referred to [the] mother as a psychopath," and said "everything she does annoys me."[86] The trial court concluded the child was "coached. His relationship is very damaged with his mother [and] it is in [the child's] best interest to have one opportunity alone with his mother and without his father."[87] The court was also very influenced by the adultification, noting it was "clear to the Court that Dad had explained, in detail, everything that went on yesterday."[88] In affirming, the appellate court quoted from the custody evaluator who testified: "[The father] has engaged in adultification of [the child] distorting the boundaries of the parent-child relationship by

---

82. Baker & Schneiderman, *supra* note 18, at 64.
83. Reichert v. Hornbeck, No. 1370, 2023 WL 3773369 (Md. Ct. App. June 2, 2023).
84. *Id.* at *1.
85. *Id.* at *2.
86. *Id.*
87. *Id.*
88. *Id.*

discussing age-inappropriate information with him in talking about the custody proceedings. He has placed [the child] in the role of an ally in the battle against [the child's] own mother."[89]

Even absent an alignment between the child and a parent, the presence of enmeshment dynamics can result in a change of custody due to its unhealthy impact on the child. In the North Dakota custody dispute case *Mayo v. Mayo*,[90] the state supreme court affirmed a change in custody of three children from the mother to the father, due to the mother's parentification of the parties' oldest child.[91] The mother suffered from ailments that forced her to "lie down at least once a month while the oldest child would care for the two younger children." The situation resulted in the oldest child describing herself as the "second mom" to the youngest.[92] At the evidentiary hearing to determine custody, the psychological evaluator testified to the "significant psychological harm," the oldest child was likely to endure, including "difficulty forming bonds with others in adulthood, as well as other psychological problems."[93] The court found that the "the simplest way to alleviate the parentification problem would be to change custody."[94]

In the Texas custody dispute case *Spence v. Davis*,[95] the father was awarded exclusive decision-making rights over the child, as well as greater time of possession, in part due to the mother's infantilization of the child.[96] In affirming the modification, discussing the infantilization and the standard for modification, the court noted "circumstances that are age-appropriate for a three-year old could be inappropriate for a six-year old and could constitute a materially and substantially changed circumstance."[97] The mother's infantilization included continuing to breastfeed the child, which may have contributed to his "difficult transition to kindergarten," and also sent "a message that the child is not safe to explore outside the mother-child relationship."[98] Other infantilizing behaviors by the mother included keeping "the child in a

89. *Id.* at *6.

90. Mayo v. Mayo, 2000 ND 204.

91. *Id.* at ¶ 1.

92. *Id.* at ¶ 4.

93. *Id.* at ¶ 7.

94. *Id.*

95. Spence v. Davis, No. 03-22-00178-CV, 2023 WL 427063 (Tex. Ct. App. Jan. 27, 2023).

96. *Id.* at *14, 18.

97. *Id.* at *8.

98. *Id.* at *9.

diaper many months after he was toilet-trained . . . in a crib for an extensive period . . . and support[ing] the child in continuing to suck his thumb and in other ways act and behave younger than his years."[99]

And in Missouri a mother had her parental rights terminated, in part, due to her FDIA.[100] In *Interest of S.R.H.*, the mother who had already lost custody of her other children was found to have engaged in "repeated medical abuse of Child."[101] This included "numerous unnecessary exams and treatments," and "transport[ing] Child in a wheelchair despite multiple medical providers not having observed a requirement for one."[102] She also gave the child medications, including Prozac and Risperidone, which she obtained from Mexico, even though "it was determined that [the] Child . . . did not require any of these medications."[103] The appellate court affirmed the termination.[104]

Spurning

Spurning is defined as "verbal and nonverbal caregiver acts that reject and degrade a child," and includes "belittling, degrading and other nonphysical forms of hostile or rejecting treatment," of the child as well as "those in significant relationships with the child such as parents, siblings, and extended kin."[105] As described in the memoir, *Lies My Mother Never Told Me*, a daughter recalls her mother telling her: "You're a mean, spoiled, and ugly girl. You bore me to death [and] I can't wait for you to grow up. You have ugly legs, not like me. I was much prettier than you when I was your age."[106] Another victim of childhood emotional abuse recalled her mother telling her: "You were pretty ugly. I was always so embarrassed when people would look at you."[107] And a third recalled hearing her mother tell her: "The Devil led us to the wrong crib."[108]

---

99. *Id.*
100. Interest of S.R.H., 589 S.W.3d 62 (Mo. Ct. App. 2019).
101. *Id.* at 70.
102. *Id.*
103. *Id.* at 69.
104. *Id.* at 66.
105. Hart et al., *supra* note 1, at 147.
106. Baker & Schneiderman, *supra* note 18, at 74.
107. *Id.* at 75.
108. *Id.*

In recounting such stories of emotional abuse, which included spurning as a form of abuse, a team of researchers provide a narrative by Rachel Sontag, who recalled her father's abusive actions:

> He would hand her a piece of paper and insist that she take dictation as he tossed out insults at her. He would throw out words such as selfish, rotten, and worthless and insist that she write them down in full sentences about herself and submit her paper for his inspection. During one of these sessions, he wanted her to write that she was the scum of the earth, like a snake, and then he threatened to kick her out of the house.
>
> Rachel's mother was often involved in these sessions as well, being commanded by her father to join him, to own his opinions as her own. "Say it Ellen. You are ashamed that she's your daughter. She can't just hear it from me."
>
> At his most cruel, he informed Rachel that he wished she had never been born.[109]

The tactics of spurning also include "shaming and/or ridiculing the child" for "showing the normal emotions of affection, grief, anger, or sorrow."[110] As one abused child recalled when she was sick and in pain and asking for medicine, her mother coldly told her "you're so neurotic."[111] Another was mocked and taunted: "Are you going to cry for us, Rachel? Are you putting on a little show?"[112]

Other forms of spurning include humiliating the child, particularly in public, "consistently singling out one child to criticize . . . punish, to perform most of the household chores, or to receive fewer rewards,"[113] and it often accompanies physical or sexual abuse or neglect, "such as telling the child that he/she is dirty or damaged due to sexual abuse," or "telling the child that he/she deserves the abuse."[114] In the Alabama custody dispute case *Hepburn v. Hepburn*,[115] the appellate court affirmed transfer of physical custody of a son to his father due to the mother's spurning, which had also affected the other child, the daughter: "[T]he mother exhibited an obvious preference for the daughter over the son and that she considered the son a

---

109. *Id.* at 69–70.
110. Hart et al., *supra* note 1, at 147.
111. Baker & Schneiderman, *supra* note 18, at 76.
112. *Id.*
113. Hart et al., *supra* note 1, at 147.
114. *Id.*
115. Hepburn v. Hepburn, 659 So. 2d 653 (Ala. Civ. App. 1995).

'brat' . . . the mother had little concern for the physical well-being of the son and she demonstrated very little affection for him. . . . [A]s a result of the mother's favoring the daughter and her lack of concern for the son, the daughter, too, had begun to belittle and berate her younger brother," which "was tolerated by the mother."[116]

In another example, an abusive "father put [his daughter] in charge of holding everyone's passports and then he derided and humiliated her for holding them in her hands rather than placing them in her fanny pack. . . . Rather than offer a constructive suggestion, he sarcastically . . . mock[ed] her hubris for risking the family's life and vacation."[117] In another instance, a "mother made [the child] walk up and down the street and confess . . . to any neighbor whose house [she] ever entered," that the child had contracted lice.[118]

Terrorizing

Terrorizing has been defined as a "behavior that threatens or is likely to physically hurt, kill, abandon, or place the child or child's loved ones/objects in recognizably dangerous or frightening situations."[119] It includes conduct such as "subjecting a child to frightening or chaotic circumstances [and] recognizably dangerous situations," "threatening to abandon [or actually abandoning] the child," "setting rigid or unrealistic expectations with threat of loss, harm, or danger if they are not met," "placing the child in a loyalty conflict" with the other parent, and "threatening or perpetuating violence against the child [or their] loved ones or objects."[120]

In the Mississippi custody case, *Bolton v. Bolton*,[121] the custody of a son was switched from the mother in California to his father in Mississippi because the mother was threatening and terrorizing the child.[122] At the custody hearing, the son testified "he was afraid of [the mother who] . . . yell[ed] and curse[ed] at him every day [and] . . . often ha[d] 'fits.'"[123] And

116. *Id.* at 655.

117. Baker & Schneiderman, *supra* note 18, at 67.

118. *Id.* at 78.

119. *Id.* at 148.

120. *Id.*

121. Bolton v. Bolton, 63 So. 3d 600 (Miss. Ct. App. 2011).

122. *Id.* ¶ 20.

123. *Id.* ¶ 13.

although the mother "had not hit him, he was afraid that she would because she threaten[ed] to do so, and she ha[d] thrown a remote control at him."[124]

As one abused child recalled: "I was asleep for only an hour when my mother came into my room and ordered me to leave the apartment. She said I couldn't use the phone to call anyone and . . . if I wasn't out of the house in fifteen minutes, she would call the police and have them take me away."[125] Another was terrified of her mother, whose behavior was outrageous: "I was having a shower. . . . She . . . fully clothed, stepped in under the drenching hot water . . . began screaming accusations at me. . . . I remember thinking that maybe she had a knife and she was going to kill me."[126]

A third mother "attempted to kill herself in front of her children. . . . 'She was my mother and she was swinging from a yellow braided laundry rope right in front of our faces with her tongue turning blacker by the second.'"[127]

Examples of violence against children's loved ones or objects includes destroying "years of handwritten stories and poems," burning a child's books, and threatening to kill a pet.[128] In a Michigan case, *Brown v. Brown*,[129] the mother won sole legal and physical custody of the parties' five children given the father's abuse of the family's pets, which included throwing a dog against the wall, kneeing another, and shooting an airsoft at the cat.[130] In affirming the custody award, the appellate court explained: "Intentionally harming an animal with whom a child . . . has a significant emotional bond could constitute engaging in [behavior] toward a family or household member" that could cause the child to "feel terrorized, frightened, intimidated, threatened, harassed, or molested."[131]

Finally, terrorizing also includes "preventing a child from having access to needed food, light, water . . . toilet," and from "needed sleep, relaxing or resting."[132] In a Missouri case, *In re G.C.*,[133] a mother's parental rights were

---

124. *Id.*
125. Baker & Schneiderman, *supra* note 18, at 79.
126. *Id.*
127. *Id.* at 82.
128. *Id.* at 83.
129. Brown v. Brown, 955 N.W.2d 515 (Mich. Ct. App. 2020).
130. *Id.* at 522.
131. *Id.* at 523.
132. Hart et al., *supra* note 1, at 148.
133. *In re* G.C., 443 S.W.3d 738 (Mo. Ct. App. 2014).

terminated, in part, because she "withheld food as punishment such that the Children would go without food for seven-to-eight hours a day."[134] As another abused child recalled: "I'm winded. I'm hungry. It's two o'clock and I haven't eaten yet today. I was going to school without breakfast, not getting any lunch money. . . . I had to do all the farm work."[135]

Exploiting and Corrupting

With this form of psychological maltreatment, the caregiver "encourage[s] the child to develop inappropriate behaviors and attitudes (self-destructive, antisocial, criminal, deviant, or other maladaptive behaviors)."[136] Caregiver behaviors include encouraging wildly inappropriate (and usually illegal) behavior such as "prostitution, performance in pornographic media, criminal activities, substance abuse, violence to or corruption of others."[137] "This reflected a narcissistic need and/or sadistic pleasure to see the child suffer or be 'bad' as a way of having the child join them and be 'bad' like them."[138]

In the Arizona custody dispute *Dunlap v. Dunlap*,[139] the father was awarded only supervised visitation of his children because of his corrupting and sadistic behaviors.[140] "Father would allow the children to drink alcohol," and "would show horror movies to the children against their wishes. He was observed coming home from work and pretending to run down [Daughter] and [Son] with his truck."[141] In addition, he once "chased Daughter, Son and a neighbor's child with a running chainsaw (with the chain removed)," and he "would encourage his children to fight each other."[142]

In another example, a foster mother enlisted her birth daughter in her abusive treatment of her foster children, "whom she would berate, humiliate, frighten, and starve."[143] As the daughter described it: "Mom puts the

---

134. *Id.* at 747–48.

135. Baker & Schneiderman, *supra* note 18, at 64.

136. Hart et al., *supra* note 1, at 147.

137. *Id.* at 148.

138. Baker & Schneiderman, *supra* note 18, at 92.

139. Dunlap v. Dunlap, No. 1 CA-CV 09-0465, 2011 WL 2176540 (Ariz. Ct. App. May 31, 2011).

140. *Id.* ¶ 5.

141. *Id.*

142. *Id.* ¶ 13.

143. Baker & Schneiderman, *supra* note 18, at 64.

flyswatter in my hand and shows me how to do it. Grab their wrists and whack the hard plastic handle over their pink baby palms."[144] And when that daughter reached the age of 16, her mother "decided . . . Julie should meet an older man and leave home. She posed Julie suggestively in a series of snapshots that she carried around in her purse."[145]

Another mother routinely arranged liaisons for her daughter with, essentially, strangers, while yet another "purchased pornography for her daughter and then referred to her as 'my little pervert.'"[146] This same mother "taught her [daughter] how to administer painkillers intravenously" at the age of ten.[147] Another became explicit in her discussions of sex with her daughter once she reached puberty: "It was as if she had been waiting impatiently for this moment and now she was eager to share. . . . One day her mother decided to introduce her to 'something very special' . . . proudly displaying a dildo. . . . 'Would you like Mummy to teach you?'"[148]

Other forms of exploitation and corruption—"encouraging betraying the trust of or being cruel to another person . . . restricting or interfering with or directly undermining the child's important relationships," and "encouraging developmentally inappropriate behavior (e.g., parentification, adultification, infantilization, living the parent's dreams)"—also fit within this category.[149]

The exploiting and corrupting tactic of psychological maltreatment includes caregiver behavior that interferes with children's education and cognitive development. For example, one mother actively encouraged her child not to do her homework, saying watching movies "is more important. I promise. You'll thank me later."[150] Another drugged her daughter prior to her taking a school entrance exam, in order to lessen her chance of attending boarding school.[151] Another "forbade her [child] to have books in the home and kept her back from school for a year," while a fourth "routinely pulled [the child] from school for shopping trips," and a fifth just said "since

144. *Id.*
145. *Id.*
146. *Id.* at 87.
147. *Id.*
148. *Id.* at 88.
149. Hart et al., *supra* note 1, at 148.
150. Baker & Schneiderman, *supra* note 18, at 90.
151. *Id.*

no one seemed to care, we didn't have to go to school anymore."[152] Such behavior could result in a loss of custody, as in the New York case *Phillip UU. v. Amanda UU.*, where the mother lost custody to her parents (grandparents of the child).[153] In that case "the child had never completed a school year without being withdrawn early and, even when the child was going to school, the mother either took him out early or failed to send him at all."[154]

Exploiting and corrupting tactics also include "extreme over-involvement, intrusiveness, or dominance, allowing little or no opportunity or support for child's views, feelings and wishes," and "manipulation (e.g., inducing guilt, fostering anxiety, threatening withdrawal of love)."[155] As Rachel Sontag recalled in *House Rules*:

> [Her] father exercised a degree of control that was excessive and inappropriate, for example, locking the phone in a metal box when he left the house and insisting on an "outline of how I would use my 'unmonitored' time at the library." When she got older, her father measured the length of her fingernails, did not allow Rachel to make any phone calls, and had strict curfews. . .. [W]hen she lost her house keys he refused to let her in the home and left her in the cold for several hours.[156]

Likewise, the stereotypical, tyrannical "stage mother" also falls within this form of PM. Consider this description of the relationship between child actor Melissa Francis and her mother:

> Missy's success was more important to her mother than Missy's feelings. . . . Her standards were impossibly high and provoked rage when not met. . . . [Her mother said]: "I am so sick of both of you. I do everything I can to help you. I've devoted my entire life to you. . . . It kills me that neither of you appreciate everything I am always doing for you. . . ." In this way she induced guilt in her children. . . . [When] Missy's stint on *Little House on the Prairie* came to an end . . . her mother reacted like someone close to her had died . . . her mother lost interest in Melissa and sank into a depressive stupor, not even remembering to . . . pick her up from school.[157]

---

152. *Id.* at 91.

153. Phillip UU. v. Amanda UU., 105 N.Y.S.3d 568, 570 (N.Y. App. Div. 2019).

154. *Id.*

155. Hart et al., *supra* note 1, at 148.

156. Baker & Schneiderman, *supra* note 18, at 66–67.

157. *Id.* at 60–61.

Finally, caregiver-fabricated illness, formerly known as Munchausen by proxy, is also a form of exploitation/corruption.[158] In *Sickened*, Julie Gregory describes her harrowing ordeal:

> The state of Julie's health was a primary preoccupation for her mother, scheduling a never-ending series of medical appointments. . . . Her mother micromanaged Julie's healthcare "with the logistical vigor of a drill sergeant." Her mother seemed to come alive in the presence of doctors, soaking up their attention and interest. However, when a doctor failed to confirm a hoped-for diagnosis, Julie's mother stalked away furious, cursing and threatening to sue. . . . In front of the doctors, Julie's mother displayed concern, worry. . . . When the doctors weren't looking, her concern turned to anger and threats, digging her nails into Julie's thighs and hissing at her to show the doctors just how sick she was.[159]

Psychologically abused in other ways, when Julie's mother finally was able to get her checked into a hospital for tests, Julie recalled feeling happy: "It's like a vacation or going away to camp, which I've always wanted to do."[160]

Emotional Unresponsiveness

In this form of PM, the caregiver "ignore[s] the child's attempts and needs to interact . . . and [shows] little or no emotion in interactions with the child."[161] Behaviors include "being detached and uninvolved through either incapacity or lack of motivation," "interacting only when absolutely necessary," "failing to express warmth, affection, caring, and love for the child," and being inattentive to the child's needs to be safe.[162]

In affirming a Massachusetts determination of unfitness and dispensing with the need for her to consent to an adoption, the appellate court there noted the following in the mother's behavior toward her young daughter, including that even during supervised visits the mother "did not focus on [the daughter's] emotional needs. . . repeatedly brought other adults or children to visit . . . was once observed reading the newspaper instead of

---

158. Hart et al., *supra* note 1, at 148.
159. Baker & Schneiderman, *supra* note 18, at 62.
160. *Id.* at 64.
161. Hart et al., *supra* note 1, at 149.
162. *Id.*

interacting with [the daughter], even refusing the child's request that the mother read to her."[163] The court concluded "the mother did not show an ability to put [the daughter's] significant emotional needs ahead of her own."[164]

Isolating

"Isolating" has been defined as "consistently and unreasonably deny[ing] the child opportunities to meet needs for interacting/communicating with peers or adults."[165] Caregiver behaviors include "confining the child or placing unreasonable limitations on the child's freedom of movement within his/her environment," and "placing unreasonable limitations or restrictions on social interactions." Examples of children subjected to isolating include preventing participation in extracurricular activities and being isolated even from family members.[166] In *Matter of K.W.*, the father's appeal of a permanent dependency order was rejected, in part, because he used parental alienation techniques to isolate the child from social contacts, which led to academic delays.[167]

Mental Health, Medical, and Educational Neglect

A caregiver's failure to "provide the necessary treatment for the mental health, medical, and education problems or needs for the child" is a form of PM. Perpetrators of this form of PM may actively refuse to provide it or simply fail to "provide treatment for serious emotional/behavioral . . . serious physical health . . . [or] serious educational problems or needs of the child."[168] In the Vermont case *In re J.B.*, the father's appeal of a court finding of medical neglect was rejected.[169] The finding was based on the evidence that the child's condition was treatable; and that "the success of a treatment plan depends heavily on a parent's consistent involvement, insight, cooperation, and encouragement in the care."[170] The father not only failed

163. Adoption of Karla, 703 N.E.2d 729, 733 (Mass. App. 1998).

164. *Id.*

165. Hart et al., *supra* note 1, at 149.

166. Baker & Schneiderman, *supra* note 18, at 84.

167. Matter of K.W., 2018-Ohio-1933, ¶ 4 (App. 2018).

168. Hart et al., *supra* note 1, at 149.

169. *In re* J.B., No. 2009-004, 2009 WL 2411937 (Vt. Apr. 16, 2009).

170. *Id.* at *1.

to do this, but refused to hospitalize the child as prescribed by his treating physician, refused to meet with a specialist, and refused to take the child to follow-up visits.[171] As the appellate court concluded, the "father's chronic failure to cooperate with either medical providers or the necessary treatment plan combined to unnecessarily prolong J.B.'s medical and emotional suffering."[172]

Likewise, in the Ohio case *Matter of K.W.*, the child was declared permanently dependent, from the father's isolation of the child, which resulted in a "lack of medical care."[173]

As for educational neglect, in *Ferguson v. Wilke*, a Missouri mother's loss of primary custody of her child was affirmed.[174] For religious reasons, the mother and the child's stepfather chose to homeschool the child and his five stepbrothers through "a course of instruction for their children," and relying at least in part on curriculum and materials that were not state approved.[175] The mother had a high school diploma as well as some college courses, and the stepfather had an associate's degree.[176] After the child was temporarily transferred to his father, it was determined that "[the child] was educationally behind the children at his grade level," and he even "crawled under the table" on his first day of public school "because he was not used to being around large groups of children."[177] In affirming the custody transfer, the court noted "the minor child . . . was and had been for several months . . . educationally neglected by the mother in that virtually no education was being provided for the child by any means."[178]

Impact and Consequences of Maltreatment

PM has been shown to result in short-term and long-lasting harm to children. The psychological or emotional nature of the maltreatment or abusive behavior does not render it less harmful than physical maltreatment or abuse. Research on brain functioning demonstrates that the pain caused

171. *Id.*
172. *Id.* at *2.
173. Matter of K.W., 2018-Ohio-1933, ¶ 4 (App. 2018).
174. Ferguson v. Wilke, 713 S.W.2d 611 (Mo. Ct. App. 1986).
175. *Id.* at 612.
176. *Id.*
177. *Id.* at 613.
178. *Id.*

from psychological wounds activates the same regions of the brain as pain caused from physical wounds.[179]

Several factors determine the impact of PM on any child, including their age, developmental period, genetic sensitivity, the environment in which they live and even "caring and competent teachers" and "strong learning ability."[180] That said, there is a "well-established dose response relationship between each of the forms of maltreatment (more severe, more frequent, longer duration) and adverse outcomes."[181]

Child emotional abuse is causally related to depressive disorders, anxiety disorders, suicide attempts, drug use, and sexually transmitted diseases or sexually risky behavior.[182] In fact, such victims are at nearly twice the "risk for adverse mental health outcomes."[183]

While an abusive parent's rejection of a psychologically maltreated child stirs a desire in the child for the parent to find her worthy, ultimately "at some point some victims of emotional abuse detach themselves from their emotionally abusive parents as a defense against the pain of rejection."[184]

Types of Impact

Broadly speaking, there are five types of impact, as described in the following subsections.

Intrapersonal

Intrapersonal problems, that is, "within the individual thoughts, feelings, and behaviors such as anxiety, depression, negative self-concept, and negative cognitive styles,"[185] includes "depression and suicidal thoughts and behaviors (e.g., pessimism, self-criticism, catastrophic thinking, immature defenses)."[186]

"Children who more often than not received the message 'how dare you be something other than what I want you to be' responded by feeling that

179. Baker & Schneiderman, *supra* note 18, at 92.
180. Hart et al., *supra* note 1, at 150.
181. *Id.* at 152.
182. *Id.* at 150.
183. *Id.*
184. Baker & Schneiderman, *supra* note 18, at 93–94.
185. Hart et al., *supra* note 1, at 151.
186. *Id.*

there was something fundamentally unacceptable about who they are."[187] Likewise, those who "are called names, put down, ridiculed, and shamed come to the same conclusion: that there is something inherently undesirable about them."[188]

In essence, abused children will turn themselves inside out to become what their parents want them to be to be accepted and loved. But in being loved for who the parent wants him to be, the child experiences a profound sense of not being loved for who he truly is.[189]

Emotional

Emotional problems and symptoms associated with PM include "substance abuse and eating disorders, emotional instability, impulse control problems, borderline personality disorder, and more impaired functioning among those diagnosed with bipolar disorder."[190] Others develop dissociative behaviors:

> As a teenager she developed an interest in theater. . . . She often found herself reverting to one of her characters in her mind in order to protect herself from her father's onslaughts and humiliations, to help her be physically present in the room with him without being fully emotionally present. It was as if her character were being humiliated and berated rather than her. . . . Many of the sessions ended with a final judgment against her. . . "I'm ashamed to say you're my daughter, disgusted and ashamed."[191]

Social

PM could result in a child developing "social competency problems and anti-social functioning," which could include "social phobia, impaired social competency, lack of empathy for others, attachment insecurity/disorganization, self-isolating behavior, non-compliance, extreme dependency, sexual maladjustment, aggressive and violent behavior, and delinquency or criminality."[192]

---

187. Baker & Schneiderman, *supra* note 18, at 92.
188. *Id.* at 93.
189. *Id.* at 96.
190. Hart et al., *supra* note 1, at 151.
191. Baker & Schneiderman, *supra* note 18, at 68–69.
192. Hart et al., *supra* note 1, at 151.

"If the consistent parental message is 'I am going to do what I please regardless of how frightening it is for you' . . . then the child's response was to feel unsafe and unprotected."[193]

On this topic, "[w]itnessing family violence and emotional maltreatment in childhood were significantly related to mothers' observed hostility toward their children."[194]

Educational

Children who are exposed to caregivers' PM may develop learning problems, which include behavioral problems in academic settings. This could result in "impaired learning despite adequate ability and instruction, academic problems and lower achievement test results, decline in IQ over time, lower measured intelligence, school problems due to non-compliance and lack of impulse control, and impaired moral reasoning."[195] Notably, "children with a psychologically unavailable caregiver or one who was hostile/verbally aggressive had more teacher/caregiver reported psychopathological behavior than other high-risk controls."[196]

Physical

Research demonstrates that children who are subjected to PM suffer significant physical and biological problems, which include "delays in almost all areas of physical and behavioral development; allergies, asthma, headaches, sleep complaints, and other respiratory ailments . . . [and] lifestyle risk behaviors in adolescence, including tobacco smoking and risky sexual behavior."[197] In addition, "deviant brain and hormonal functioning have been tied to children experiencing severe forms of PM."[198]

Severity Considerations

Severity of PM is measured by considering: "(a) the intensity, extremeness, frequency, and chronicity of the caregiver PM behavior; (b) number of PM subtypes and other forms of maltreatment the child is experiencing;

---

193. Baker & Schneiderman, *supra* note 18, at 94.
194. Hart et al., *supra* note 1, at 151.
195. *Id.* at 151–52.
196. *Id.* at 152.
197. *Id.*
198. *Id.*

(c) degree to which the caregiver/perpetrator-child relationship is pervaded by PM; (d) salience of the type(s) of PM for the developmental period(s) in which it occurs and the developmental periods that will follow; (e) extent to which harm to the child has occurred, is developing, or is likely; (f) influences that may mitigate the consequences of PM . . . and (g) the willingness and capacity of the caregiver to abandon PM behaviors and improve his or her parenting."[199]

Developmental Considerations

Research suggests that certain forms of PM are more harmful at some ages than others.[200] "Spurning and terrorizing separately and in combination . . . are particularly damaging in the first two years of life through middle childhood."[201] These two "are uniquely related to both internalizing disorders (anxiety disorders, particularly social phobia, depression, suicidal behavior) and externalizing disorders (conduct problems, delinquency as well as personality disorders)."[202] When spurning and terrorizing are "pervasive," this "constitute[s] toxic stress," which is a "significant threat to healthy development."[203]

Moreover, "[e]motional unresponsiveness . . . is particularly devastating from birth through 5 years of age and then again in adolescence," and it "is related to dramatic drops in IQ, language delays, attachment disorders, and early onset of both internalizing and externalizing problems."[204] And in "adolescence it is related to [an] increase in depression and suicidality as well as substance abuse."[205]

Prevalence and Incidence

It is difficult to determine the prevalence and incidence of PM because: (1) at times it is hard to tell the difference between poor or sub-optimal parenting and PM; (2) when other maltreatment is present, such as physical

199. *Id.* at 153.
200. *Id.*
201. *Id.*
202. *Id.*
203. *Id.*
204. *Id.* at 153–54.
205. *Id.* at 154.

abuse, sexual abuse, or neglect, PM may not receive much notice even though present; and (3) child protective services or social workers focus more on physical and sexual abuse.[206]

That said, "incidence data . . . for emotional abuse and neglect indicate a rate of less than 1% of children in the United States,"[207] and less than that worldwide.[208] On the other hand, self-report data indicates lifetime prevalence of PM ranging from "13% to 25% in community samples, and 19% to 32% in clinical samples."[209] Experts opine that the "large difference between legal cases of PM and self-report data are likely due to vague, limited, or missing definitional systems in many jurisdictions and the underreported nature of all maltreatment. . . . The true prevalence of PM is probably much higher than generally recognized."[210] It is "estimated that domestic violence in the United States is observed by as many as 10 million children each year," and this "is primarily a PM experience for the observing child." This data "suggests that approximately one-third of children in the United States experience some form of PM in their lifetime and 10% to 15% experience severe and chronic forms."[211] In her memoir, *Sickened*, Julie Gregory describes such an event:

> [Mom] would block [Dad's] view and provoke him out of his stupor until he raged at her, bashing her head against the wall, frightening the children. Mom's screams swallow my head. Julie and her brother flailed at their father while their mother played the role of the victim. "Let him kill me, Julie, just let him put me out of my misery and kill me!" The whole family screamed and thrashed about until the situation subsided.[212]

Intervention Considerations

Interventions to protect children from PM and to treat them requires a coordinated effort by child protective services workers, legal professionals, and mental health clinicians. An effective intervention could be a combination of putting appropriate safeguards in place, which would provide immediate

206. *Id.*
207. *Id.* at 154–55.
208. *Id.* at 155.
209. *Id.*
210. *Id.*
211. *Id.*
212. Baker & Schneiderman, *supra* note 18, at 64.

protection and stop the PM, provide educational tools to the caregivers to allow them to understand the impact of PM, provide treatment to the child-victim to build resiliency and heal trauma, and maintain oversight of the case to ensure that a child is not revictimized.

Three-Tiered Approach

The three tiers of intervention in this area are "(a) all children, (b) children at risk, and (c) children experiencing maltreatment."[213] This is implemented by "raising normative standards (emphasis tier 1), mobilizing bystander action, and strengthening child agency (emphasis tiers 2 and 3) and for shifting child protection primary service responsibilities to child health professionals and school communities."[214]

Experts recommend that the prevention of mistreatment and child well-being overall can be advanced in all sectors of the social ecology by encouraging respect for children's rights and dignity, attention to their perspectives, and support for their well-being."[215] They suggest "public awareness-education campaigns should be conducted with emphasis on these themes and the nature of and proscriptions for PM."[216] Examples include "promotion and training of all present and potential caregivers, including teachers and coaches," to "establish a base of shared values and expectations."[217] Other efforts should include "[p]rosocial skills, social competency, and conflict resolution programs for children, adolescents, and parents."[218] Finally, they recommend "training for all child protection services personnel and community mental health personnel on PM, preferably based on APSAC standards, models, and guidance on child rights."[219]

Multitier Applications to Existing Interventions

Experts also recommend existing interventions be effectively modified to work within a multitier approach.[220] They recommend incorporating into

213. Hart et al., *supra* note 1, at 156.
214. *Id.*
215. *Id.*
216. *Id.*
217. *Id.*
218. *Id.* at 157.
219. *Id,*
220. *Id.*

tier 1 "home visits, education, connection with resources, and encouragement . . . to all families in preparation for and to sustain good child care."[221] For tier 2, they opine "alerts from any family member, including the child, could lead to guided family . . . meetings, planning, action and evaluation loops."[222] And for tier 3, they suggest "a modified 'Multi-Systemic Treatment' approach . . . including time and results limited 24/7 monitoring, planning and networking with family and community."[223]

Public Health Approach

"Evolving wisdom at the international level regarding child maltreatment has encouraged movement to a child rights-informed public health approach that would include multi-tier components."[224] The public health approach pushes toward a child rights-based approach that emphasizes a child's right to be free from PM, rather than the conventional child protection approach, which allows and awaits the maltreatment to occur and the damage it inflicts prior to taking remedial action. This approach "proactively supports the child's right to be free from maltreatment."[225]

As the APSAC Handbook on Child Maltreatment reminds us: "The fact that psychological maltreatment is an attack on the essential psychological needs and potentials of persons, which when fulfilled undergird health, and, as noted, that these needs have been denied and corrupted for perpetrators of violence and maltreatment, should place [PM] in the forefront of primary and secondary prevention objectives."[226]

---

221. *Id.*
222. *Id.*
223. *Id.*
224. *Id.* at 158.
225. *Id.*
226. *Id.*

Chapter 4

Alienation and Brainwashing: Weaponizing Children

A divorce aspires for a healthy closure of a marriage. For a couple with children, a post-divorce parent-child relationship continues to exist, which necessitates the parents, despite their divorce, to continue to co-parent their children. At the healthiest end of this spectrum, after the divorce, a child has positive relationships with *both* parents and desires and spends time with *each* parent. The majority of post-divorce children fit into this category. At the other end of this spectrum is an unhealthy, toxic, and often pathological situation wherein a child rejects a parent. When the rejection is unequivocal, strident, without guilt or ambivalence, absolute and unjustified, a phenomenon known as "parental alienation" may exist.

More often than not, the first signs of the corrosive legacy of parental alienation are contact refusal or visitation interference, which could manifest as: "The children refuse to see their mother!" or they refuse to leave their mother's house and get in the car when the father shows up for his parenting time. Or "I am 16 years old and no judge is going to tell me whether or not I want to see my father!" Such scenarios confound and frustrate judges, lawyers, guardians ad litem, child representatives, child custody evaluators, parenting coordinators, child therapists, mediators, and, last but not least, rejected parents who are entangled in the intricate web of family court litigation dynamics. Court professionals often report being stymied by children's refusals to cooperate and abide by the court-ordered parenting time schedules.[1]

---

1. Richard Warshak, *Parental Alienation: Overview, Management, Intervention, and Practice Tips*, 28 J. Am. Acad. of Matrim. Lawyers 181, 182 (2015).

For frustrated litigants—fathers, mothers, grandparents—who are entangled in the tentacles of an alienation monster and attempt to seek redress from the family court system, the words of actor Alec Baldwin ring true: "To be pulled into the American family law system in most states is like being tied to the back of a pickup truck and dragged down a gravel road late at night. No one can hear your cries and complaints, and it is not over until they say it is over."[2]

Parental Alienation: Old Wine in a New Bottle

Parental alienation is not a new phenomenon; this mental condition has existed for years. It has been described in legal cases since the early 19th century and in the scientific literature since the 1940s.[3] The concept of parental alienation has been acknowledged and addressed by English-speaking courts for the past 200 years. Family law judges, attorneys, guardians ad litem, and mental health professionals routinely deal with cases involving parental alienation, even though they may be unaware of the condition or be unfamiliar with the term, its origin, or its implications.

What Is Parental Alienation?

Scientists and mental health experts have defined parental alienation in several different ways. One of the most widely accepted definitions is: Parental alienation is a "mental condition in which a child—usually one whose parents are engaged in a high-conflict separation or divorce—allies himself or herself strongly with an alienating parent and rejects a relationship with the 'targeted' parent without legitimate justification."[4] At the core of this definition are three key features: One, parental alienation can be conceptualized as a mental condition present in a child, resulting in the child's distorted or false belief that the rejected or disfavored parent is evil, dangerous, or unworthy of love or affection. Two, the child's rejection of the

---

2. Alec Baldwin, A Promise to Ourselves 3 (2008).

3. *See, e.g.*, Lawrence Stone, *Westmeath v. Westmeath*: *The Wars Between the Westmeaths, 1812–1857, in* Broken Lives: Separation and Divorce in England, 1660-1857, at 284 (Lawrence Stone, 1993); David M. Levy, Maternal Overprotection 153 (1943).

4. Demosthenes Lorandos, William Bernet & Richard Sauber, *Overview of Parental Alienation, in* Parental Alienation: The Handbook for Mental Health and Legal Professionals 5 (Demosthenes Lorandos et al. eds., 2013).

alienated or targeted parent lacks legitimate justification.[5] Three, although the rejected parent might have contributed to the child's dislike or hatred of him or her, by reacting to the alienation dynamic in frustration or even anger, that *reaction*, however, should not be confused as *causation* of the alienation.[6]

Aside from the mental health professionals, family courts too have defined the phenomenon of parental alienation. The courts' definitions encapsulate the key features of the condition as defined by mental health professionals.

One of the most succinct but comprehensive summaries of the judicial definitions of parental alienation can be found in the book *Parental Alienation: The Handbook for Mental Health and Legal Professionals* (2013). In his chapter summarizing North American law on parent alienation "distilled from 3,000 parental alienation cases in the United States and Canada," attorney-psychologist Demosthenes Lorandos provides the reader with representative examples of parental alienation cases from the United States and Canada and provides brief but accurate descriptions of many alienation cases across a 25-year period.[7] From thousands of U.S. and Canadian courts' decisions over a 25-year period, Dr. Lorandos concluded that the North American courts not only acknowledged parental alienation but decisively intervened to provide appropriate mental health and legal interventions.[8] Updating his research and findings, in 2020, Dr. Lorandos published his chapter—Parental Alienation in U.S. Courts, 1985 to 2018—in the book *Parental Alienation—Science and Law*.[9] From his research, Dr. Lorandos found thousands of cases across the United States in which the

5. This is an important distinction: If there is a documented history of the rejected parent being abusive or severely neglectful, the child's rejection of that parent could be legitimate and if so, it would not be a case of parental alienation.

6. As the essential feature of parental alienation, the child's rejection of the alienated parent is disproportionate to anything that the alienated parent has done.

7. Demosthenes Lorandos, *Parental Alienation and North American Law, in* PARENTAL ALIENATION: THE HANDBOOK FOR MENTAL HEALTH AND LEGAL PROFESSIONALS 348 (Demosthenes Lorandos et al. eds., 2013).

8. Demosthenes Lorandos, William Bernet & S. Richard Sauber, *Overview of Parental Alienation, in* PARENTAL ALIENATION: THE HANDBOOK FOR MENTAL HEALTH AND LEGAL PROFESSIONALS 5 (Demosthenes Lorandos et al. eds., 2013).

9. DEMOSTHENES LORANDOS & WILLIAM BERNET (EDS.), PARENTAL ALIENATION: SCIENCE AND LAW (2020).

term "parental alienation" or "alienation" or a variant thereof was discussed. By limiting the query to focus on cases in which an independent evaluating expert testified on parental alienation (whether or not the expert found parental alienation), or cases in which the court ruled on whether parental alienation existed (with or without expert testimony), Dr. Lorandos and his team identified 1,181 cases in which the construct of parental alienation was determined to be material, probative, relevant, admissible, and discussed.[10] For a practitioner who doubts American family courts' acceptance of the phenomenon of parental alienation and desires supporting evidence, the entire list of the 1,181 cases that recognize parental alienation, by both trial and appellate courts, is in the appendix of *Parental Alienation—Science and Law*.

Attempting to simplify the issues, eschew esoteric terminology, and perhaps inject common sense in dealing with the practical matters at hand, family court judges have acknowledged that "[p]arental alienation is the flipside of a concept long used by the . . . courts to decide disputed custody matters; i.e., the 'willingness to foster a relationship between the child and [the opposite] parent.'"[11] In analyzing this bedrock concept of American custody law, courts have generally focused on "interference" by one parent in the other parent's relationship with the children in a manner inconsistent with the best interests of the children.[12] In parental alienation cases, an alienating parent's interfering conduct—sometimes defined as *parental alienating behaviors*—is identified, usually through the lens of expert testimony, but also through judicial fact-finding after an evidentiary hearing or trial.[13]

While the detractors continue to attempt to undermine the concept of parental alienation, American courts have unhesitatingly accepted the phenomenon, defined it, and intervened when they found evidence of alienating behaviors.

---

10. Demosthenes Lorandos, *Parental Alienation in U.S. Courts, 1985 to 2018, in* Parental Alienation: Science and Law 370–71 (Demosthenes Lorandos & William Bernet eds., 2020).

11. J.F. v. D.F., 61 Misc. 3d 1226(A), 2018 N.Y. slip op. 51829(U), 2018 WL 6530810, at *3, n.4. (citing Matter of Sweeney v. Daub-Stearns, 2018 NY App. Div. Lexis 7923 (3d Dep't 2018)).

12. Musachio v. Musachio, 137 A.D.3d 881 (2d Dep't 2016).

13. J.F. v. D.F., 61 Misc. 3d 1226(A), 2018 N.Y. slip op. 51829(U), 2018 WL 6530810.

Parental alienation is defined by both appellate and trial courts. For instance, in *Meadows v. Meadows*, the Michigan Court of Appeals defined parental alienation as "[t]he process of one parent trying to undermine and destroy to varying degrees the relationship that the child has with the other parent."[14] In that regard, the *Meadows* court focused more on the "process"—the alienating behaviors through which the alienating parent attempts to "undermine and destroy" the child's relationship with the targeted parent.

On the other hand, in *McClain v. McClain*, the Tennessee Court of Appeals, in defining parental alienation, focused on the mental condition of the child and defined the phenomenon as "primarily a description of the psychological condition of [a] child."[15] Recognizing the prevailing essential feature of parental alienation among mental health professionals, the *McClain* court asserted: "The essential feature of parental alienation is that a child . . . allies himself or herself strongly with one parent (the preferred parent) and rejects a relationship with the other parent (the alienated parent) without legitimate justification."[16]

At the trial court level, a New York trial court affirmed the existence of parental alienation and then went on to define the term. It concluded: "[T]here is no doubt that parental alienation exists."[17] After affirming the existence of parental alienation, the court wrestled with the somewhat amorphous concept of "unjustified behavior" of an alienating parent. It struggled to create a "more demanding definition of parental alienation to more explicitly describe the concept of what constitutes 'unjustified behavior.'"[18] By considering the elements of the tort claim, intentional infliction of emotional distress, the New York court defined the parental alienation condition to require that "(1) the alleged alienating conduct, without any other legitimate justification, be directed by the favored parent, (2) with the intention of damaging the reputation of the targeted parent in the children's eyes or which disregards a substantial possibility of causing such, (3) which proximately causes a diminished interest of the children in spending time

14. Meadows v. Meadows/Henderson, 2010 WL 3814352 (Mich. App.) (Unpublished).

15. McClain v. McClain, 539 S.W.3d 170, 182 (2017).

16. *Id.*

17. *J.F.* v. D.F., 61 Misc. 3d 1226(A), 2018 N.Y. slip op. 51829(U)), 2018 WL 6530810, at 8.

18. *Id.*

with the targeted parent and, (4) in fact, results in the children refusing to spend time with the targeted parent either in person, or via other forms of communication."[19]

Despite the different ways the family courts have defined parental alienation, one consensus is that that there are certain *behaviors*, which, when manifested by an alienating parent, damage a child's relationship with the other parent. These behaviors need not be intentional; they could be reckless or even inadvertent but still cause significant damage to a parent-child relationship. On occasions, family court judges have even personally witnessed such alienating behaviors. A long-serving domestic-relations judge from the Cook County Circuit Court in Illinois[20] observed alienating behavior by a mother after a court proceeding. As the judge recalled:

> One day in court, a mother was seeking an increase in child support from her former husband. The father testified that his income had declined dramatically. After the case was over, I was riding down the elevator with the mother and the parties' teenage daughter. They did not notice I was there or did not recognize me out of my black robe. The mother was sharing details of the case with the daughter, as I would not let the daughter come into the courtroom. The mother was telling her what a liar and manipulator her father was, fully expecting the daughter to agree. I doubted this child would ever be able to hear her father's side of the story. Even if the father was lying, I wondered why the mother could not share her frustration with her sister, her neighbor, or even the cashier at the corner store; anyone but the child. I was saddened because I knew that sharing this information with the daughter might forever affect the way the girl viewed her father and ultimately how she viewed men in general. Would they all be liars and manipulators to her? The daughter had no way to defend her trust in her father against this onslaught; she would certainly question it and probably cease to rely on it. Could the mother be sure the daughter would heal from believing her father is manipulative, uncaring, and a liar?

---

19. *Id.* In reviewing the literature and judicial opinions, one finds that the terms "target parent," "targeted parent," and "favored parent" are used interchangeably to describe the parent who is the victim of parental alienation.

20. Michele Lowrance is a former Domestic Relations Division judge in Cook County, Illinois. She has written and presented extensively on the topic of parental alienation and judicial interventions.

> I don't believe the mother considered the long-term effects. If she had, would she have intentionally hurt her daughter?[21]

Some alienating parents, as the courts have found, proactively undermine their children's relationships with the targeted parent. In *Sukul v. Sukul*, the mother moved her children from New York to Georgia, without the father's consent and in violation of the parties' divorce decree, asserting: "[T]his is a free country."[22] Critical of the mother's alienating behaviors, the New York appellate court affirmed the transfer of custody to the father, declaring:

> [S]he did not tell the father she moved to Georgia or provide him with an address . . . the father texted one of the children after the move to find out "where they lived." Moreover . . . mother also stated that the father is "no good" and she did not believe he should ever see the children.[23]

While proactive steps by one parent may cause alienation, casual, insensitive, and unguarded remarks by a parent lacking impulse control can also cause the same effect. In a custody dispute case in Michigan, *Martinez v. Martinez*, the mother was jailed for four days and fined $100 for failing to comply with the parenting time order.[24] In dismissing the appeal for lack of jurisdiction (grounds unrelated to custody or alienation), the court highlighted the mother's damaging remarks. When the parties first broke up, the mother remarked to the father in front of children: "You're not divorcing me, you're divorcing your family." Moreover, she refused to resolve any parenting time disputes amicably or do anything to encourage father's parenting time other than have a conversation with the teenage child.[25]

Because courts are increasingly aware of the enormous and long-lasting damage that parental alienation may cause, most intervene before the child is fully alienated. In *Hanna v. Hanna*, the Arkansas appellate court noted: "When a trial court finds a custodial parent is attempting parental alienation,

---

21. Michele Lowrance, *A Judge's Perspective on Parental Alienation, in* PARENTAL ALIENATION: THE HANDBOOK FOR MENTAL HEALTH AND LEGAL PROFESSIONALS 507 (Demosthenes A. Lorandos, William Bernet & Richard Sauber eds., 2013).

22. Sukul v. Sukul, 151 N.Y.S.3d 684, 687 (N.Y. App. Div. 2021).

23. *Id.*

24. Martinez v. Martinez, No. 359759, 2023 WL 2542279, at *1–2 (Mich. Ct. App. Mar. 16, 2023).

25. *Id.* at *1–3.

it is not necessary that he or she complete the process before the trial court is justified in changing custody."[26] The court explained: "Our focus was . . . on the actions of the custodial parent to destroy the relationship with the noncustodial parent. We can think of nothing more detrimental to a caring relationship."[27]

The damage from parental alienation, as shown in *Dixon v. Dixon*, can occur swiftly and cause a lasting effect.[28] In affirming a modification that awarded an alienated mother greater custody, the Nebraska appellate court reversed the lower court's refusal to find severe parental alienation due to a procedural mistake.[29] As the court highlighted, within a nine-month period, the mother and children's previous healthy relationship turned tumultuous:

> [Oldest son] "kneed" [Mother] in the side . . . . [T]he children would sit in front of their bedroom doors to keep [Mother] from being able to enter their rooms . . . the children were on the phone "nonstop' with [Father] . . . the conversations had increased so much . . . a lot of times they wouldn't even come to dinner . . . [the children] began to withdraw from [Mother] and their extended family . . . they stopped talking to [Mother], removed photographs and family memorabilia from their rooms, and threw their personal belongings and newly purchased school clothes into garbage bags . . . the children refused to ride in a car with [Mother], would not communicate with her in any way and would record videos of her inside her home.[30]

In a Pennsylvania custody modification case, *Kovalchuk v. Kovalchuk*, the mother's manipulation and her uncredible behavior resulted in the trial court granting father's contempt and modification petitions, and awarding him sole legal and physical custody with mother only having supervised visitation.[31] In affirming, the appellate court found compelling that mother "[was] deemed to have interfered and manipulated children to a degree that her household [was] not appropriate [for the children] . . . absent a supervised setting . . . until she [was] capable of demonstrating refrain from continued manipulation."[32]

---

26. Hanna v. Hanna, 377 S.W.3d 275, 284 (Ark. Ct. App. 2010).
27. *Id.*
28. Dixon v. Dixon, No. A-21-492, 2022 WL 2035983 (Neb. Ct. App. June 7, 2022).
29. *Id.* at *20–21.
30. *Id.* at *6.
31. Kovalchuk v. Kovalchuk, 296 A.3d 587 (Table), 2023 WL 2397386, at *2 (Pa. Super. Ct. Mar. 8, 2023).
32. *Id.* at *4.

Different Terms Used to Describe Parental Alienation

In litigating cases involving parental alienation, it is important to not get fixated on the term "parental alienation"; what is more important are the *behaviors* that are demonstrated by a parent, which raise the concern that a child is being alienated from a parent. Mental health professionals and experts have used different terms to describe parental alienation behaviors.[33] For example, Dr. Stanley Clawar, a sociologist, and Brynne Rivlin, a social worker, use the terms "programming," "brainwashing,"[34] and "indoctrination" when describing the behaviors that cause a child to reject a parent without legitimate justification and due to the favored parent's undue influence.[35] The authors explain that these "brainwashing" and "programming" behaviors:

> [H]inder the relationship of the child with the other parent due to jealousy, or draw the child closer to the communicating parent due to loneliness or a desire to obtain an ally. These techniques may also be employed to control or distort information the child provides to a lawyer, judge, conciliator, relatives, friends, or others, as in abuse cases.[36]

Dr. Richard Warshak, a clinical professor of psychiatry, has used the term "pathological alienation" to describe the outcome of such alienating behaviors:

> a disturbance in which children, usually in the context of sharing a parent's negative attitudes, suffer unreasonable aversion to a person or persons with whom they formerly enjoyed normal relations or with whom they would normally develop affectionate relations.[37]

---

33. *See* the discussion in Demosthenes Lorandos et al., *Overview of Parental Alienation*, *in* Parental Alienation: The Handbook for Mental Health and Legal Professionals 8 (Demosthenes Lorandos et al. eds., 2013).

34. Jennifer H. v. Paul F., 800 N.Y.S.2d 348, 2004 WL 3131979, at *10 (Suffolk Co., N.Y. Fam. Ct. June 9, 2004).

35. Stanley S. Clawar & Brynne Valerie Rivlin, Children Held Hostage: Dealing with Programmed and Brainwashed Children (1991); *see also* Stanley S. Clawar & Brynne Valerie Rivlin, Children Held Hostage: Identifying Brainwashed Children, Presenting a Case, and Crafting Solutions (2d ed. ABA, 2013).

36. Clawar & Rivlin, Children Held Hostage, *supra* note 35, at 15.

37. Richard Warshak, *Social Science and Parental Alienation: Examining The Disputes and the Evidence*, *in* The International Handbook of Parental Alienation Syndrome: Conceptual, Clinical and Legal Considerations 361 (R.A. Gardner, S.R. Sauber & D. Lorandos eds., 2006).

At times, judges have used non-parental alienation terms to address and characterize the underlying behaviors of the parental alienation condition. For instance, in *Martin v. Martin*, the Nebraska Supreme Court found a custodial parent to have used "passive aggressive techniques" in undercutting the noncustodial parent's relationship with the children.[38] Although the term "parental alienation" was not used by the Nebraska Supreme Court, the court's detailed discussion of the custodial parent's alienating behaviors and strategies confirm that the court was indeed addressing the parental alienation condition. In summary, the consensus among the courts, experts, and mental health professionals appears to be that the parental alienation condition involves "a child's reluctance or refusal to have a relationship with a parent without a good reason" along with evidence of certain behaviors by the favored parent that have been identified as parental alienating behaviors in case law and scientific literature.[39]

Regardless of the varying definitions of parental alienation, or even the nomenclature (as discussed earlier), this consensus among the mental health and legal professionals was aptly observed by the New York Supreme Court: "There is no doubt that parental alienation exists."[40]

Existence, Severity, and Forms of Parental Alienation

In determining the existence of parental alienation, Dr. Amy J. L. Baker and her colleagues' Five Factor Model of parental alienation is one tool that is used and accepted by some courts and mental health professionals to determine the existence of parental alienation.[41] As one of the five factors that

38. Martin v. Martin, 294 Neb. 106 (2016).

39. William Bernet, Marianne Z. Wamboldt & William E. Narrow, *Child Affected by Parental Relationship Distress* 55 J. Am. Academy of Child & Adolescent Psych. 575 (2016).

40. *J.F.* v. D.F., 61 Misc. 3d 1226(A), 2018 N.Y. slip op. 51829(U), 2018 WL 6530810.

41. Amy Baker & Paul Fine, *Educating Divorcing Parents: Taking Them Beyond the High Road, in* Working with Alienated Children and Families: A Clinical Guidebook (Amy Baker & S. Richard Sauber eds., 2013). However, *see* Benjamin D. Garber, *A Structured Rubric for Evaluating the Many Systemic Variables That Can Contribute to Parent-Child Contact Problems (PCCP)*, Fam. Ct. Rev. (2024), DOI:10.1111/fcre.12785. In his article, Dr. Garber cautions against improper use of the Five Factor Model and advocates using a structured rubric to avoid binary arguments of alienation versus estrangement.

needs to be carefully evaluated before making a diagnosis of parental alienation, Dr. Baker describes 17 alienating strategies by the alienating parent that are most prevalent in the alienation process. They include badmouthing, limiting contact, confiding in the child, asking the child to spy on the targeted parent, referring to the targeted parent by first name, withholding important information from the targeted parent, and undermining the authority of the targeted parent. Not all strategies have to be present for alienation to occur. Parental alienation can exist, even severe parental alienation, with less than half of the 17 strategies put into play.

In terms of the severity of the symptoms or behaviors that are manifested in the child, parental alienation can be termed as mild, moderate, or severe.[42] Mild parental alienation "means that the child resists contact with the target[ed] parent but enjoys the relationship with that parent once parenting time is underway."[43] Moderate parental alienation "means that the child strongly resists contact and is persistently oppositional during parenting time with the target[ed] parent."[44] Severe parental alienation "means that the child persistently and adamantly refuses contact and may hide or run away to avoid being with the target[ed] parent."[45]

A 2023 study[46] of 1,049 interdisciplinary family law professionals from the U.S., Canada, Australia, New Zealand, Europe, and Asia addressing parent-child contact problems (PCCP) and parental alienation as a "valid and widespread phenomenon versus a legal strategy to counter IPV and child abuse allegations" produced rather interesting findings that confirm parental alienation is abusive to the children involved: 90.88 percent agreed parental alienation behaviors range from mild to severe, 86.56 percent believed parental alienation was one of many factors to explain PCCP, 78.70 percent identified bad mouthing in front of the child is always harmful, 75.81 percent agreed that parental alienation is a form of child abuse, 74.28 percent favored parental alienation testimony in family court, 65.75 percent agreed that alienated children repeat lies and misinformation, 62.66 percent believed the alienating parent's intention impacted parental

---

42. Demosthenes Lorandos et al., *supra* note 33.

43. *Id.*

44. *Id.*

45. *Id.*

46. Marsha Kline Pruett, Janet R. Johnston, Michael Saini, Matt Sullivan & Peter Salem, *The Use of Parental Alienation Constructs by Family Justice System Professionals: A Survey of Belief Systems and Practice Implications*, 61 Fam. Ct. Rev. 372, 372–94 (2023).

alienation, 55.14 percent identified that its cause is multifactorial, 47.33 percent agreed it can occur without active undermining, 39.98 percent of respondents felt parental alienation parents have personality disorders, and 11.63 percent claimed parental alienation is "junk science."[47] In addition, 26.30 percent agreed that parental alienation is a defensive strategy against abuse allegations.[48]

In analyzing these findings, researchers of the 2023 study identified consensus among professionals around the construct of parental alienation, although most also rejected it as a medical syndrome; likewise, the researchers found that the "high consensus among the practitioners for the admission of testimony about PA behaviors . . . suggests their concern for the child not getting lost in the demanding cases PA concerns engender."[49] And while a majority expressed concerns about parental alienating behaviors, there were mixed reactions as to how much to weight them, and that this depended on the particular family and child.[50] In addition, most felt that while parental alienation was difficult to measure, testimony about it was valuable and that family courts are able to sort it out; moreover, most respondents felt that interventions to reconnect should occur—even in cases of trauma.[51] To sum up, researchers of the 2023 study found that parental alienation is a valid construct and, when present, is highly destructive within the family. It has the potential to wreak long-term harm to a child.

Severe Parental Alienation Is Child Abuse

In its severest forms, parental alienation is an emotional, psychological and mental child abuse that causes serious consequences for the children and their custody. In a Connecticut case, *In re Jazmin S.*, the alienating mother's abusive behavior caused her to lose custody of her children.[52] In determining neglect and ordering supervised visitation, the court noted: "Mother appears to be oblivious to [one child's] emotional anxiety which has been caused by mother's conduct and words as well as the emotional anxiety caused to

47. *Id.*
48. *Id.*
49. *Id.* at 387.
50. *Id.*
51. *Id.*
52. *In re* Jazmin S., Nos. H12CP1214515A, H12CP1214514A, 2012 WL 5519573, at *6 (Conn. Super. Oct. 9, 2012).

[another child]. . . . Mother's primary concern, indeed, her sole concern, appears to be with alienating the children from Father."[53]

In another Connecticut case, the court found an alienated child was "being seriously harmed by the conflict between his parents and his mother's campaign to alienate him from his father. [The child] engaged in at least one suicide attempt and [had] harmed family pets. His mental state fluctuate[d] from . . . improving to deteriorating."[54]

In a California dependency adjudication case, *In re J.W.*, a child was removed from the mother and placed with the father upon receiving an "emotional abuse referral" where the minor child disclosed a pattern of abusive behavior wherein "[the] mother called [the] father and the paternal grandmother 'bitch, dummy, stupid, a liar, and full of shit.'"[55] Mother's alienating behaviors also included recording the minor's conversations with the father and telling the child "to lie and accuse father of sexual abuse," as well as to tell him his last name was not his father's.[56] This abusive behavior resulted in the minor being "extremely distraught after returning from mother's home, to the point of vomiting."[57] Determining "the minor was suffering severe emotional damage," and "there were no reasonable means to safeguard his emotional health absent removal," he was placed in father's care with mother having only supervised visitation.[58]

Consider also the Connecticut custody dispute case, *Wallace v. Wallace*, in which the court found "[a]ll of the credible evidence supports almost to an absolute certainty that the [father's] behavior resulted in the emotional and financial abuse of his wife as well as in the alienation of his two older children from their mother."[59] The father demonstrated a pattern of alienating behaviors, which included (1) "repeatedly and routinely told the children [that] their mother was crazy and the sole person responsible for the breakup of the family"; (2) "arranged situations in which he knew he could manipulate [mother] into an overreaction that would support and reinforce

53. *Id.*

54. *In re* Matthew M., No. F04CP11009363A, 2013 WL 4734892, at *4, *6 (Conn. Super. Oct. 12, 2013).

55. *In re* J.W., No. C090430, 2020 WL 4280659, at *1 (3d Dist. Cal. July 27, 2020).

56. *Id.*

57. *Id.*

58. *Id.*

59. Wallace v. Wallace, No. FSTFA104018720, 2012 WL 3089710, at * 1 (Conn. Super. Apr. 18, 2012).

his claims . . . to the girls"; (3) "routinely violated parenting arrangements to the detriment of the [mother]"; (4) "took [the children] on a week-long vacation without consent depriving [mother] of her parenting time," and when they returned to the mother's "scheduled weekend time, that too was usurped by surprise tickets to a Lady Gaga concert followed by plans for the following day—Easter Sunday—that had been previously allocated to [mother]"; (5) "delayed seeking emergency medical care for [Oldest Daughter] initially . . . did not inform the [mother] of the very serious event despite the fact that he finally did take her to the hospital and he did not inform the school" of it; and (6) during oldest child's mental health evaluation, "attempted to text his daughter . . . that these events were her mother's doing and he would protect her."[60]

The results were tragic:

> The oldest child . . . has deteriorated significantly while the litigation has been pending. She has been hospitalized several times for various mental health treatments and currently is being tutored as a homebound student . . . [mother] was told that the child could not return to school before being evaluated [which] . . . the school urged, should take place immediately. The girl ended up being hospitalized for three days.[61]

And yet, despite all of this damage, the court did not lessen the father's parenting time because: "Given the ages of the two older children and their current and heavily biased views of their mother, the court may not be in a position to safely order an appropriate access schedule and will have to rely necessarily on the defendant's compliance with its orders."[62] It is because of such dynamics—aging of the alienated children, which may increase the complexity of a court intervention—it is advisable to seek court intervention at the earliest opportunity. Time is the enemy in cases involving evidence of parental alienating behaviors.

In *Thaner v. Thaner*, the determined mother worked unceasingly to reacquire custody of her children.[63] Mother's scorched-earth campaign to denigrate their lives with father included: "interference with, and failure to support the children's home [at their father's house] . . . including their

60. *Id.* at *3.

61. *Id.*

62. *Id.* at *6.

63. Thaner v. Thaner, No. HHDFA074034225, 2016 WL 4071878, at *3 (Conn. Super. June 30, 2016).

schooling, enrichment activities, sporting events and religious commitments," which, as the court found, "is not in the children's best interest."[64] Shortly after the court's findings, mother refused to return the children from visitation, "unilaterally attempted to enroll them in school" in mother's town and refused to take them to their actual school by father's house.[65] Only after the mother was arrested and charged with custodial interference and a no-contact order was entered were the children returned to the father.[66]

Undeterred and remarkably persistent, as mother's campaign progressed, the children became increasingly resistant to parenting time with father, to the point that while mother was under arrest, the children were placed with her aunt.[67] This pattern repeated; as the court described it: "Despite father's request for return of the children; police involvement, criminal arrest, four charges of custodial interference; family court orders . . . juvenile court involvement; and DCF involvement, [mother] persistently refused to return the children, claiming the children didn't want to go, and she was not going to force them."[68] In fact, to return the children to the father required mother being incarcerated again, and "the effort of several people and several hours to get the children in the plaintiff's [father's] car."[69]

After all of this, mother enlisted the help of a third party and an adult son who emailed the children, attempting to further alienate them from the father.[70] This resulted in one child leaving the father's home for mother, and this child eventually worked with the adult child to abduct another minor child from father's home.[71] After more inappropriate conduct, mother's access to her three youngest children was restricted to one supervised hour every two weeks.[72]

In *Weaver v. Sena*, the alienated father with nearly no access to his child was awarded joint legal custody and much greater visitation.[73] Mother's alienation included (1) insisting that the father's visitation occur in her

64. *Id.*

65. *Id.* at *6.

66. *Id.*

67. *Id.* at *7.

68. *Id.* at *8.

69. *Id.* at *10.

70. *Id.* at *11–12.

71. *Id.* at *14.

72. *Id.* at *21.

73. Weaver v. Sena, No. FA084107935S, 2012 WL 4377779, at *2 (Conn. Super. Aug. 29, 2012).

living room where she "control[ed] all aspects of the visit and made normalized visitation uncomfortable for the father and child and nearly impossible"; (2) being "overly controlling and manipulative and seek[ing] to undermine or sabotage the father's attempts to have a relationship with his child"; (3) "reschedul[ing] doctor's appointments for the child at the last minute, knowing that the father intended to attend"; (4) "prohibit[ing] the doctor's office and daycare facility from disclosing information to the father"; and (5) keeping "the child home from daycare on occasions when she knew the father was intending to visit."[74]

In the California custody dispute, *In re Marriage of Murr Ingels*, the court found that the mother's alienating behaviors resulted in "psychological maltreatment" of the parties' child.[75] Those behaviors included years of increasingly dramatic false allegations of domestic violence against the father, kidnapping the child and turning her against the father by making statements such as:

> (1) [Mother] is the only parent who loves [daughter] and that daughter needs mother to feel good about herself, (2) that father is dangerous and unavailable, and (3) that pursuing a relationship with father would jeopardize daughter's relationship with her mother.[76]

The appellate court affirmed the lower court's award of sole legal and physical custody to the father and supervised visitation for the mother.[77]

False allegations of abuse and sexual abuse were the weapon of choice in the Minnesota custody dispute *SternJohn v. John*.[78] In that case, levying such charges with child protection in two different counties allowed the mother to deprive the father of access to their children for well over year, during which time she "coached the children to report abuse," and "used these proceedings and her position as the children's sole caretaker to stoke the children's fear of father, exacerbating the rift that exists between" them.[79] As a consequence, the father was awarded sole legal and physical custody of

---

74. *Id.* at *1.

75. *In re* Marriage of Murr Ingels, No. C087789, 2020 WL 7639219, at *9 (3d Dist. Cal. Dec. 23, 2020).

76. *Id.*

77. *Id.* at *10.

78. SternJohn v. John, No. A18-1838, 2019 WL 30000751 (Minn. Ct. App. July 1, 2019).

79. *Id.* at *4.

the parties' son, and mother's parenting time was suspended pending her participation in therapy.[80]

In the Connecticut custody dispute *Stancuna v. Stancuna*, the alienating father used a unique tool—mother's immigration status—to manipulate the children and keep them from their mother.[81] After mother traveled home to Russia during the dispute, father made a "false allegation to federal immigration authorities" that resulted in her being separated from the children for ten months.[82] And he used this time to alienate them from their mother on false accusations, the situation described by the court as:

> The ineluctable implication of that finding [mother is credible] is the subsidiary finding that her separation from the children for ten months while she was in Russia, the damage to her parental bond with the children during that time, the need thereafter to reintroduce herself to the children as their mother through supervised therapeutic visitations, and the restrictions on her access to the children because of her husband's claims that she ha[d] untreated mental problems and would flee with them to Russia have all resulted from efforts by the father to alienate the children from their mother on a groundless basis.[83]

Mother was ultimately successful in re-establishing her relationship with her children, and the court ordered that, eventually, the parties would share parenting time with the children.[84]

In the Florida custody dispute case, *Schumaker v. Schumaker*, the alienating father's parenting time was limited to every other weekend.[85] On appeal, the court affirmed the trial court's refusal to award father parenting time during holidays and school breaks because of the father's conduct in degrading the mother. The court summarized:

> The Father has throughout these proceedings attempted to parentally alienate the minor children and the Court has grave concerns about the children having primary residence ever with the Father. The Father has consistently made degrading and obscene comments about the Mother . . . and routinely refers to the Mother in derogatory terms. The Father has

---

80. *Id.* at *2.

81. Stancuna v. Stancuna, No. FA0540113133S, 2007 WL 2570428, at *3 (Conn. Super. Aug. 22, 2007).

82. *Id.*

83. *Id.* at *5.

84. *Id.* at *9.

85. Schumaker v. Schumaker, 931 So. 2d 271, 272–73 (Fla. 5th DCA 2006).

> told the minor son . . . that he does not have to listen to his mother and made derogatory statements about . . . half sister . . . the Court has serious concerns about the moral fitness of the Father in consideration of his actions in alienating the children from the Mother. It found that [Father] . . . blamed [Mother] because she cannot afford to pay for or carryout such a promise [of private school]. It found that [Father] further alienated [Mother] by having the children count out the money for temporary attorney's fees the court awarded to her. . . . It concluded that [Father] is in need of in-depth parental alienation counseling.[86]

Some parental alienating behaviors could be more insidious. In the Connecticut custody dispute case *Sapper v. Sapper*, father's alienation of his children began when they were very young. Father "repeatedly and hatefully belittled Wife in front of their children, throughout their childhood . . . for her housekeeping skill, for imagined infidelity and for staying home with the children. . . . This loutish behavior was witnessed, then mimicked, by the children, much to the delight of their father."[87] However, as the children were 17 and 15, the court allowed them to choose where and how they would have contact with each parent.[88]

In a case of alienation whiplash, the alienating father ended up alienated from his children in *Ruggiero v. Ruggiero*.[89] It involved father "coaching his minor child to say negative things about [mother] and to report false accusations," causing an evaluator to describe him as having an "inability to have any insight or, give any thought to the impact that his coaching would have on his children," describing his conduct as "reprehensible."[90]

Recent scholarship has demonstrated that alienating behaviors like those just described are often accompanied by "co-occurring forms of abuse as part of a pattern of coercive control."[91] In *Findings of Abuse in Families Affected by Parental Alienation*, a peer-reviewed study of 492 appellate court cases in which parental alienation was found by either the court or an independent expert, researchers determined that "there is an 86.05% greater likelihood

86. *Id.* at 274–75.

87. Sapper v. Sapper, No. FA044003773S, 2006 WL 3114318, at *3 (Conn. Super. Oct. 18, 2006).

88. *Id.* at *4.

89. Ruggiero v. Ruggiero, 819 A.2d 864, 867–68 (Conn. Ct. App. 2003).

90. *Id.*

91. Amanda E. Sharples, Jennifer J. Harman & Demosthenes Lorandos, *Findings of Abuse in Families Affected by Parental Alienation*, J. of Fam. Violence (June 2023).

of finding an unsubstantiated abuse claim against an alienated parent as compared to an alienating parent who had a substantiated finding of abuse." The study also revealed that "alienating parents had an 82.18% greater likelihood of having a finding of non-emotional abuse against them than an alienated parent."[92] As the researchers concluded: "This finding directly contradicts claims made by critics of [parental alienation] research that it is the parent (fathers specifically) who alleges being a victim of [parental alienation] [and] who is the abusive parent. . . . We found that it is the *alienating parent* who is more likely to have other findings of abuse."[93] The authors concluded: "This finding indicates that false, or exaggerated claims of abuse or neglect may be a strategy used by alienating parents to make it appear the other parent is abusive."[94]

Alienation Versus Estrangement

Not all cases in which a child rejects a parent or refuses to see a parent after separation or divorce involve parental alienation. While the common denominator in both parental alienation and parental estrangement is the child's refusal to have a relationship with a parent, one distinguishing feature of parental alienation is that the child's rejection of the target parent is *without legitimate justification*. If, for example, a rejected parent has a documented history of family violence, abuse, or neglect, the child's rejection of that parent could be justified.[95] Most mental health professionals call this legitimate rejection of a parent by a child an estrangement or realistic estrangement.

Courts too have distinguished alienation from estrangement. For example, here's how the Tennessee Court of Appeals, in *McClain v. McClain*, differentiated alienation from estrangement:

> Alienation and estrangement . . . are not interchangeable or synonymous concepts. The difference between estrangement and alienation resides in the presence vs absence of a reasonable objective basis for a child's severe and persistent rejection and denigration of a parent. Rejection and

92. *Id.*

93. *Id.*

94. *Id.*

95. Joan B. Kelly & Janet R. Johnston, *The Alienated Child: A Reformulation of Parental Alienation Syndrome* 39 Fam. Ct. Rev. 249, 253 (2001).

denigration of a parent with a reasonable objective basis is estrangement; rejection and denigration without such basis is parental alienation.[96]

Accordingly, the *McClain* court, in its attempt to distinguish alienation from estrangement, was careful to point out that not only does there have to be a legitimate justification in estrangement for a child's rejection of a parent, but such justification has to be considered from an "objective" basis. Family law practitioners should keep this distinction in mind and not let unfounded or undocumented allegations of "abusive" behavior on the part of the rejected parent provide an easy justification for a child's rejection of a parent.

In addition, while estrangement may also result in a child rejecting a parent and may necessitate court and therapeutic intervention, it does not necessarily negate the existence of parental alienation. The existence of the former does not necessarily mean the absence of the latter. At times, despite a pattern of abuse or neglect demonstrated by a rejected parent, there may *also* exist evidence of alienating behaviors. These cases are known as "hybrid" cases. And it's possible that what was once a hybrid case may turn into an alienation case with the passage of time coupled with the improved behavior from one parent and no change from the other.

Consider the Michigan case, *Martin v. Martin*, in which the Michigan Court of Appeals affirmed the trial court's finding that the father, who in the past was found to have been "controlling," changed his behavior while the mother, despite the change in the father's behavior, continued to interfere with and obstruct the children's relationship with their father:

> Since at least 2010, [mother] has denigrated her now ex-husband . . . to their three children. [Father] was not blameless, and the trial court found in 2012 that he was controlling and misused corporal punishment in times of anger. During a four-year period during which [mother] effectively prevented any parenting time, [father] engaged in extensive counseling and showed marked improvement. Even so, [mother] continued to obstruct her children's counseling and parent-child reunification efforts, adding to the strain on [father's] relationship with his children. . . . We discern no error in the circuit court's conclusion that awarding [father] sole custody and preserving that parent-child relationship was in the child's best interest.[97]

---

96. *McClain*, 539 S.W.3d at 182.

97. Martin v. Martin, No. 349261 (Mich. Ct. App. Jan. 28, 2020).

In evaluating a case for presence of alienation or estrangement, the evaluation must include an analysis of the objective evidence supporting the reason for rejection. If abusive or neglectful behavior is alleged of a parent, the determination includes a review of independent evidence corroborating such behavior. The review should include an examination of the relationship, as it existed *prior* to the divorce and/or separation. For example, if the father is being accused of having an anger problem, was this complaint made by the child (*not* the spouse) before the separation or divorce? If the mother is being accused of neglect, did this problem manifest before the divorce or separation? Were there any findings made by the child protective services or by an independent fact-finder such as a jury or a judge in an ancillary proceeding that corroborated the allegations of such abusive behavior? Are there witnesses who have witnessed the alleged abusive behavior of the accused parent? *Why* is it important to thoroughly investigate the allegations of abusive behavior that arguably led to the rejection of the parent by the child? It is important to do so for several reasons.

First, it is important to thoroughly investigate the allegations of abusive behavior because in a forensic setting—such as a courtroom—a fact finder is asked to determine a more objective "truth" than what practicing clinicians and therapists are asked to evaluate behind closed doors. Second, it is dangerous to simply assume the abuse allegations to be true. The argument of some special interests groups—for example, "the fact that there is no evidence doesn't mean it didn't happen"—has no place in a courtroom, especially an American courtroom, where an accused has a presumption of innocence. Allegations of physical, sexual, or other kind of abusive behavior can have life-changing ramifications for the accused, his or her reputation, career, and, more importantly, his or her access to the children. Third, it's a common alienating strategy for the alienating parent to falsely accuse or orchestrate the false allegations against the targeted parent. Such repeated false allegations of "domestic violence" or "abuse" that lead to investigations by protective services or the police have been seen by courts as an "abusive use of conflict," which is an alienating strategy.[98] Fourth, young children, adolescents, and even adults can be coached or manipulated into making false allegations of "abuse"—a fact supported both by legal and scientific

98. *See* Delekta v. Delekta, 2019 WL 2711294 (Mich. Court of Appeals) (Unpublished); *In re* Marriage of Reichert v. Reichert-Randazzo, 2 Wash. App. 2d 1063 (2018) (Unpublished).

literature.[99] Fifth, alienators attempt to triangulate, misuse, and often abuse the court process, child protective services' investigations, and law enforcement resources to further solidify parental alienation by denigrating the parent who has been falsely accused of abuse in the eyes of the child (and the world at large) and deprive the accused parent access to the children.[100]

When confronted with solid evidence of their alienating behaviors—behaviors that have been shown to severely harm a parent-child relationship—alienators often resort to making unfounded claims in an attempt to obfuscate the issues. One claim, made often, argues that the theory of parental alienation is nothing but a litigation strategy used to protect abusive men from being held accountable for their actions. Sometimes this strawman argument is taken to absurd levels. For example, one of the well-known deniers of parental alienation wrote a letter to the Diagnostic and Statistical Manual, Fifth Edition (DSM-5) Task Force alleging that advocates of parental alienation include "father's rights' groups who don't like to be interfered with when they are sexually abusing their children."[101] The denier subsequently withdrew his outrageous statement, saying, "I apologize for suggesting that all fathers who accuse mothers of [parental alienation syndrome] are sexually abusing their children. That was clearly an overstatement that I retract. . . . I do not deny that parental alienation occurs and that a lot of people are hurt when there is an alienator."[102]

Allegations of abuse should be thoroughly investigated. "Determining when a child's negative feelings about one parent are rational or irrational is more often than not quite challenging. In some respects, the process is similar to differentiating a non-bizarre delusion from a persistent, justified worry."[103] A child who has been alienated typically "has a false belief that the

---

99. Sternjohn v. John, 2019 WL 3000751 (Court of Appeals of Minnesota) (Unpublished); Elizabeth Ahern, et.al., *Young Children's Emerging Ability to Make False Statements* 47(1) Dev. Psych. 61–66 (2011); Steven Ceci et al., *Repeatedly Thinking About Non-Events: Source Misattribution Among Preschoolers* 3 Consciousness and Cognition 388 (1994); Quin Chrobak et.al., *Inventing Stories: Forcing Witnesses to Fabricate Entire Fictitious Events Leads to Freely Reported False Memories* 15 Psychonomic Bull. & Rev. 1190–95 (2008).

100. *Sternjohn*, 2019 WL 3000751.

101. William Bernet, *Parental Alienation, DSM-5, and ICD-11, in* Parental Alienation: The Handbook for Mental Health and Legal Professionals 494 (Demosthenes Lorandos et al. eds., 2013).

102. *Id.*

103. Lorandos, *supra* note 10, *citing* to Stephen Ceci et al., *Repeatedly Thinking About a Non-Event: Source Misattributions Among Preschoolers*. 3(3–4) Consciousness & Cognition 388–407 (1994).

rejected parent has been abusive or neglectful. Children with false beliefs about events that never actually occurred may develop false memories . . . memories of non-events."[104] In evaluating the presence of alienation and/or estrangement, the court-appointed evaluators and/or experts must investigate whether the reasons given for contact refusal are true, accurate, and/or justified. Fortunately, available research publications provide guidance on how to conduct investigations.[105]

A thorough and robust investigation into allegations of abuse is necessary not only to rule out the possibility of estrangement but also to check for the presence of any alienating behaviors. Domestic violence is about control and domination. A perpetrator of domestic violence is likely to continue his or her "violent" pattern by controlling the children also. Research has demonstrated that "abusive ex-partners are likely to attempt to alienate the children from the other parent's affection (by asserting blame for the dissolution of the family and telling negative stories), sabotaging family plans (by continuing criticism or competitive bribes) and undermining parental authority (by explicitly instructing the children not to listen or obey).[106] A parent who has been found to be abusive or controlling and domineering is more likely to continue his or her harassing and controlling pattern by manipulating the children to turn against the victim parent.[107]

Another differentiating aspect between estrangement and alienation is the level or magnitude of rejection of a parent by the child. An alienated child is polarized in his or her views of the rejected parent: The child views the world in black and white. The targeted parent is often characterized as "horrible"; the preferred parent is praised as "perfect." The level of polarization in severe alienation cases is pathological. While non-alienated children recover quickly from whatever caused their resentment, alienated children "never," "ever" want to see the target parent. Though it sounds

---

104. Lorandos, *supra* note 10, at 577.

105. *See e.g.* William Bernet & Bradley W. Freeman, *The Psychological Assessment of Contact Refusal, in* PARENTAL ALIENATION: THE HANDBOOK FOR MENTAL HEALTH AND LEGAL PROFESSIONALS 47-73 (Demosthenes Lorandos et al. eds., 2013). Leslie Drozd & Nancy Olesen, *Is It Abuse, Alienation, and/or Estrangement? A Decision Tree* 1 J CHILD CUSTODY 65-106 (2004).

106. Peter Jaffe P, Johnston J, Crooks C, Bala N., *Custody Disputes Involving Allegations of Domestic Violence: Toward a Differential Approach to Parenting Plans*, 46(3) FAM. CT. REV. 500–23 (2008).

107. Richard Warshak, *Family Bridges: Using Insights from Social Science to Reconnect Parents and Alienated Children* 48(1) FAM. CT. REV. 48–60 (2010).

counterintuitive, research shows that an alienated (and non-abused) child may be *more* negative toward the rejected parent than a child who was actually abused:

> It is remarkable that abused children frequently remain attached to their abusive parents, whom they might perceive as charming and charismatic. . . . a maltreated child may have ambivalent feelings toward the abusive parent; however, the alienated child almost always has highly negative attitudes toward a non-abusive parent.[108]

Last but not least, family practitioners should be wary of the binary trap: the either/or choice between abuse and alienation. Alienation and estrangement should not be seen as mutually exclusive alternatives, but rather as family dynamics. Litigation often involves zealous advocacy and a deliberate haste to reach a finding in favor of one parent or another. In some instances this could mislead a trier of fact to reach for simplistic solutions that ignore complex relationship dynamics.

Parental Alienation Versus "Parental Alienation Syndrome"

Courts often get dragged down the rabbit hole of being asked to adjudicate whether the "parental alienation syndrome" has sufficient scientific validity and reliability or general acceptability among the scientific community to be admissible as expert evidence. A parent who is accused of engaging in alienating *behaviors* may attempt to obfuscate the issues by presenting expert opinion that parental alienation syndrome has no scientific underpinning and, therefore, the court must disregard any and all evidence of parental alienating *behaviors*. This is a red herring, and family law practitioners who represent the alienated parents in court should correspondingly reframe the issue for the court. The focus of the fact-finder must not be on the "syndrome"; it must be on the alienating *behaviors*. But first, it's important to understand this controversy.

The term *parental alienation syndrome* was formulated by the child psychiatrist Richard Gardner. As Dr. Gardner, who was certified in psychiatry and child psychiatry by the American Board of Psychiatry and Neurology, explained:

---

108. Lorandos, *supra* note 10 at 577.

> [T]he parental alienation syndrome is a disorder that arises primarily in the context of child-custody disputes.. . . It results from the combination of a programming (brainwashing) parent's indoctrinations and the child's own contributions to the vilification of the target parent[.][109]

Dr. Gardner's formulation of parental alienation syndrome was lauded by some and criticized by others. The criticisms included "*ad hominems* and shoddy scholarship," which found Dr. Gardner pilloried.[110] However, since Dr. Gardner's formulation of the parental alienation syndrome in the mid-1980s, several mental health professionals and researchers, working *independently* of Dr. Gardner in studying alienating behaviors, reached a consensus that parental alienation is real and it constitutes "child abuse."[111] As described in this chapter elsewhere, the Clawar-Rivlin findings that were published by the American Bar Association in their book entitled *Children Held Hostage*, Dr. Warshak's description of a pattern of coercive control and domination by a parent, Leona Kopetski's research, Barry Bricklin's work, and Johnston-Kelly's paper referring to parental alienation as "an insidious form of emotional abuse of children that can be inflicted by divorced parents," *all* ultimately culminated into a proposal that parental alienation be included in the DSM-5.[112]

The difference between the term *parental alienation* and *parental alienation syndrome* is that Dr. Gardner's definition of parental alienation syndrome focuses solely on the *child's* behavior after he or she has been successfully alienated from the targeted parent. Whereas parental alienation "focuses on the behavior and actions of the aligned parent, rejected parent, and the child."[113] The fact that there may be some controversy surrounding the former does not negate the robust science underlying the latter. As the Connecticut Superior Court acknowledged in *Mastrangelo v. Mastrangelo*, the "strategies" of alienation are "scientifically present and reliable, and thus

---

109. Demosthenes Lorandos, *Parental Alienation, in* HANDBOOK OF FORENSIC SOCIOLOGY AND PSYCHOLOGY 323 (S. Morewitz & M. Goldstein eds., 2013).

110. *Id.*

111. *Id.* at 324.

112. *See* William Bernet, *Parental Alienation Disorder and DSM-5* 36 AM. J. FAM. THERAPY, 349, 366 (2008); WILLIAM BERNET, PARENTAL ALIENATION, DSM-5, AND ICD-11 (2010).

113. Mastrangelo v. Mastrangelo, 55 Conn. L. Rptr. 245 (2012) (unreported).

pass the . . . *Daubert* test."[114] They also pass the *Frye* test.[115] In an informal poll of members of the Association of Family and Conciliation Courts (AFCC) conducted in 2010, 98 percent of the 300 respondents agreed with the question: "Do you think that some children are manipulated by one parent to irrationally and unjustifiably reject the other parent?"[116] While the term *parental alienation syndrome* may continue to generate irrelevant controversy, the courts and mental health professionals agree on the phenomenon of parental alienation and the toxic *behaviors* manifested by the alienating parent, which cause significant harm to the targeted parent's relationship with the child.

Family courts have increasingly refused to get drawn into the meaningless controversy surrounding parental alienation syndrome and instead focused their attention on alienating parent's behaviors. For instance, in *Martin v. Martin*, the Michigan Court of Appeals, refusing to take the bait on adjudicating the controversy over the "syndrome," held:

> [Mother] . . . essentially contends that "parental alienation" is junk science. While there may be a dispute in the scientific community about whether there is diagnosable, pathological condition called parental alienation syndrome . . . there is no reasonable dispute that high-conflict custody disputes frequently involve acts by one parent designed to obstruct or sabotage the opposing parent's relationship with the child.[117]

Experts do not dispute the existence of parental alienation but some allege alienation claims are used as a tactic to obtain or retain custody. They are not entirely wrong; the claimed misuse of the phenomenon of parental alienation does occur. For instance, in *Matter of Doe I*, the mother appealed the termination of her parental rights, claiming that because her child was alienated, she was unable to comply with court plans to avoid termination.[118] The appellate court rejected the claim, stating: "The claim of parental alienation is not a defense in this case. Parental alienation did not occur. . . . The fact that the child 'found her voice' . . . and began to vocalize her feelings and opinions with Mother during visits is not parental

---

114. *Id.*

115. H.L.J. v. R.G.J., Jr., No. 2014 MDA 2019 (Super. Ct. Pa. July 28, 2020).

116. Amy Baker, Peter Jaffee, William Bernet & Janet Johnston, *Brief Report on Parental Alienation Survey* 30(2) The Association of Family and Conciliation Courts eNEWS (2011).

117. Martin v. Martin, Michigan Court of Appeals No. 349261 (Jan. 28, 2020), n. 2.

118. *Id.* at *6.

alienation."[119] Despite the fact that courts see through these unreasonable attempts to hide behind false claims of parental alienation, detractors point to them as support for their inflated and unsupported claims that most (if not all) assertions of parental alienation are made by actual abusive fathers against pure-hearted, protective mothers.

Take, for example, the Harman-Lorandos critique of the 2019 study by Joan Meier and colleagues (Meier study) in which they claimed that "mothers who claimed their children were abused were more likely to lose custody of their children and their legal cases than were fathers," and that "fathers who claimed they were alienated were more likely to get custody of their children, even if they were proven to be abusive.[120] In a follow-up study to test the durability of these findings, Dr. Harman (an award-winning scientist-researcher) and Dr. Lorandos found 30 conceptual and methodological flaws with the Meier study, including that it lacked peer review, the samples used in the study were cherry picked, and the codes were not clearly defined.[121] For instance, Ms. Meier's team "coded protection orders and arrests as evidence of guilt despite the fact that such allegations could later be proven false or unsubstantiated."[122]

As a corrective measure, Dr. Harman and Dr. Lorandos conducted their own peer-reviewed study and found: (1) No data supported the hypothesis that "mothers who are perceived to be . . . alienating their children are more likely to get a decrease in parenting time, lose custody . . . and lose her case"; (2) there was no data to support the assertion that such a reduction would occur "even if the accusing or alienated parent was found to have been abusive"; (3) the data did not support the hypothesis that "when a mother claims intrafamilial abuse and the father claims [parental alienation], her reports of abuse will be deemed unfounded more often than if the father claimed abuse and the mother claimed [parental alienation]"; (4) "when mothers claim intrafamilial abuse and the father claims [parental

119. Matter of Doe I, No. 50515, 2023 WL 3735067, at *6 (Idaho Ct. App. May 31, 2023).

120. Jennifer Harman & Demosthenes Lorandos, *Allegations of Family Violence in Court: How Parental Alienation Affects Judicial Outcomes,* Psych., Pub. Pol'y & Law, ISSN: 1076-8971 (*citing* Meier, J.S., Dickson, S., O'Sullivan, C., Rosen, L., & Hayes, J. (2019) *Child Custody Outcomes In Cases Involving Parental Alienation and Abuse Allegations* (GWU Law School Public Law Research Paper No. 2019-56)).

121. Harman & Lorandos, *supra* note 120, at 184.

122. *Id.*

alienation], she will be more likely to have a decrease in parenting time or lose all custody than if the father claimed abuse and the mother claimed she was being alienated," was also not supported by the data; (5) neither was the hypothesis that "if a GAL [guardian ad litem], court-appointed psychologist or custody evaluator were to identify or find [parental alienation] in a case, mother will lose more parenting time or custody than will fathers"; (6) there was no data to support the hypothesis that "when a mother claims that both child abuse and sexual abuse occurred and one or both were corroborated, she is more likely to be penalized than are fathers by getting a decrease in parenting time or lose all custody"; but (7) the hypothesis that "the more unfounded claims of abuse that were made against a parent, the more the accused parent was likely to get a decrease . . . in parenting time—increased parenting time favored the accuser," was supported by the data.[123]

In a yet another recent peer-reviewed study, results indicate that there is an illusory correlation between family court cases involving both allegations of abuse and parental alienation, and that mothers are generally not losing custody to abusive fathers.[124] While there may be anecdotal cases of family courts dismissing allegations of abuse (or alienation), there is no systematic pattern of family courts around the country "dismissing" allegations of domestic violence or child abuse in favor of claims of parental alienation.

False Positives When Identifying Parental Alienation

Complications can occur when evaluators or fact finders make erroneous findings of parental alienation. "False positive identifications of parental alienation can occur with respect to a parent's alienating behaviors, a child's alienation from a parent, or both."[125] In his peer-reviewed academic article published by the American Psychological Association, Dr. Richard Warshak identifies three types of false positives: "erroneously concluding that a child is alienated . . . failing to recognize that a child's rejection of a parent is a justifiable response . . . and wrongly concluding that the parent has engaged

123. *Id.*

124. Hesam Varavei & Jennifer Harman, *The Illusory Correlation Between Parental Alienation and Other Forms of Family Violence*, Int'l J. Social Welfare 1–13 (2024), DOI: 10.1111/ijsw.12692.

125. Richard Warshak, *When Evaluators Get It Wrong: False Positive IDs and Parental Alienation,* 26(1) Psych., Pub. Pol'y & Law 54, 57 (2019).

in a campaign of alienating behavior."[126] Dr. Warshak asserts that these false positives are due to several factors, such as a poor understanding of parental alienation and a rush to judgment that does not "consider the context in which the behaviors occurred and their frequency, severity and duration."[127] Another factor that may contribute to false positives is when an evaluator makes insufficient efforts to reduce their own cognitive biases.[128]

To avoid false positives, Dr. Warshak articulates seven criteria to distinguish irrationally alienated children from those whose rejection is *not* due to alienation.[129] Thus, a child who has moderate to severe parental alienation will display each of the following characteristics:

1. The behavior is chronic rather than temporary and short-lived.
2. The behavior is frequent rather than occasional.
3. The behavior occurs in most situations rather than only in certain situations.
4. The behavior occurs without displays of genuine love and affection toward the rejected parent.
5. The behavior is directed at only one parent.
6. The behavior does not reflect typical dynamics for the child's stage of development.
7. The behavior is disproportionate to, and not justified by, the rejected parent's past or current behavior.[130]

Dr. Warshak also provides seven examples of situations where there is negative treatment of a parent by a child, but not parental alienation:

> (a) normal reactions to parental separation; (b) behavior reflecting a difficult temperament or emotional problems; (c) reluctance to leave a parent who need emotional support; (d) situation-specific resistance to being with a parent; (e) feeling closer to or having more rapport with one parent; (f) feeling more comfortable in one parent's home, either because of differences in parenting styles or in the emotional atmosphere of the home; and (g) typical adolescent psychological functioning.[131]

---

126. *Id.* at 62.
127. *Id.* at 63.
128. *Id.*
129. *Id.*
130. *Id.* at 58.
131. *Id.*

Dr. Warshak's concerns about false positives in identifying parental alienation have been mirrored by family courts, wherein they have discredited claims of parental alienation that lack evidentiary support. For instance, in *Stacy V. v. Frank B.*, a California appellate court affirmed a superior court's denial of the father's motion to modify custody based on claims of parental alienation.[132] Despite the father's claim and the social workers' assessments that "mother in 2019 engaged in concerning behaviors such as speaking negatively of father in front of the children, coaching the children, and maintaining excessive contact" with one child, the court found allegations of emotional abuse to be unfounded. Father failed to present expert testimony to support his claim of parental alienation, and the court refused to acknowledge and credit such claim.[133]

Similarly, a New York appellate court affirmed a trial court's finding of no parental alienation, despite the trial court's finding that the mother was a "contributor to some of the difficulties," and had involved the children in some inappropriate discussions as their "favorite parent."[134] In rejecting the claim of parental alienation, the court gave weight to the testimony of the court-appointed psychologist who reasoned the mother's behaviors did "not signify parental alienation," and that "this [was] not a case in which parental alienation [was] the core of the problem in the family dynamic."[135]

In an Illinois case, the father who claimed parental alienation was unable to prove it in the face of "multiple witnesses to [father's] abuse of one or more of the children," and expert testimony that "abuse of one of the children or of the other parent [by father] eliminates the possibility of parental alienation."[136] The court also noted "the testimony of [mother's] friends and the e-mails [mother] sent to the children suggesting that [mother] was encouraging them to maintain a relationship with their father."[137]

Similarly, an Illinois mother's rights under a shared parenting plan were terminated, despite her claims that parental alienation was afoot.[138] While there were clear signs of estrangement from her children, and a

---

132. Stacy V. v. Frank B., No. B316943, 2023 WL 225796, at *11 (2d Dist. Jan. 18, 2023).

133. *Id.* at *9.

134. Reynolds v. Reynolds, 279 A.3d 1240 (Table), 2022 WL 1447714, at *7 (Pa. Super. Ct. May 9, 2022).

135. *Id.* at *7.

136. *In re* Marriage of Yazeji and Assaf, 2022 IL App (3d) 190197-U, ¶¶ 22, 39.

137. *Id.* at 39.

138. Hrabovsky v. Axley, 2014-Ohio-1168, ¶¶ 12, 15 (5th Dist. App.).

court-ordered evaluator found "parental alienation," the court refused to credit it; this was in large part because of the mother's conduct that the children didn't like, and the evaluator's admission that "parental alienation could be caused by that parent's own conduct."[139] As the court concluded: "The evidence presented demonstrated mother's conduct could be a source of the children's strained relationship with mother, as opposed to father's conduct as the sole reason for the children to feel negatively about mother."[140]

Parental Alienation and DSM-5

Another argument lobbed against parental alienation is that it is not included in the American "bible" of mental disorders—the DSM-5, which is the 2013 update to the Diagnostic and Statistical Manual of Mental Disorders, the taxonomic and diagnostic tool published by the American Psychiatric Association. Therefore, the argument goes, it must not be good science. This is another red herring. Prior to the publication of DSM-5, "there was a proposal to include parental alienation disorder as a new diagnosis."[141] The members of the DSM-5 Task Force "never said that they doubted the reality or the importance of parental alienation."[142] "However, they concluded that parental alienation did not meet the standard definition of a mental disorder, that is, 'the requirement that a disorder exists as an internal condition residing within an individual.'"[143] Accordingly, the DSM-5 Task Force said that "parental alienation should be considered an example of a relational problem because it involves a disturbance in the child's relationship with one or both parents."[144]

In 2016, two contributing authors to the DSM-5, Dr. Marianne Wamboldt and Dr. William Narrow, along with Dr. William Bernet of Vanderbilt University School of Medicine, published a paper in the peer reviewed Journal of the American Academy of Child & Adolescent Psychiatry.[145] The authors pointed out that "one of the new terms introduced in the DSM-5 was 'child affected by parental relationship distress' (CAPRD)."[146]

139. *Id.* at 33.
140. *Id.*
141. Bernet, Wamboldt & Narrow, *supra* note 39, at 575.
142. *Id.*
143. *Id.*
144. *Id.*
145. *Id.* at 571–79.
146. *Id.* at 571.

The authors elaborated that their purpose in publishing the article was "to explain how clinicians and researchers can use the new terminology of CAPRD."[147] They pointed out that "since two of the authors [of DSM-5]" wrote the chapter on "Other Conditions," their article was consistent with the structure, content, and intentions of the DSM-5.[148] The authors proposed that the CAPRD category be used by clinicians "when the focus of clinical attention is the negative effects of parental relationship distress on a child in the family, including effects on the child's mental or medical disorders."[149] The term *parental relationship distress*, the authors pointed out, includes behaviors such as "persistent disparagement of one or both parents by the other parent."[150] Typically, as a result of such behaviors, "a child affected by parental relationship distress displays impaired functioning in behavioral, cognitive, affective, and/or physical domains. Examples of behavioral problems include oppositionality and the child's reluctance or refusal to have a relationship with a parent without a good reason (parental alienation)."[151] Examples of "cognitive problems" may include the child "adopting the false belief that the rejected parent is evil or dangerous (parental alienation)."[152] The authors clarified that "children who experience parental alienation almost always fulfill the definition of CAPRD."[153]

The concept of parental alienation is covered by DSM-5 under three specific diagnoses: (1) child affected by parental relationship distress (V61.29), (2) parent-child relational problem (V61.20), and (3) child psychological abuse (995.51).[154]

The psychological damage associated with parental alienation has been well researched and documented.[155] Heeding the clarion call of anguished parents and frustrated mental health professionals, family courts around the country have intervened in the cases involving parental alienation and taken

147. *Id.* at 572.

148. *Id.*

149. *Id.*

150. *Id.*

151. *Id.*

152. *Id.*

153. *Id.* at 575.

154. *See* DSM-5 (5th ed., 2013), at 715–16, 719.

155. J. Wallerstein & S. Blakeslee, Second Chances: Men, women, and children a decade after divorce (1989); *see also* Amy Baker, *The Long-Term Effects of Parental Alienation on Adult Children: A Qualitative Research Study* 33 Am. J. of Fam. Therapy 289 (2005).

remedial action.[156] This has resulted in thousands of judicial opinions that acknowledge the phenomenon of parental alienation. In the three decades since Dr. Richard Gardner first published his formulation of a parental alienation syndrome, American courts have seen a significant increase in parental alienation cases. It is imperative that the professionals, from both legal and mental health professions, understand the solid research in the area of parental alienation. Given extensive scientific research and legal literature that supports parental alienation, diligent professionals can easily and effectively refute any claim that the phenomenon doesn't exist or cannot be accepted by courts because of alleged insufficient corroborating data.

Recent scholarship has affirmed this in the DSM-5-TR.[157] For example, "parent-child relational problem" (PCRP) is defined as: "negative attributions of the other's intentions, hostility toward the other, and unwarranted feelings of estrangement," and describes the relationship between alienated children and their parents.[158] Likewise, "child affected by parental relationship distress" (CAPRD) similarly applies, as it is defined as: "negative effects of parental relationship discord (e.g. high levels of conflict, distress, or disparagement) on a child in the family."[159]

Depending on the severity of the family dynamics, parental alienating behaviors could constitute to be "child psychological abuse," which is defined in the DSM-5-TR as "harming/abandoning people or things that the child cares about," such as the other parent.[160] In addition, a number of very troubling diagnoses may arise, including "delusional symptoms in the context of relationship with an individual with prominent delusions" and "factitious disorder imposed on another," in discussing the delusions and

---

156. Matter of Marriage of Reichert, No. 48783-7-II, 2018 WL 1393794, at *7 (Wash. Ct. App. Mar. 20, 2018); *In re* HM, No. G057128, 2019 WL 3522043, at *26 (Cal. Ct. App., Aug. 2, 2019); Hiller v. Hiller, 919 N.W.2d 548, 558 (S.D. 2018); SternJohn v. John, No. A18-1838, 2019 WL 3000751, at *5 (Minn. Ct. App. July 1, 2019); Delekta v. Delekta, No. 345006, 2019 WL 2711294, at *3 (Mich. Ct. App. June 27, 2019); Geary v. Geary, 27 N.E.3d 877, 895 (Ohio Ct. App. 2015); McClain v. McClain, 539 S.W.3d 170, 223 (Tenn. Ct. App. 2017); Rodman v. Friedman, 33 A.D.3d 400, 401, 826 N.Y.S.2d 1, 2 (2006); Bergin v. Bergin, No. HAN-19-77, 2019 WL 3788326, at *3 (Me. Aug. 13, 2019).

157. William Bernet & Amy J.L. Baker, *Parental Alienation in the DSM-5-TR, But Not the Actual Words: APA Experts Agree*, Parental Alienation International, Parental Alienation Study Group (PASG) (2023).

158. *Id.*

159. *Id.*

160. *Id.*.

factitious disorder of the alienating parent.[161] Finally, "identity disturbance due to prolonged and intense coercive persuasion" can also occur.

Despite the fact that parental alienation is a valid and supported construct, its deniers remain undeterred, pushing misinformation and disinformation in courtrooms to mislead the courts and compromise judicial outcomes. At times, ideological positions may supersede common sense and well-established scientific literature. For instance, consider the recent push by some professionals to use the gender-oriented term *child and mother sabotage* (CAMS) instead of the term *parental alienation*. As its adherents openly admit, they prefer CAMS because it clarifies "how perpetrator fathers intentionally sabotage the child-mother connection."[162] This preference completely ignores the fact that mothers, too, have been found to have engaged in alienating behaviors; as demonstrated by overwhelming judicial fact findings and scientific literature, parental alienating behaviors do not fall under the monopoly of one gender.[163]

A recent joint statement by the Association of Family and Conciliation Courts (AFCC) and the National Council of Juvenile and Family Court Judges (NCJFCJ) underscores the key issues that are discussed in this chapter. The joint statement was informed by a survey of 1,049 members of both organizations, and it integrated the available social science on parent child contact problems (PCCPs).[164] In prioritizing the safety of children and parents, the joint statement offered considerations and recommendations to family court professionals. Included in these recommendations are the risk factors identified as parental alienating behaviors (PABs). The term *parental alienation* is unequivocally mentioned as a family dynamic that is relevant to family court professionals who work with PCCPs.[165]

---

161. *Id.*

162. Dr. Elizabeth Dalgarno, *From Parental Alienation to ['Abusers'] Child and Mother Sabotage (CAMS) as a preferent term for how perpetrator fathers intentionally sabotage the child-mother connection*, Shera Research Group (Oct. 23, 2023) https://www.shera-research.com/latest-news/from-parental-alienation-to-abusers-child-and-mother-sabotage-cams-as-a-preferable-term-for-how-perpetrator-fathers-intentionally-sabotage-the-child-mother-connection.

163. *See supra* notes 78 and 156.

164. Matthew Sullivan, Marsha Kline Pruett & Janet Johnston, *Parent-Child Contact Problems: Family Violence and Parental Alienating Behaviors Either/Or, Neither/Nor, Both/And, One in the Same?* Fam. Ct. Rev. (2023), DOI 10.1111/fcre.12764.

165. AFCC and NCJFCJ, Joint Statement on Parent-Child Contact Problems (2022).

Chapter 5

Stereotypes, Shame, and Silence: Intimate Partner Violence Against Men

In the late spring of 2022, the world tuned in as Johnny Depp played a recording in a Fairfax County Virginia courtroom that gave a voice to an often-overlooked social problem. In this recording, Defendant Amber Heard was heard to say: "Tell people it was a fair fight and see what the jury and judge think. Tell the world, Johnny. Tell them, 'I, Johnny Depp, I'm a victim, too, of domestic violence, and it was a fair fight,' and see if people believe or side with you."[1]

Heard's words emphasize a meme echoed in our halls of justice and social institutions that only men can inflict intimate partner violence over their female victims and that only men can be perpetrators and never the victims. Intimate partner violence (IPV) is a subset of domestic violence involving coercion; psychological, physical, and sexual aggression; and the use of children of one intimate partner against the other. The impact of IPV is far reaching—leaving partners, their children, and the community grappling for solutions. While the legal and mental health communities adjust their treatment and enforcement models, it is important not to lose focus on what groups of people are endangered.

Research demonstrates that both men and women are capable of inflicting intimate partner violence on their partners. A recent 2025 empirical study validates the importance of considering IPV as a complex and

1. Kalhan Rosenblatt, *Male Domestic Violence Survivors Say They Feel the Depp-Heard Trial Is a Turning Point*, NBC News, May 24, 2022, https://www.nbcnews.com/pop-culture/pop-culture-news/male-domestic-violence-survivors-say-feel-depp-heard-trial-turning-poi-rcna29742.

nuanced phenomenon likely to occur with both partners engaged in violence—initiatively or reactively—during relationships.[2] But while 30 years of research has documented this effect, "little research has examined men's experiences in such relationships."[3] Men's struggle with victimization has been largely discounted by our courts, social institutions, and mainstream social science research.[4] This meme exists partly because of our need to fully understand and address IPV. For instance, when social institutions were tasked with finding "shelter houses for female victims as well as mandatory treatment for male perpetrators,"[5] the resulting science research regarding intimate partner violence was "based in many cases on samples drawn from those shelters (woman-victims) or court-mandated treatment groups (male-perpetrators)."[6] Coupled with the prevailing ideology at the time, "the notion evolved that spouse assault was exclusively male perpetrated or that female intimate violence, to the extent that it existed at all, was defensive or inconsequential."[7]

The perspective that has framed the science literature on intimate partner violence suggests that "men systematically and intentionally use violence to maintain a power system in which men are dominant and women are subordinate."[8] This paradigm is the result of a combination of "[g]roup think" and "belief perseverance" where "perpetrators are viewed as exclusively or disproportionately male."[9] Some social scientists and researchers believe that the goal of righting "an imbalance against women" has resulted in misdirecting "social and legal policy, to misinform custody assessors, police, and judges, to disregard data sets contradictory to the prevailing theory, and to mislead attempts at therapeutic change for perpetrators."[10]

---

2. Alexandra Lysova et al., *Bidirectional and Unidirectional Intimate Partner Violence: A Comprehensive Review*, 16 Partner Abuse 1 (2025).

3. Denise A. Hines & Emily M. Douglas, *A Closer Look at Men Who Sustain Intimate Terrorism by Women*, 1 Partner Abuse 3, 286 (2010).

4. *Id.* at 50.

5. Donald G. Dutton & Tonia L. Nicholls, *The Gender Paradigm in Domestic Violence Research and Theory: Part 1 – The Conflict of Theory and Data*, 10 Aggression & Violent Behavior 6, 681 (2005).

6. *Id.*

7. *Id.*

8. Denise A. Hines & Emily M. Douglas, *Intimate Terrorism by Women Towards Men: Does It Exist?*, 2 J. Aggression, Conflict & Peace Rsch. 3, 37 (2010).

9. Dutton & Nicholls, *supra* note 5, at 682.

10. *Id.*

Unfortunately, this meme persists despite the research showing that "[w]omen are at least as likely as men to engage in partner aggression."[11] In fact, research regarding women's perpetration of violence has been met with criticism, "especially by the activist-research community" and "[d]ata surveys similarly met with criticism, especially by feminist researchers who were committed to the view that intimate violence was the by-product of patriarchy and hence, an exclusively male activity."[12] In reality, women engage in violence at least at the same rates as men do.[13] So much so, that a "Center[s] for Disease Control survey of young adults found that in cases of one-way partner aggression, women were the instigators in 71% of cases."[14] In a sample of men and women who sought help for victimization, the female perpetrators of male abuse "used five-to[-]six times the frequency of physical and severe psychological aggression, and controlling [behaviors]; in addition, the female partners' rates of these types of aggression were twice as high as their male partners."[15] Additionally, physical aggression is mutual in half of all reported cases, with only a small percentage accounting for self-defense. In fact, studies typically show that self-defense or retaliation is among the least cited reasons that women provide for their use of IPV.[16] In the sample of help-seeking—where a victim of IPV has attempted to seek help for victimization—men and women, "the help-seeking men had significantly higher rates of injuries than their female partners: among those men and women who sustained injuries, the men were injured at approximately twice the frequency as their female partners."[17] This data contradicts the long-held belief that women do not cause physical injury to men, and, if they do, it is inconsequential.

Recent research strives to answer three important questions relating to gender issues in IPV: (1) What is the directionality of IPV? (2) What motives cause IPV? (3) Is IPV related to essentially the same risk factors? The answers to these questions have tremendous implications for our family

---

11. Coalition to End Domestic Violence, Myths of the ABA Commission on Domestic Violence: Summary Report, Special Report, at 5, https://endtodv.org/wp-content/uploads/2021/08/Myths-of-ABA-Commission-Summary.pdf (last updated 2021).

12. Dutton & Nicholls, *supra* note 5.

13. Coalition to End Domestic Violence, *supra* note 11.

14. *Id.*

15. Hines & Douglas, *supra* note 8, at 51–52.

16. *Id.* at 38.

17. *Id.* at 51–52.

law system. For example, family violence is an important factor in determining child custody, parenting time and visitation orders, and, in some cases, distribution of the marital estate. A court's ability to understand gender dynamics in family violence ensures proper decision-making and intervention for at-risk families. In *Partner Abuse Worldwide*, a study designed to answer the three questions at a global scale, the researchers found that "[m]ost intimate partner abuse is bidirectional, perpetrated by both parties, driven by similar motives, and related to essentially the same risk factors."[18] In fact, most Western industrialized countries show that "one-third to one-half of all IPV victims are men."[19] Men's victimization is not isolated to psychological aggression but also includes "physical and sexual violence, psychological aggression, financial abuse, legal and administrative abuse, and homicide."[20]

Men Too Are Victims of IPV

Researchers in the field of social science posit that IPV is motivated by "intimacy and psychopathology rather than gender[.]"[21] This becomes clear when data from same-sex couples is compared with opposite-sex couples.[22] "[A]busiveness in intimate relationships occurs for both genders and that certain psychological features increase risk for individuals independent of gender."[23] For instance, a 1991 study of lesbian relationships reported higher abuse rates "for all forms of abuse in relationships with women: physical, sexual, emotional."[24] A consensus in the literature shows that "intimate violence is not specific to men and cannot be explained on the basis of gender or gender roles."[25] Instead, IPV may stem from a number of causes, including "psychopathology, attachment, anger, arousal, alcohol abuse, skills

---

18. Esteban Eugenio Esquivel-Santovena et al., *Partner Abuse Worldwide*, 4 Partner Abuse 1, 8 (2013).

19. Alexandra Lysova et al., *"How Can I Be a Victim When I Have Children?" Abused Men's Perceptions of Their Children's Exposure to Domestic Violence*, 33(1) J. Aggression, Maltreatment & Trauma 67, 67 (2023), DOI: 10.1080/10926771.2023.2186300.

20. *Id.* at 68.

21. Dutton & Nicholls, *supra* note 5, at 684–85.

22. *Id.*

23. *Id.*

24. *Id.*

25. *Id.*

deficits, head injuries, biochemical correlates, attitudes, feelings of powerlessness, lack of resources, stress, and family of origin sources for male intimate violence."[26] Additionally, "anxious attachment and angry temperament predicted dating violence in both sexes."[27]

The IPV sustained by men is "quite severe and both mentally and physically damaging."[28] When victimized, men's "most frequent response to their partner's IPV is to get away from her."[29] However, men often stay in an abusive relationship for much the same reason women do—"strong psychological and emotional ties to their partners and especially their children."[30] In our courts and social institutions, help-seeking men have the additional burden of not only proving they were subject to violence by their female partners, but also that the violence they sustained was damaging to them. The Centers for Disease Control (CDC) has recognized the problem of access to services for survivors of violence and has stated that "[o]ne strategy to improve access is co-located, multi-disciplinary service centers that include mental health, legal, economic, housing and other related services for survivors."[31] The CDC has stressed the importance of designing services "to meet the needs of a wide range of different populations such as teens, older adults, men, gay, lesbian, bisexual, and transgendered people."[32]

So, when making decisions relating to domestic violence, our courts must understand that intimate partner violence "takes place within a dyadic system and the system works in such a way as to maintain those dysfunctional interactional styles."[33] Since violent interactions often are bidirectional, interventions must work "to change the system in which that person belongs."[34] This is especially important considering that men who sought

26. *Id.*

27. *Id.*

28. Denise A. Hines & Emily M. Douglas, *A Closer Look at Men Who Sustain Intimate Terrorism by Women*, 1(3) Partner Abuse 286 (2010).

29. *Id.*

30. *Id.*

31. Michele C. Black et al., *The National Intimate Partner and Sexual Violence Survey (NISVS): 2010 Summary Report.* (National Center for Injury Prevention and Control, Centers for Disease Control and Prevention, Atlanta, GA) (2011), at 91.

32. *Id.*

33. Denise A. Hines et al., *Using Dyadic Concordance Types to Understand Frequency of Intimate Partner Violence*, 11 Partner Abuse 79 (2020).

34. *Id.* at 79.

help for victimization "described situations of their own abuse being intertwined with the experiences of their children."[35] In a research study titled *How Can I Be a Victim When I Have Children?" Abused Men's Perceptions of Their Children's Exposure to Domestic Violence*, the researchers report that "[t]his theme includes abuse in front of children, use of children to abuse victim, parental alienation, eye-opener to abuse, and continuation of abuse involving children after separation."[36] In custody determinations, it is critical to demonstrate how violence in a relationship unfolds and how the immediate and future consequences of the violence affect the child's best interests.

Prevalence of Violence Against Men and Boys

To better address IPV against men in court, it is first necessary to understand its prevalence. General U.S. population surveys show all genders experience violence at a rate of "8.4% to 18.4% for any type of physical violence and from 3.2% to 5.5% for severe physical violence, with approximately equal rates of male and female perpetration."[37] Tellingly, IPV is bidirectional.[38] The scientific literature provides ample reports and surveys detailing the prevalence of women aggressors against men.[39] As early as 1974, research has shown that "the eruption of conjugal violence occurs with equal frequency among both husbands and wives."[40] Since this early research, reports and surveys "show that between 25% and 50% of victims of IPV in a given year in the United States are men."[41] For instance, in its 2016/2017 National Intimate Partner and Sexual Violence Survey, the CDC reported that "[m]ore than 40 percent (44.2% or 52.1 million) of U.S. men reported [a form of] contact sexual violence, physical violence, and/or stalking by an intimate partner in their lifetime."[42] Of those reporting any contact sexual violence, "[l]ess than 1% (0.5% or 560,000) reported rape, 2.8% (3.3 million) being

35. Lysova et al., *supra* note 19, at 77.
36. *Id.*
37. Hines et al., *supra* note 33, at 77.
38. *Id.*
39. Hines & Douglas, *supra* note 8, at 37.
40. *Id.*
41. *Id.*
42. Kathleen C. Basile et al., *The National Intimate Partner and Sexual Violence Survey: 2016/2017 Report on Intimate Partner Violence.*, (National Center for Injury Prevention and Control, Centers for Disease Control and Prevention, Atlanta, GA) (2022), at 4.

made to penetrate, 5.0% (5.9 million) sexual coercion, and 2.1% (2.5 million) of men reported unwanted sexual contact by an intimate partner during their lifetime."[43] Of those reporting physical violence, "[b]eing slapped, pushed, or shoved by an intimate partner in their lifetime was reported by 39.0% of men (46.1 million), and 24.6% (29 million) reported experiencing any severe physical violence, including 16.9% of adult men reporting being hit with a fist or something hard, 12.2% being kicked, 7% who were slammed against something, 6.8% hurt by hair pulling, and 5.0% who were beaten."[44] Over six million men "reported being stalked by an intimate partner in their lifetime."[45] Psychological aggression was reported as the most prevalent type of violence perpetrated by women against men, with 45.1 percent or 53.3 million men reporting "psychological aggression by an intimate partner in their lifetime."[46] Additionally, "[e]xpressive aggression by an intimate partner in their lifetime was reported by 1 in 5 men (20.2%), and 2 in 5 men (42.8%) reported coercive control and entrapment, including 26.7% who reported that a partner kept track of them by demanding to know where they were and what they were doing, 23.8% that a partner destroyed something important to them, and 20.9% that a partner made decisions for them that should have been theirs to make."[47]

Family conflict studies provide additional data on "violence by women toward men in the US . . . [through] the Conflict Tactics Scales (CTS)."[48] These studies demonstrate men are victims 50 percent of the time.[49] National studies project rates of severe assaults against men to be "2.6 million men per year." These men "sustained IPV that had a high likelihood of causing an injury."[50]

Even though the scientific literature is replete with research demonstrating women use intimate partner violence against men, a myth persists that "men do not sustain IPV from their women partners, unless it is because their partners are acting in self-defense or retaliation."[51] This

---

43. *Id.*
44. *Id.* at 5.
45. *Id.*
46. *Id.* at 6.
47. *Id.*
48. Hines & Douglas, *supra* note 8, at 37.
49. *Id.*
50. *Id.*
51. Hines & Douglas, *supra* note 28, at 287.

myth persists on the belief that IPV "is an issue of men maintaining power and control over their women partners, it is not possible for women to be perpetrators of IPV."[52] The research, however, shows that men, too, are victimized and suffer from IPV at the hands of women. For instance, in data extrapolated from help-seeking samples of men and women, "female partners were reported by the male participants to have used all types of IPV at significantly higher rates than the male participants."[53] In fact, women were reported by the help-seeking samples to have used aggression up to six times more than men.[54] This differs from reports from community samples, who report "[m]ale participants and female partners engaged in minor psychological, severe psychological, sexual, minor physical and total physical aggression at relatively equal rates, although female partners were reported to have engaged in significantly higher rates of controlling [behaviors] and severe physical aggression."[55] Comparing community samples with help-seeking samples, researchers theorize that female partners of help-seeking samples are more likely to engage in "intimate terrorism" (IT) compared to violence that just gets out of hand. For instance, in the help-seeking samples, researchers found females were one and half times more likely to use sexual and severe physical aggression against their male partners and 3.75 times more likely to use controlling behaviors against their male partners.[56] Additionally, "men in the help-seeking sample were injured at higher rates and frequencies than men in the community sample—help-seeking men were close to 90 times more likely to have sustained an injury in the past year than men from the community sample."[57]

In studies assessing intimate violence not focused on crime victim statistics, researchers found that "[m]en reported greater victimization and more severe assaults than did women."[58] This research demonstrated that "[t]he majority (55%) of assaults on men were perpetrated by spouses, partners, or former partners."[59] Additionally, another study using a sample of couples seeking marital therapy, researchers found:

---

52. *Id.*
53. Hines & Douglas, *supra* note 8, at 44.
54. *Id.* at 44.
55. *Id.*
56. *Id.* at 52.
57. *Id.*
58. Dutton & Nicholls, *supra* note 5, at 692–96.
59. *Id.*

> 61% of the husbands and 64% of the wives were classified as aggressive, 25% of the husbands and 11% of the wives were identified as mildly aggressive, and 36% of husbands and 53% of wives were classified as severely aggressive. Sixty-eight percent of couples were in agreement with regard to husbands' overall levels of aggression and 69% of couples were in agreement on wives' overall levels of aggression. Aggression levels were identified as "nonviolent, mildly violent, or severely violent."[60]

Interestingly, men were more likely to underreport than to overreport aggression by women[61] and "[w]omen reported receiving lower levels of violence than they perpetrated for overall, minor, and severe violence."[62] A similar study of U.S. participants found that "more women than men had been physically violent towards their partners (44% vs. 31%)."[63] In Canada, "[t]hirty-nine percent of female participants in the survey reported 'participation in some form of spouse abuse' and 16.2% reported severe violence perpetration."[64] These studies also found that "[t]he risk factors for female participation were being young, having high scores on the Eysenck psychoticism scale [which measures two pervasive, independent dimensions of personality], neuroticism index, and MacAndrews alcoholism scale [which measures a relatively stable trait common to many alcoholics]."[65] In other words, gender was not a factor that predicted violence—psychological disturbance and alcohol abuse were.[66]

Research studies also indicate that when women reported incidents of violence, men and women perpetrated violence at an equal rate (1 percent difference, males higher), but when males report incidents of violence, women perpetrated violence at a much higher rate (9 percent).[67] This is not a new development or statistic. Back in 2004, in a study of "abuse alleged in same- and opposite-gender litigants applying for abuse prevention orders,"[68] the researchers concluded that despite widespread belief that intimate abuse involves an abusive male and a victimized female, male and female plaintiffs

60. *Id.*
61. *Id.*
62. *Id.*
63. *Id.*
64. *Id.*
65. *Id.*
66. *Id.*
67. *Id.*
68. *Id.*

alleged very nearly identical behaviors by male and female defendants.[69] More than two decades ago, in 2001, the U.S. National Comorbidity Survey confirmed "there was no significant gender difference in the prevalence of minor physical victimization reported by the women (17.4%) and the men (18.4%)."[70] Additionally, this same survey confirmed that "[m]en reported significantly less severe violence perpetration (2.7%) than women reporting severe violence victimization (6.5%)."[71] In 2001, another study questioned reciprocal aggression.[72] This national survey replicated previous findings that violence is reciprocated in men and women.[73] This subset was defined as "those that required intervention by any professional (e.g., hospital, police, lawyers)."[74] For those who perpetrated abuse, they "evidenced signs of personality disturbance," for instance "the women had aggressive personalities and/or adolescent conduct disorder."[75] This research counters prior findings that assume "if clinical abuse was ascertained in epidemiological samples, it would be primarily man-to-woman, explained by patriarchy rather than psychopathology."[76] These gender-biased assumptions are a disservice as they do not consider alternative causes of violence. Without addressing the alternative causes, improper interventions are put in place and family systems could be led astray. Research suggests instead that "psychological factors in both genders predicted aggression: anxious attachment and angry temperament influenced the need to control one's partner which in turn predicted use of aggression."[77] In fact, "personality disorder symptoms were most predictive of IPV for both sexes."[78]

Types of Violence Experienced by Male Victims

The ways men are victimized in IPV are similar to the ways women are victimized. IPV can either directly or indirectly target the victim. Generally, there are five different types of IPV experienced by men: (1) coercion,

69. *Id.*
70. *Id.*
71. *Id.*
72. *Id.*
73. *Id.*
74. *Id.*
75. *Id.*
76. *Id.*
77. *Id.*
78. *Id.*

(2) emotional abuse, (3) physical abuse, (4) sexual abuse, and (5) through weaponization of children. Additionally, as shown earlier, men are impacted by IPV at approximately the same rate women are.

The CDC defines IPV as "physical violence, sexual violence, threats of physical or sexual violence, stalking and psychological aggression (including coercive tactics) by a current or former intimate partner."[79] The CDC further states that "[i]ntimate partner violence may occur among cohabitating or non-cohabitating romantic or sexual partners and among opposite or same sex couples."[80] IPV is "a serious, preventable public health problem that affects millions of Americans."[81] While men experience many types of violence similar to women, there are other forms of violence that are typical of male victims. For instance, "[w]hen considering physical violence female perpetrators are more likely to use accessible weapons rather than physical strength alone, this might include boiling water, mobile phones, knives and household objects."[82]

Of men seeking help for IPV victimization, the most common physical acts of violence perpetrated against them by females were "hitting, pushing, kicking, grabbing and punching."[83] However, the physical aggression was sometimes severe, and "[o]ver 20% of the sample reported violence that could be considered life threatening (e.g. choking, using a knife)."[84] Most of the help-seeking males were fearful of their partner's violence.[85] Regarding emotional abuse, the help-seeking males reported a variety of psychologically aggressive behaviors:

> [C]lose to 95% of the callers reported that their female partners used controlling [behaviors], including threats and coercion (e.g. Threatening to kill herself or him, threatening to leave; 77.6%), emotional abuse (e.g. calling him names, humiliation; 74.1%), intimidation (e.g. instilling fear by smashing things, destroying property, abusing pets, displaying weapons; 63.3%), blaming the male caller for the violence, denying the violence (59.9%), misusing the judicial system (e.g. using the court system to gain

---

79. Black et al., *supra* note 31, at 37.

80. *Id.*

81. National District Attorneys Association, *National Domestic Violence Prosecution Best Practices Guide*, Update 2020, at 6.

82. Luke Martin & Ippo Panteloudakis, Toolkit for Work with Male Victims of Domestic Abuse 12 (3d ed. 2019).

83. Hines & Douglas, *supra* note 8, at 40.

84. *Id.*

85. *Id.*

> sole custody of children; falsely obtaining a restraining order against the male caller; 49.0%), isolating the caller from family and friends (41.5%), controlling the household finances and not allowing the caller to see or use the cheque book or credit cards (38.1%) and using the children to keep the caller in the violent relationship (64.5%).[86]

Regarding directionality of perpetration, research studies demonstrate "[of] physical PV [partner violence], severe psychological PV, and controlling behaviors, bidirectional PV was the most common, followed by female only perpetration."[87] These researchers further explain that "[w]ithin bidirectionally aggressive relationships, women committed significantly more physical PV and controlling behaviors; there were no sex differences in frequency of PV perpetration for these three forms of PV for male-only versus female-only PV."[88] The study also found that men perpetrated more verbal sexual aggression than women.[89] Incidents of bidirectional aggression also tend to be the most aggressive type of violence.[90] These researchers suggest that when family courts and mental health practitioners assess victimization and perpetration, a family systems perspective is needed to understand the IPV.[91] This is because it is important to have "an accurate understanding of the dynamics within the couple."[92] In fact, "early indications are that both physical and psychological injuries are more severe among both men and women who experience bidirectional violence compared to those who experience unilateral violence."[93] The same researchers reason this is so because "mental health problems are also more severe among both men and women who experience bidirectional severe psychological PV and controlling behaviors."[94]

Coercion, Intimidation, and Threats

Coercion, intimidation, and threats are a rather insidious form of violence. They include controlling behaviors that are designed to intimidate or

---

86. *Id.*
87. Hines et al., *supra* note 33, at 76–77.
88. *Id.*
89. *Id.*
90. *Id.*
91. *Id.*
92. *Id.*
93. *Id.*
94. *Id.*

threaten a victim. Some examples reported by men include (1) threatening violence, especially when the victim does not do what the perpetrator wants him to do; (2) threatening to call authorities and make false allegations against him; (3) threatening various legal proceedings; (4) denying access to medical care; (5) intimidating with threatening gestures; (6) destroying the victim's personal items; (7) telling the victim that nobody will believe him because he is a man; (8) threatening the victim with weapons; (9) threatening to deny visitation with his children; and (10) forced sleep deprivation.[95]

Coercion is legally defined as "the intimidation of a victim to compel the individual to do some act against his or her will by the use of psychological pressure, physical force, or threats."[96] Coercive control is grounded in concepts derived from the Power and Control Wheel[97] and includes "intimidation; emotional abuse; isolation; minimizing, denying, and blame; using children and male privilege; economic abuse; and coercion and threats."[98]

In some instances, partners use false allegations against their victims to intimidate and control a victim.[99] In fact, in a research study, *A Closer Look at Men Who Sustain Intimate Terrorism by Women*, a team of researchers report, "[O]ver half of the men reported that their women partners made false accusations against them, which included that he hit or beat her, that a restraining order was filed against him under false pretenses, or that he physically and/or sexually abused the children."[100] These researchers conclude that "[t]hese findings are also consistent with a study of families undergoing custody disputes in the courts, which showed that 21% of women made allegations of physical child abuse against their husbands, 23% of sexual child abuse, and 55% of IPV. Only 6%, 6%, and 41% of the accusations,

---

95. Martin & Panteloudakis, *supra* note 82, at 6–7.

96. Ashish Joshi, *"Coercive Control: What Family Practitioners Should Know About This Insidious Form of Mental Abuse,"* 51 Mich. Fam. L.J. 9, 17 (2021) (citing Coercive. (n.d.) West's Encyclopedia of American Law, edition 2 (2008), https://legal-dictionary.thefreedictionary.com/coercive.

97. Alexis Chavis & Melanie Hill, *Integrating Multiple Intersecting Identities: A Multicultural Conceptualization of the Power and Control Wheel.* 32 Women & Therapy 121 (2009). 10.1080/02703140802384552.

98. Kristy Candela, *Protecting the Invisible Victim: Incorporating Coercive Control in Domestic Violence Statutes*, 54(1) Fam. Ct. Rev. 112–15 (2016).

99. Andreia Machado et al., *Male Victims of Female-Perpetrated Partner Violence: A Qualitative Analysis of Men's Experiences, the Impact of Violence, and Perceptions of Their Worth*, 21(4) Psychology of Men & Masculinities 618 (2020).

100. Hines & Douglas, *supra* note 28, at 306.

respectively, were substantiated by the courts."[101] Researchers report that men are particularly vulnerable to legal abuse—"when one partner uses the legal and administrative system to the detriment of the other partner."[102] In other instances men are stalked by women perpetrators.

Emotional Abuse

Emotional abuse includes all types of psychological aggression, or the "use of verbal and non-verbal communication with the intent to harm another person mentally or emotionally, and/or to exert control over another person."[103] Some examples of emotional abuse reported by men have been: (1) put-downs and humiliating the victim in front of others, (2) calling the victim names, (3) gaslighting, (4) blaming the victim for the abuse, (5) giving the victim the "the silent treatment," and (6) telling the victim he is not the children's father.[104] Research shows that "100% of women partners were reported by their men partners to have used minor psychological aggression, 96.0% used severe psychological aggression, 93.4% used controlling behaviors, and 41.1% used sexual aggression."[105] Research also shows that there are significant gender differences in the perpetration of psychological abuse, as women perpetrate "significantly more psychological aggression than males."[106]

In interviews with male victims of female perpetrated partner violence, men reported their experiences to include "denial of [child] visitation (. . .) there is . . . constant derogatory comments and intimidation" and a "disregard [of] all my suggestions and ridiculed me for being so weak."[107] The effects of emotional abuse are similar to physical abuse. Male victims have reported that "[w]hat women lack in muscle strength they more than make up in deceit and cunning . . . just as violent in their ways if not much more."[108] As one male victim reported, "[m]y abuser never hit me hard

101. *Id.* at 307.

102. Machado et al., *supra* note 99, at 615.

103. *Id.* at 618.

104. Martin & Panteloudakis, *supra* note 82, at 6–7.

105. Hines & Douglas, *supra* note 28, at 295.

106. Denise A. Hines & Kimberly J. Saudino, *Gender Differences in Psychological, Physical, and Sexual Aggression Among College Students Using the Revised Conflict Tactics Scales*, 18(2) Violence & Victims 198 (2003).

107. Machado et al., *supra* note 99, at 618.

108. *Id.*

enough to draw blood or send me to the emergency room, but the near constant emotional abuse sure felt like terrorism to me."[109]

Physical Abuse

The CDC defines physical violence as "the intentional use of physical force with the potential for causing death, disability, injury, or harm,"[110] and can include (1) hitting, punching, slapping, kicking the victim; (2) using objects to hurt the victim, sometimes in the groin area; (3) using knives or other sharp objects to attack the victim; (4) pouring boiling water on the victim; and (5) attacking the victim when he's asleep.[111] In a 2003 study examining female perpetrators from a community sample, "women reported the following physical abuse frequencies directed at their male partners: kicking (20.2%), choking/strangling (9.1%), physically attacked the sexual parts of his body (7.1%), used a knife or gun against him (7.8%)."[112] For those women who used physical violence, they reported the repeated use of violence.[113] Help-seeking males have also reported their experiences with physical violence. One male reported "I was viciously attacked in my house, knocked out, concussion, thrown through the front window of my residence."[114] Another male reported "[my wife] tried to stab me in the back with both knives (. . .) I had seen the reflection in the mirror and spun around at the last moment, so the knives didn't go deep. Some blood spattered on the mirror and white wall next to it."[115]

Sexual Abuse

The CDC subdivides sexual violence into five different categories: (1) "rape or penetration of victim";[116] (2) "victim made to penetrate someone else";[117] (3) "non-physically pressured unwanted penetration";[118] (4) "unwanted

109. *Id.*

110. Black et al., *supra* note 31, at 37.

111. Martin & Panteloudakis, *supra* note 82, at 6–7.

112. Dutton & Nicholls, *supra* note 5, at 692–96.

113. *Id.*

114. Machado et al., *supra* note 9, at 618.

115. *Id.*

116. Black et al., *supra* note 31, at 37.

117. *Id.*

118. *Id.*

sexual contact";[119] and (5) "non-contact unwanted sexual experiences."[120] Unwanted sexual contact occurs when the perpetrator intentionally touches the victim or makes "the victim touch the perpetrator, either directly or through clothing . . . without the victim's consent."[121] Likewise, non-contact unwanted sexual experiences occur when the victim is exposed to "sexual situations (e.g., pornography); verbal or behavioral sexual harassment; threats of sexual violence to accomplish some other end; and/or unwanted filming, taking, or disseminating photographs of a sexual nature of another person."[122] Help-seeking males who have been victimized by sexual violence have reported that females have (1) coerced or threatened the victim overtly into sex; (2) coerced the victim into using objects or using objects on him during sex, against his wishes; (3) coerced the victim to perform sexual acts that he does not want; (4) mocked the victim's sexual behavior in front of others; (5) threatened consequences unless the victim participates in sex; and (6) coerced the victim to participate in sexual activities with others against his will.[123] Some male participants in research studies have disclosed acts of sexual aggression that consist of "She talked about me being poor in sex"[124] and "Demanded sex from me or she would ban me from seeing our children (a threat which she actually followed through with)."[125]

Weaponizing Children

As an indirect form of abuse, the use of children is particularly troublesome. Children may be used as a weapon of abuse by (1) isolating the victim from the children, (2) instilling fear of the victim in the children, (3) undermining the victim's parental authority, (4) stripping the child of symbolic and emotional connection with the victim, and (5) encouraging the child to betray the victim. Help-seeking males have identified this type of abuse as the perpetrator sending the victim messages through the children, the perpetrator excluding the victim from activities with the children, and the perpetrator belittling the victim's attempts to take care of the children.[126]

---

119. *Id.*
120. *Id.*
121. *Id.*
122. *Id.*
123. Martin & Panteloudakis, *supra* note 82, at 6–7.
124. Machado et al., *supra* note 99, at 618.
125. *Id.*
126. Martin & Panteloudakis, *supra* note 82, at 6–7.

Additionally, in a peer-reviewed research study, researchers reported that participants described "instances where their partners used their children as 'weapons' to harm or manipulate them."[127] One participant reported that "denial of visitation should be considered a form of abuse, as 'doing that is doing that for a reason, doing that to hurt you emotionally.'"[128] Another participant "described this form of abuse 'so many times' as 'she has just denied all contact with the children, on a whim, just using them as weapons. I can't see them on Father's Day, talk to them on the phone, you name it.'"[129] Eleven participants in this study felt alienated from their children by their partners.[130] A UK participant "described his time away from his children as 'the worst abuse that [he] experienced.'"[131] Another U.S. participant reported "[w]e separated with false claims of domestic violence, and she used that to take her [our daughter] and stay at a friend's house, and she wouldn't tell me where she was at, or where my daughter was or how I could contact her on the phone, and that's pretty much been the theme ever since she left."[132]

In addition to children being used as abusive weapons, abuse that occurs in front of children—where the children are forced to watch a parent being humiliated, beaten, degraded—is incredibly damaging. Researchers have found "two primary forms of abuse that occur[] in front of their children—physical violence and psychological abuse."[133] One participant reported physical abuse such as "once driving in the car with [his] four little children in the back and being punched in the side of the head while . . . driving on the highway."[134] The use of weapons was also identified as an abusive strategy. For instance, one participant reported being "'stabbed in the arm with a fork' in front of his daughter,"[135] while another described a dinnertime incident: "I had come home after work and my wife said, 'Watch the potatoes' and went to get some food. I started playing with the kids and the potatoes boiled over. She threw the pot of boiled potatoes at me. I ducked out of

127. Lysova et al., *supra* note 19, at 78.
128. *Id.*
129. *Id.*
130. *Id.*
131. *Id.*
132. *Id.* at 78–79.
133. *Id.*
134. *Id.*
135. *Id.*

the way and was not hurt."[136] Another participant reported that his partner "poured hot dinner plates over me with the dinner still on"[137] and "this happened quite often and in front of the children as well."[138]

Participants also reported psychological abuse. One U.S. participant stated:

> The kids are really the Achilles heel. I never really felt that my ex penetrated, no matter how violent she was or how irrational, no matter how much humiliation was heaped on. I never felt that she was able to penetrate my armor until the kid came along and she was able to able to embarrass me, humiliate me in front of my own child. And that was when I really began to suffer.[139]

Another participant explained "that abuse in front of his daughter was 'much more traumatic for me . . . than being punched in the face.'"[140] This participant "decided to leave his abusive relationship when the children started to be involved as '[he] didn't want her putting [him] down anymore in front of the children.'"[141]

Men's Perpetration of IPV as a Response to "Intimate Terrorism"

In a research study, *A Closer Look at Men Who Sustain Intimate Terrorism by Women*, researchers found that the most common response men have to physical violence perpetrated by women was to "get away from her or go to another room. . . . The next common response was to yell or curse . . . , followed by calling a friend or family member . . . , crying . . . , calling the police . . . , and grabbing/shoving/pushing/hitting her back."[142] Additionally, the research found that the "most common qualitative response was to ask her to calm down or attempt to reason with her."[143] Male study participants

136. *Id.*
137. *Id.*
138. *Id.*
139. *Id.*
140. *Id.*
141. *Id.*
142. Hines & Douglas, *supra* note 28, at 299.
143. *Id.*

described that they "[t]ried to talk to her about it calmly, saying 'now, if I did that to you, you'd call it abuse.' She answered that she was defending her honor."[144] Additionally, participants reported that "I tell her that it is not acceptable for her to hit me, or yell at me, especially in front of the children. I also ask her to apologize."[145] Another participant described his response as:

> I have never hit my wife, but today I came close to doing this. It should be noted she has hit me more times than I can remember and kicked me. I grabbed her arms in self-defense and held her to the floor. I am a very big and strong man, my wife is tall but thin, not strong at all. I know I will be the one who goes to jail even though she is the one hitting and kicking.
>
> I asked her why she hit me, and she said, "because you're bigger than me." I just felt vengeful for a second and slapped her back. It was the only time I hit her, ever. I cried because I was raised not to hit women, and I felt disappointed in myself that I had crossed that line.[146]

However, when men used severe physical IPV, it was found that those men had "sustained more frequent acts of severe psychological aggression from their female partners within the past year than men in the other two groups who did not differ from each other."[147] Additionally, those men who "used severe physical IPV also experienced more physical IPV from their female partners than men who did not use physical IPV in the previous year; they were more likely than the men in the other two groups to have sustained a severe injury in the previous year, and they were more likely than men who used minor physical IPV only to have sustained sexual aggression in the previous year."[148]

Experts who study family violence posit that "it could be that male victims of I[ntimate] T[errorism] who choose to use physical IPV as a response to their partner's aggression have deficits in executive cognitive functioning, which contributes to both their aggressive responses and their drinking problem."[149]

---

144. *Id.*

145. *Id.*

146. *Id.*

147. Denise A. Hines & Emily M. Douglas, *Understanding the Use of Violence Among Men Who Sustain Intimate Terrorism*, 2(3) Partner Violence 272 (2011).

148. *Id.* at 272.

149. *Id.* at 275.

Gender and Perpetration of Violence

Difference in Men's Use of IPV

The CDC reports that prevalence estimates of IPV "differ from those reported in other similar national surveys." The prevalence of IPV is higher for both men and women, but particularly for physical violence victimization of men. In addition to the previously mentioned changes related to the measurement of stalking and sexual violence, which are components of IPV, another key factor may account for the differences in prevalence estimates.[150] For instance, "[m]ale rape victims and male victims of non-contact unwanted sexual experiences reported predominantly male perpetrators. Nearly half of male stalking victims also reported perpetration by a male. Male victims of other forms of violence reported predominantly female perpetrators."[151] Interestingly, previous national surveys aimed to study the prevalence of IPV framed questions in a way that made the relationship between the perpetrator and victim unclear. For example, "some previous national surveys have asked respondents to identify whether they have experienced physical violence by any perpetrator, and then respondents are subsequently asked whether the perpetrator was an intimate partner."[152] More recent surveys, including the National Intimate Partner and Sexual Violence Survey, ask whether victims have "experienced physically violent acts specifically by a romantic or sexual partner."[153] This key difference has increased our understanding of IPV between genders and within relationship types.

Difference Between Men Who Use Physical IPV Versus Those Who Do Not

Research studies have found that "[t]here were several significant differences in the men's use of various forms of IPV in the previous year."[154] For men who perpetrated severe IPV, it was found that they were "significantly more likely to have used controlling behaviors in the previous year and to

150. CDC, National Center for Injury Prevention and Control, Division of Violence Prevention, National Intimate Partner and Sexual Violence Survey, 2010 Summary Report, at 84.

151. *Id.*

152. *Id.*

153. *Id.*

154. *Id.*

have used these behaviors significantly more frequently, than men in the other two groups who did not differ from each other."[155] These men also "used significantly more physical IPV, in terms of frequency, than men who used minor physical IPV only (men who did not report using IPV were not included in this analysis because there was no variability in their use of physical IPV)."[156] The female victims in this group were also more likely "to have reportedly sustained a serious injury in the previous year than the female partners of men in the other two groups."[157] Of the men who did not use physical intimate partner violence, they were "significantly less likely to have used severe psychological aggression and to use it significantly less frequently, than men in the other two groups who did not differ from each other in either the prevalence or frequency of severe psychological aggression."[158] Interestingly, it was also found that "men who use physical IPV (either minor or severe) engage in other maladaptive behaviors with their female partners as well."[159] For instance, these men "engaged in significantly more severe psychological IPV (both in prevalence and in frequency) and were more likely to insist on engaging in sex when their partners did not want to."[160] Additionally, research demonstrates that men who do not use physical intimate partner violence are more likely to seek help by calling the police, going to the emergency room, or going to a shelter.[161] "[W]hen men call the police or go to a shelter for help, it is unlikely that he is the real abuser in this relationship, an accusation that male help-seekers often encounter by domestic violence agency workers and police."[162]

Difference Between Men Who Use "Minor Physical" IPV Versus "Severe" IPV

Studies show that men who used severe physical intimate partner violence compared to men who used minor physical intimate partner violence "were more likely to use controlling behaviors and used them significantly more

155. *Id.*
156. *Id.*
157. *Id.*
158. *Id.*
159. *Id.*
160. *Id.*
161. *Id.* at 275.
162. *Id.*

often in the previous year."[163] This explains the trend toward mutual violent control, a behavior that is described as "two intimate terrorists battling each other for control."[164] Notably, the men who used severe physical intimate partner violence "still reportedly engaged in much fewer of these behaviors than their female partners."[165] Even though these men used severe physical IPV, they were still "considered victims of I[ntimate] T[errorism] who engage in violent resistance," according to a classification criteria established by some researchers.[166]

Demographically, the men who used physical IPV were generally younger than the men who did not use physical IPV.[167] Studies have found no differences "between men who used physical IPV and men who did not in ethnicity, education, income, or disability status of either the participant or his partner."[168] Moreover, there were no differences found in "childhood history of abuse, or mental illnesses including PTSD."[169] Instead, it was discovered that "[t]he major characteristic that seems to differentiate men who use minor physical IPV only from men who use severe physical IPV is substance abuse."[170] These researchers found that "men who used severe physical IPV were more likely to engage in substance abuse and used substances significantly more often than the other two groups of men—no IPV and minor IPV groups (who did not differ from each other)."[171]

Consequences of Violence: Adverse Childhood Experiences (ACE) Study

The consequences of violence are profound. Even when controlling for demographics and adverse childhood experiences, researchers have found that "increasing levels of dating violence was associated with anxiety, depression, and PTSD in boys[.]"[172] While the meme persists that female victim-

163. *Id.* at 276.
164. *Id.*
165. *Id.*
166. *Id.*
167. *Id.* at 273.
168. *Id.*
169. *Id.* at 275.
170. *Id.* at 276–77.
171. *Id.*
172. Dutton & Nicholls, *supra* note 5, at 692–96.

ization is more severe, "research shows that [physical violence] against men is associated with a range of negative physical and mental health outcomes."[173] For instance, in the 2016/2017 *National Intimate Partner and Sexual Violence Survey*, the CDC reported that the impact of contact sexual violence, physical violence, and/or stalking by an intimate partner on male victims commonly led to injury, PTSD symptoms, fear, concern for safety, needing legal services, missing at least one day of work, and needing help from law enforcement.[174] The CDC reported that:

> [t]he most frequent forms of injury reported by male victims were minor bruises or scratches, mental or emotional harm, and cuts, major bruises, or black eyes. In the 12 months prior to taking the survey, 40.5% of male victims of intimate partner violence experienced contact sexual violence, physical violence, and/or stalking and at least one impact related to intimate partner violence. . . .
>
> Overall, 11.1% of male victims who reported experiencing contact sexual violence, physical violence, and/or stalking by an intimate partner in their lifetime also reported experiencing a recent impact related to intimate partner violence in the past 12 months; this includes [those] who were not victimized in the past 12 months but who still reported an impact related to intimate partner violence in the past 12 months[.][175]

Men who are victims of intimate terrorism "are at exponentially increased risk for exceeding a clinical cut-off for PTSD."[176] Family violence researchers found that 60 percent of men who sought help for abuse exceeded this cut-off, a percentage that is similar to what samples of battered women typically show.[177]

Not only does violence impact the person it is targeted to, but violence also impacts the entire family system. For instance, children exposed to intimate partner violence are at risk for a variety of physical and mental health impairments. Researchers explain this "trajectory from adverse childhood experiences to adult morbidity . . . by the influence of toxic stress

---

173. Machado et al., *supra* note 99, at 612–21.

174. Basile et al., *supra* note 42, at 12.

175. *Id.*

176. Denise A. Hines & Emily M. Douglas, *Symptoms of Posttraumatic Stress Disorder in Men Who Sustain Intimate Partner Violence: A Study of Helpseeking and Community Samples*, 12(2) Psych, of Men & Masculinity 123 (2011).

177. *Id.*

and allostatic load."[178] These researchers explain that a "high allostatic load occurs when toxic stress causes excessive activation of stress hormones, which can damage the metabolic, cardiovascular, immune, and nervous systems."[179] This could result in "cognitive, behavioral, social, and mental and physical health challenges, which in turn increase the risk for unhealthy behaviors."[180] In fact, research has "consistently found detrimental effects of exposure to IPV on children, such as affective problems, anxiety, attention-deficit/hyperactivity, conduct problems, oppositional defiance, pervasive developmental issues, and somatic problems."[181] In addition to the consequences of exposure to violence in the home, children of victims are indirectly impacted by the victim's subsequent mental health. Victims who are experiencing "higher rates of post-traumatic stress symptoms, depression, suicidal ideation, psychosomatic symptoms, cardiovascular disease, general psychological distress, poor overall health, isolation and loneliness, and job loss"[182] ultimately impact the entire family system. This may lead to male victims of violence reported loss of "custody of their children and being a target of false accusations of child abuse."[183] Horrifically, threats and actual false allegations of abuse are "sometimes used by abusive women to dominate their male partners."[184] For instance, researchers have found that "when male victims of IPV file complaints against their female partner, there is a high probability of the women filing a false allegation against men, which may lead to their arrest."[185]

Men who complained of being subjected to IPV described their "children as 'mirroring' their partner's abusive behaviors."[186] For instance, one UK father said that his son "one day mirrored some behavior that he had seen his mother did to me. Basically, he chucked some dinner over [him] a few days after he had seen his mum did it."[187] A Canadian participant

---

178. Leah K. Gilbert et al., *Childhood Adversity and Adult Chronic Disease: An Update from Ten States and the District of Columbia, 2010*, 48(3) Am. J. of Preventive Medicine 346 (2010), https://doi.org/10.1016/j.amepre.2014.09.006.

179. *Id.* at 346.

180. Hines & Douglas, *supra* note 147, at 272.

181. Lysova et al., *supra* note 19, at 69.

182. Machado et al., *supra* note 99, at 613.

183. *Id.* at 615.

184. *Id.*

185. *Id.*

186. Lysova et al., *supra* note 19, at 75.

187. *Id.*

"discussed how his partner's verbal abuse influenced his 3-year-old son's first words: His first words were, you know, 'daddy has a small dick,' and so this was the kind of stuff that would go on, while his older son would '[kick] and [beat] on [him] every day in response because that was what he always saw.'"[188] This study's participants also described their children as having emotional problems caused by the exposure of abuse. Another Canadian participant stated "his partner [was] leaving the children with 'nightmares' so that his youngest son 'wouldn't even speak and he just stopped talking.'"[189] Another participant "specifically noted that his partner's child 'started developing emotional problems that started to become apparent because of the hate he was starting to exhibit against her because of her constant abuse.'"[190] Other participants of studies focused on men being victims of IPV felt they were estranged from their children. For instance, a U.S. participant noted "a precursor to full blown estrangement as planted by his partner: I said that she still had presents under the tree. She looked at me and said, 'But daddy, mommy said you were bad and didn't give me any Christmas presents.' And I told her, 'Well that's not true, sweetie.'"[191] Another U.S. participant explained that his son "won't have anything to do with [him] after fighting with his partner in the courts."[192]

Shame/Humiliation Factor

Reshaping how we view victimization can go a long way in providing solutions for male victims. In the United States, "men tend to be taught to suppress emotions, avoid vulnerability, and not ask for help."[193] This has a silencing effect on male victims, who may feel ashamed to report abuse. For instance, in a research study titled *'I'm a Red-Blooded Male': Understanding Men's Experiences of Domestic Abuse Through a Feminist Lens*, researchers explain that our society has shaped our idea of how a man should behave. They describe these behaviors as the "Man Box." The seven pillars of the

---

188. *Id.*

189. *Id.*

190. *Id.*

191. *Id.* at 75–76.

192. *Id.*

193. National Sexual Violence Resource Center, *Understanding Male Socialization, Stigma, and Reactions to Sexual Violence*, https://www.nsvrc.org/working-male-survivors-sexual-violence/Understanding (last visited Dec. 3, 2025).

Man Box are "(1) be self-sufficient; (2) act tough; (3) be physically attractive; (4) stick to rigid gender roles in the home; (5) be heterosexual; (6) be hypersexual and (7) use aggression where needed and have control over women."[194] When males attempt to behave in a way contrary to the Man Box they are socially shamed. For instance, male victims who called the helpline explained that showing "vulnerable emotion in response was met with ridicule and more abuse," and one victim stated: "She pissed herself laughing when I told her [I was scared]."[195] Other callers "felt ashamed and panicked when faced with their female partner's violence: 'I feel shameful talking about this as I am [a] bit of a macho guy, but she would slap me round the face . . .' and 'she self-harms and punches herself in the face. It makes me ill and it brings on a panic attack, and she says how can I be having a panic attack when I am a man.'"[196] Once the help-seekers began speaking about the violence they endured, they began opening up those vulnerable feelings and expressed "I am scared of her, and I don't care if this makes me less of a man. I have decided to speak up as I am now worried about my daughter and need help."[197]

Some say that the *Depp v. Heard* trial became a catalyst for men to talk about intimate partner violence. Kalhan Roosevelt reports in *Male Domestic Violence Survivors Say They Feel the Depp-Heard Trial Is a Turning Point*, "some men and male-presenting people who have survived violent relationships and experts who work with survivors say the trial feels like a turning point in the stigma against male survivors."[198] A program viewer expressed that "he was finally able to open up to friends about what he had endured. Feelings of humiliation are just a part of the stigma that has prevented so many men from coming forward to share their stories."[199] Critically:

---

194. Nicole Westmarland & Stephen R. Burrell, *'I'm a Red-Blooded Male': Understanding Men's Experiences of Domestic Abuse Through a Feminist Lens*, 0 Criminology & Criminal Justice 1 (2023), https://doi.org/10.1177/17488958231210985.

195. *Id.* at 1.

196. *Id.*

197. *Id.*

198. Kalhan Rosenblatt, *Male Domestic Violence Survivors Say They Feel the Depp-Heard Trial Is a Turning Point*, NBC News, May 24, 2022, https://www.nbcnews.com/pop-culture/pop-culture-news/male-domestic-violence-survivors-say-feel-depp-heard-trial-turning-poi-rcna29742.

199. *Id.*

> [A]ll people, including victims, must work to relearn what it means to be masculine and how a masculine person should behave when confronted with a domestic violence situation. Stereotypes about how men should act and how they should cope with violent partners, especially in heterosexual relationships, are inaccurate and lead more victims to stay silent[.][200]

Research on shame and/or humiliation as a factor of both female perpetration of abuse and male response to victimization is crucial to understanding why this abuse occurs and how we may better support male victims.[201]

Substance Abuse and Its Impact on Violence by and Against Men

In cases of IPV, substance abuse plays a big role. If a partner who is intoxicated is provoked, "the intoxicated person may not be able to access higher order social problem-solving skills to resolve conflict."[202] When this happens, the intoxicated partner "is attending to immediate cues (i.e., provocation by his partner) and is unable to attend to more distal, inhibitory information (e.g., possibility that he could be arrested for engaging in IPV) or to figure out alternative means to conflict resolution other than aggression."[203]

In studying cases involving IPV acts committed by men and women's IPV that drives men's maladaptive behavior, researchers have found few differences in the behaviors of female partners. They found that "it may not be the women's IPV that drives the men's maladaptive behavior but something about the men that leads them to react with IPV."[204] This "something" appears to be alcohol abuse.[205] That is to say, "men who used both minor and severe physical IPV were intoxicated significantly more often and were more likely to be categorized as abusing alcohol in the past year than men who did not use physical IPV."[206] In their study, a team of researchers found that "during the last physical argument that was instigated by the female

200. *Id.*

201. Westmarland & Burrell, *supra* note 194, at 1.

202. Denise A. Hines & Emily M. Douglas, *Understanding the Use of Violence Among Men Who Sustain Intimate Terrorism*, 2(3) Partner Violence 274, 274–75 (2011).

203. *Id.*

204. *Id.*

205. *Id.*

206. *Id.*

partner, male participants who reported that they used any physical IPV in the previous year were significantly more likely to have been drinking than male participants who reported no use of physical IPV in the previous year."[207] Consequently, this may show that the "man's intoxication contributed to his use of physical IPV when physically provoked by his female partner."[208]

Reporting: Do Men Report Less than Women?

Men report their victimization on crime victim surveys less than women do.[209] As discussed earlier, some men face many roadblocks in reporting intimate partner violence. For instance, men are less likely to be believed by law enforcement, men are less likely to be taken seriously, and men are more likely to be accused of perpetrating the violence.[210] Men also face social stigma in appearing vulnerable and less "manlike." In *Male as a Victims: Domestic Violence from a Different Perspective*, researchers looked at the response of male reporting around the world and found that:

> in the Netherlands . . . men don't report the abuse to law enforcement, because men didn't believe law enforcement would act on the report . . .
>
> In the United Kingdon . . . "male victims of women perpetrators are more often ignored by the police,"
>
> . . . the Australian police have told victims to "grow some balls."[211]

Additionally, "[w]hen men are injured, female perpetrators are arrested only 60.2% of the time, compared to 91.1% of cases involving in the reverse situation."[212] Female perpetrators are less likely to be arrested and when no one was injured, men were more likely to be arrested than women. The scientific literature suggests that men are no less likely to suffer from serious injury than women. For instance, in Detroit, "male victims reported three times the rate of serious injury as their female counterparts, 38% compared

207. *Id.*

208. *Id.* (noting that the temporal associations do need to be investigated in more detail, such as through the diary studies conducted by Fals-Stewart (2003)).

209. Dutton & Nicholls, *supra* note 5, at 680.

210. Aleksandar Jovanoski & Kire Sharlamanov, *Male as a Victims: Domestic Violence from a Different Perspective*, 12(3) INT'L J. SCI. & ENG'G RSCH. 904 (2021).

211. *Id.*

212. Dutton & Nicholls, *supra* note 5, at 692–96.

to 14%."[213] Consequently, when intimate violence is based on crime report data, male victimization is underestimated due to the systemic dismissal of female perpetrated violence.

Limitations of Research on Men Being Victims of IPV

Intimate partner violence is a looming community health and legal problem that deserves further investigation. While the current research documents both men and women's experience with intimate partner violence, there are limitations in the research on men as victims of intimate partner violence. These limitations frustrate both litigators' and mental health practitioners' attempts to find real solutions for their male clients. There are several memes that persist in our society that disable efforts to provide a healing environment for men. For instance, there is a dominant paradigm that "IPV experienced by men is less frequent, severe, and consequential than IPV experienced by women."[214] Because of this, men's experience of intimate partner violence was "studied primarily in comparison to women."[215] The research is clear that "comparing male victims to female victims has implied that men do not suffer to the same degree, which may erroneously trivialize men's experiences of violence."[216]

Some limitations on research boil down to "[d]iffering theoretical perspectives about the nature of the IPV, inconsistent definitions of violence used, measures employed, and populations sampled."[217] These limitations have "contributed to highly variable estimates of the prevalence and severity of IPV victimization in men."[218] For example, in population studies, researchers conclude that "gender symmetry"[219] exists based on data that "men and women experience IPV at the same rate."[220] However, in these studies, gender is defined as sex, "and is reflective of a continued and

213. *Id.*

214. Kelly Scott-Storey et al., *What About the Men? A Critical Review of Men's Experiences of Intimate Partner Violence*, 24(2) Trauma, Violence, & Abuse 865 (2023).

215. *Id.*

216. *Id.*

217. *Id.*

218. *Id.*

219. *Id.*

220. *Id.*

pervasive misunderstanding of gender."[221] Other researchers have expressed concerns "in the decontextualized way in which IPV is measured and consequently studied, especially among populations other than cis-gendered woman."[222]

Yet another limitation in the research data is the availability of data relating to the partner of the victim. A commonly used survey, the Conflict Tactics Scale, has been used in several population-based surveys. While the data from these surveys has furthered the prevalence of research of male victims, it does little to show who victimized these males.[223] Another inherent limitation in using crime victim surveys is the underreporting of males in these systems. Coupled with the likelihood of males being arrested in bidirectional claims of violence, the data from these sources may not be reliable. Researchers also emphasize caution when examining reports from help-seeking communities, as the sample size is limited to those who seek help for victimization, which can skew estimations.

Moreover, researchers have argued that "instruments that only assess whether a particular act of violence (e.g., hitting) is experienced (yes/no) 'lack specificity to capture other core elements of IPV (e.g., control, patterning of abuse, intimidation).'"[224] For instance, some researchers point out that "the limitations of merely focusing on acts of violence suggesting that, 'this view assumes that a slap or a push by a man is equivalent to a slap or a push by a woman and fails to measure the different consequences of those acts, which may reveal gender asymmetry in IPV outcomes.'"[225] These researchers support use of newer surveys, such as the Composite Abuse Scale Revised Short Form [CASR-SF], which show "promise for disentangling patterns between and among men and women experiencing IPV in various types of relationships."[226]

Addressing these limitations may reduce the meme that "(1) men are the primary perpetrators of abuse, and their women partners use violence in self-defense or retaliation; (2) men are physically dominant and can therefore easily strike back, restrain their partner, or leave the premises without being physically restrained; (3) the IPV that men sustain is trivial, humorous, or

---

221. *Id.*
222. *Id.*
223. *Id.* at 862.
224. *Id.* at 863.
225. *Id.*
226. *Id.*

of no consequence; (4) men have greater socioeconomic resources than their women partners and, thus, have the ability to leave relationships that pose a danger to them and that this ability is bolstered by their weaker psychological investment in their marriage and children as compared to women."[227]

Male Victims of IPV and Family Courts: Case Law Discussion

In mid to late 1990s, family courts appeared to view men's claims of being victims of IPV with skepticism. For instance, a Maryland court remarked "[a]lthough we recognize that men can also be victims of domestic abuse, it is clear that in the vast majority of cases, the victims are female."[228] In another instance, a North Dakota court[229] determined that the mother did not commit domestic violence upon the father's application for custody. The father asked the court to consider the mother's conduct of violence against third parties that the mother had intimate relationships with. North Dakota statute provides that if the court "finds credible evidence that domestic violence has occurred, this evidence creates a rebuttable presumption that a parent who has perpetrated domestic violence may not be awarded sole or joint custody of a child."[230] This statute triggers a change in circumstances warranting a change in custody, with domestic violence as the principal factor.[231] The court determined this conduct did not constitute domestic violence under North Dakota's statutes. The trial court reasoned that the abuse was not directed toward the father or the child, therefore, did not constitute domestic violence. The father appealed. The appellate court, in its reversal of the trial court, held that "ex-wife's conduct did not constitute domestic violence was inconsistent with statute setting forth presumption against awarding custody to perpetrator of domestic violence."[232] In its hold-

227. Denise A. Hines & Emily M. Douglas, *A Closer Look at Men Who Sustain Intimate Terrorism by Women*, 1 Partner Abuse 3, 289 (2010).

228. Coburn v. Coburn, 342 Md. 244, 251, 674 A.2d 951, 955 (1996) (*citing* Developments in the Law—Legal Responses to Domestic Violence, 106 Harv. L. Rev. 1498, 1501 n.1 (1993); Catherine F. Klein & Leslye E. Orloff, *Providing Legal Protection for Battered Women: An Analysis of State Statutes and Case Law*, 21 Hofstra L. Rev. 801, 808 (1993)).

229. Anderson v. Hensrud, 548 N.W.2d 410 (N.D. 1996).

230. N.D. Cent. Code Ann. § 14–09–06.2(1)(j) (West 2023).

231. *See generally* Bruner v. Hager, 547 N.W.2d 551 (N.D. 1996).

232. Anderson v. Hensrud, 548 N.W.2d 410 (N.D. 1996).

ing, the appellate court reasoned that the trial court's reading of the domestic violence statute was too narrow and stated that the North Dakota statute defines "family or household member," to include, in addition to a parent or child, "persons who are in a dating relationship," or "persons who are presently residing together or who have resided together in the past."[233]

In the past two decades, courts appear to have acknowledged the reality of men being victims of IPV. In 2008, a New Jersey court[234] found "sufficient credible evidence to support a trial judge's finding that a wife committed an act of domestic violence, as required for the issuance of a final restraining order against the wife under the Prevention of Domestic Violence Act (PDVA)." Husband complained that "on November 7, 2007, [wife] came to his home, screamed profanities, and struck him in the face. He also alleged that on November 29, 2007, [wife] stole [husband's] work equipment from a storage locker. [Husband] claimed that [wife] had committed an assault, burglary, criminal trespass, and harassment. [He] also claimed that. . . [wife] had threatened to cut off his genitals."[235] The trial court found this conduct contrary to domestic violence statute and issued a restraining order.[236] Wife appealed. The appellate court was satisfied that Husband met his burden of proving evidence of domestic violence, holding that domestic violence occurs when an assault is "inflicted upon a person protected"[237] under the New Jersey domestic violence statute, finding that the husband was a "victim of domestic violence" because he had been subjected to "domestic violence by [his] spouse."[238]

In 2010, a Florida court was affirmed in its issuance of a domestic violence protection order. However, the appellate court clarified that: "Abuse of court processes and filing false reports with law enforcement are serious matters, to be discouraged indeed, or even prosecuted. However, the statutorily created actions for injunction against violence are not the proper remedies to sanction these acts. Unfounded reports to authorities or requests for judicial relief, even if repeated or for malicious purposes, do not support the entry of an injunction against domestic or other violence."[239]

---

233. *Id.*
234. Herko v. Muzyka, 2008 WL 4329878 (N.J.).
235. *Id.*
236. N.J. Stat. Ann. §§ 2C:12-1, 2C:25-17 *et seq.*, 2C:25-19(a) (West 2023).
237. *Herko*, *supra* note 234.
238. *Id.*
239. Olin v. Roberts, 42 So. 3d 841, 842 (Fla. Dist. Ct. App. 2010).

In 2019, in Alaska, a trial court changed custody to the father after determining he had rebutted the mother's claims that the father perpetrated domestic violence.[240] Upon father's filing of divorce, mother was awarded interim sole legal and primary physical custody based on her claims that father "had a history of perpetrating domestic violence."[241] At the hearing for final custody determination, father presented evidence that he had "applied for a batterers' intervention program, [and] during an examination by an expert as part of the intake process for the program it was determined that husband was not recommended for the program as he was the victim of domestic violence, and a custody investigator reported the same conclusion that husband was the victim and that wife engaged in 'intimate partner stalking behaviors' and 'ongoing harassment behaviors'"[242] contrary to Alaska statute.[243] The trial court ruled it was in the child's best interest for the father to have sole custody.

In 2019, in an Oregon case, the Department of Human Services placed the minor child in foster care due to bidirectional abuse between father and mother. Father appealed the trial court's decision to change the child's reunification plan to an adoption plan. The appellate court held that "[1] DHS's efforts to provide services to father were not related to ameliorating jurisdictional basis for permanency hearing; [2] referral for father to domestic violence shelter was not a reasonable effort by DHS to provide services to father; and [3] father's reluctance to utilize DHS services did not provide evidence that DHS's efforts to provide services were reasonable."[244] In its holding, the appellate court reasoned that the services provided to the father were not tailored to ameliorating jurisdictional basis for a permanency hearing in this case, and instead were "typically provided in every case and were unrelated to father's chaotic relationship with mother."[245]

After finding that the father was a victim of domestic violence, DHS recommended father seek services from a women's shelter "Womenspace." The appellate court held "[s]pecifically regarding Womenspace, although DHS provided pamphlets to father after it became clear that he was a domestic-violence victim, DHS provided little or no evidence concerning

240. Joy B. v. Everett B., 451 P.3d 365 (2019).

241. *Id.*

242. *Id.*

243. Alaska Stat. §§ 25.24.150(g), 25.24.150(h) (2023).

244. Matter of M. M. R., 301 Or. App. 436 (2019).

245. *Id.*

precisely what programming Womenspace offered, or how that programming served to ameliorate father's "chaotic relationship" or prevented that chaotic relationship from endangering the child. From that lack of evidence, the juvenile court could not reasonably infer that Womenspace has the capability to provide relevant services for father."[246]

In 2017, a New Mexico court found that a university professor's female friend had perpetrated domestic abuse by "[sending] threatening email messages, made threatening telephone calls, left threatening voice messages, and posted slanderous and derogatory statements about professor on her website and social media page."[247] The friend appealed. The appellate court affirmed in part, holding that "as matter of first impression, [the] term 'severe emotional distress,' as that phrase is used in the Family Violence Protection Act (FVPA), means great harm to a person's mental health and well-being[.]"[248]

In a criminal prosecution out of Kentucky, in 2017, the husband was sentenced to prison for 15 years for killing his wife. The husband appealed this decision, claiming he was a victim of domestic violence perpetrated by his wife. During husband's trial, "four witnesses testified that they were aware of possible domestic violence committed against [husband] by his wife"[249] and "[a]n investigating detective also testified that [the husband] displayed visible signs of physical abuse at the time of his arrest."[250] On appeal, the husband argued that the trial court "failed to sufficiently find whether he was more likely than not to have been a domestic violence victim as required" under Kentucky law.[251] The appellate court agreed with the husband and remanded the case "with instructions to make specific findings as to the validity of [the husband's] domestic violence claim,"[252] as these findings ultimately would impact husband's parole determinations.

A rather insidious consequence of IPV perpetrated against males is the forced liability of child support on male rape victims. In *Fatherhood by Conscription: Nonconsensual Insemination and the Duty of Child Support*, law professor Michael J. Higdon describes a case where the male rape victim was forced to accept liability of the resulting child. In doing so, the court noted,

---

246. *Id.*
247. Best v. Marino, 404 P.3d 450 (N.M. 2017).
248. *Id.*
249. Crowe v. Commonwealth, 2017 WL 3129204, 1 (Ky.).
250. *Id.*
251. *Id.*
252. *Id.*

"[t]here is an important distinction between a party who is injured through no fault of his or her own and an injured party who willingly participated in the offense about which a complaint is made. The court placed [Complainant who was a minor] in the latter category given that he voluntarily engaged in sexual intercourse with [the perpetrator]. It does not necessarily follow that a minor over the age of [14] who voluntarily engages in sexual intercourse is a victim of sexual abuse."[253] Interestingly, the court held that despite the child victim being a minor and unable to consent to sexual activities with an adult, he was still liable for the resulting child. Higdon explains that this case is not alone in its reasoning. A Michigan court held that a 14-year-old child "participated in the act of sexual intercourse that resulted in the conception of [the child] . . . [and] is not absolved from the responsibility to support the child because [the mother] was technically committing an act of criminal sexual conduct."[254] In Kansas, the Kansas Supreme Court held that a 12-year-old was liable for child support, stating, "This State's interest in requiring minor parents to support their children overrides the State's competing interest in protecting juveniles from improvident acts, even when such acts may include criminal activity on the part of the other parent. . . . This minor child, the only truly innocent party, is entitled to support from both her parents regardless of their ages."[255] This sends a chilling message to boys and mimics the "Man Box" described earlier in this chapter—men and boys are not supposed to be vulnerable.

In cases where mothers weaponize and use children to abuse the child's father, courts will sometimes change custody to the targeted parent. For instance, in a 2015 Indiana case,[256] the appellate court reversed the trial court's denial of the father's petition to modify custody. The trial court had made numerous findings that the mother was, without justification, harming the father–child relationship. In fact, the lower court accepted most of the findings of its guardian ad litem, who had identified a pattern of false allegations by Mother, her resistance to Father's relationship with the children, and her undermining of the Father's access to and relationship with the children.[257] She had made at least six unsubstantiated abuse

253. Michael J. Higdon, *Fatherhood by Conscription: Nonconsensual Insemination and the Duty of Child Support*, 46 GA. L. REV. 407, 425 (2012).

254. *Id.*

255. *Id.*

256. Maddux v. Maddux, 40 N.E.3d 971 (Ind. Ct. App. 2015).

257. *Id.*

allegations to authorities, which had resulted in the Father remaining under a "no-contact" order with the children. Despite this, the trial court made strangely inconsistent findings, including, after "illustrating Mother's audacious and successful attempts to alienate Father from the Children . . . [it found that] such conduct 'does not warrant a change of the custody.'"[258] The trial court also found "the Children are developing well,"[259] despite the fact that one had suicidal thoughts that the Mother failed to address (or even worry about). Remarkably, the trial court expressly found that Mother "had irreparably harmed [the Children's] emotional wellbeing,"[260] but inexplicably refused to find a change in custody was in their best interests. Luckily, for the children, the appellate court reversed.

This sentiment is echoed in other claims as well. For instance, in 2004, in Maine, a male victim claimed that police officers deprived him of "his rights to due process and equal protection in implementing Cumberland County's policy or custom of providing less protection to male victims of domestic violence than female."[261] The male victim claimed that "police view male victims as second class citizens; there is a cultural bias against male victims in which the police always believe female complainants but just 'take a report' of male; there is more funding available for female victims than male; and it is more politically correct to protect females than males."[262]

A female perpetrator of domestic violence who was arrested in Colorado claimed that police officers discriminated against domestic violence victims as a class. As the woman was arrested, she claimed that the man she lived with had also perpetrated violence against her. The Colorado court reasoned that the arresting officers had properly determined probable cause did not exist to arrest the male subject and that the female was not denied equal protection when the officer's failed to make the arrest.[263]

In a federal case out of Indiana, the plaintiff (male victim) filed a 42 U.S.C. section 1983 claim based on gender discrimination. The plaintiff provided the court "[o]ut of approximately 123 domestic reports the

---

258. *Id.*

259. *Id.*

260. *Id.*

261. Bloomquist v. Albee, No. CIV.03-276-P-S, 2004 WL 2287758, at *4 (D. Me. Oct. 7, 2004).

262. *Id.*

263. Eckert v. Town of Silverthorne, 25 Fed. App'x 679, 685, n.1 (Colo. Ct. App. 2021).

Bartholomew County Sheriff's Department responded to in 2000, only 17 listed the victim as a male, which equates to approximately 13%. Out of those 17 reports that listed the victim as a male, at least 7 reports dealt with a male to male altercation (instead of a male to female). Consequently, such statistics would lower the above referenced percentage to roughly 10%. Consequently, 90% of the time the Sheriff Deputies responded to a domestic violence call dealing with a male/female altercation, they cited the victim as a female and the aggressor as a male."[264] However, granting defendant's motion to strike, the court held:

> that the Bartholomew County Sheriff's Department's police records for domestic disputes between a man and a woman only list the man as the victim 10% of the time does not demonstrate gender discrimination. Disparate impact does not equal disparate treatment, the latter being the concern in equal protection claims.[265]

Finally, in the Virginia case, *Depp v. Heard*, Depp alleged that Heard had falsely accused him of domestic violence, constituting defamation. He specifically alleged that "Ms. Heard falsely yelled 'stop hitting me Johnny,' in addition to stating that [Depp] struck her with a cell phone, hit her, and destroyed the house, before she 'presented herself to the world with a battered face as she publicly accused Mr. Depp of domestic violence and obtained a restraining order against him.'"[266] The court held that "[t]he implication that Mr. Depp abused Ms. Heard is defamatory per se because it imputes to Plaintiff [Depp] 'the commission of some criminal offense involving moral turpitude, for which the party, if the charge is true, may be indicted and punished.'"[267]

---

264. Miller v. Whipker, 2004 WL 1622212 (Indiana).

265. *Id. See also* Anderson v. Cornejo, 355 F.3d 1021, 1024 (7th Cir. 2004) (*citing* Washington v. Davis, 426 U.S. 229, 96 S. Ct. 2040, 48 L. Ed. 2d 597 (1976)). "[D]isparities that cannot be chalked up to random variance may have causes other than race, sex, or another proscribed ground of decision." *Id.* For example, it is common knowledge that domestic violence is much more frequently perpetrated against women than against men. See U.S. Dep't of Justice, Bureau of Justice Statistics Factbook, Violence by Intimates: Analysis of Data on Crimes by Current or Former Spouses, Boyfriends, and Girlfriends 4 (1998) ("[F]emales are 5 to 8 times more likely than males to be victimized by an intimate.").

266. Depp v. Heard, 104 Va. Cir. 377 (2020) (*See*, Complaint at ¶ 19).

267. *Id. See also* Tronfeld v. Nationwide Mut. Ins. Co., 272 Va. 709, 713 (2006) (*citing* Fleming v. Moore, 221 Va. 884, 889 (1981); *see also* Va. Code § 18.2-57.2 (2020); Cal. Penal Code § 243(e)(1) (2016).

Conclusion

A common misconception of IPV is that women rarely use violence against romantic partners or men, and when they do, this is usually in self-defense.[268] However, evidence demonstrates that women are just as likely as men to commit IPV, and our courts and communities are ill-equipped to provide support and solutions for male victims. In litigation, family law practitioners who represent men claiming to be victims of female-driven IPV should be prepared to present evidence demonstrating the prevalence of male victimization, how it affects families, and proper interventions. Understanding and acknowledging that IPV is bidirectional and driven by similar motives, gender can be taken out of the equation and courts can focus on effective intervention based on the psychological aspects of the parties and the needs of the case.

268. Ailsa McGrath, et al., *The Impact of Childhood Adversity on Female-Perpetrated Intimate Partner Violence in Young Adulthood*, Legal & Criminological Psych. (2023), DOI: 10.1111/lcrp.12259.

Chapter 6

Fallacies, False Positives, and Fake News: Mis- and Disinformation About Family Violence

The landscape of family violence, whether it be a case of domestic violence, coercive control, child psychological maltreatment, or weaponization and alienation of a child against a parent, is rife with myths and fallacies. Domestic violence cases are not only chock-full of allegations and accusations that require careful sifting through facts but they also involve confronting, challenging, and rebutting in litigation commonly held misconceptions about how family violence occurs, its effect on the family system, and the underlying research in mental health and social sciences.

Between 1880 and present, there has been considerable discussion and debate regarding domestic violence issues in mental health and legal professional literature, which has led to disagreements between social scientists and legal experts regarding how domestic violence is motivated. Scholars, practitioners, and researchers have engaged in a dialogue regarding several issues that permeate the field of family violence, particularly related to domestic violence or intimate partner violence. For instance, there has been a robust exchange of ideas and research to determine the criteria for finding domestic violence, the pathways by which domestic violence comes about, and the relative culpabilities of the victim and perpetrator, the prevalence of domestic violence in custody and parenting time litigation, appropriate and effective interventions, role of professionals, and preventive measures.

Despite the robust exchange of ideas, the discussion of domestic violence at times has been a lightning rod for controversy, vitriol, and ad hominem attacks on professionals, and it has featured an unusual level of misinformation and deceptive propaganda. For instance, in peer-reviewed literature, *Feminist Contributions to Understanding Woman Abuse: Myths, Controversies, and Realities*, Professor Walter DeKeseredy found that studying abuse against women sometimes divided social scientists and resulted in "frequent vitriolic attacks on feminist scholarship, some of which include assaults on researchers' professionalism and integrity."[1]

Professor DeKeseredy's research discovered that abuse of women in intimate relationships takes different shapes and forms and is a worldwide public health problem. "Many journalists, activists, and researchers, however, minimize the extent of woman abuse, sharply criticize feminist empirical, theoretical, and policy work on this issue, and disseminate myths about feminism."[2] The primary goal of this peer-reviewed research publication was to refute these myths and respond to criticisms of feminist scholarship (an interdisciplinary academic endeavor that aims to advance gender equality).[3]

An overwhelming majority of mental health and legal professionals accept the basic premise that domestic violence is a pervasive social problem. Similarly, every state has some type of codified law prohibiting some forms of domestic violence—usually physical, but some states have included prohibition against emotional or psychological abuse and coercive control as well. Nevertheless, mis- and disinformation about domestic violence continues to compromise outcomes and treatment in cases involving divorce and separation, child custody, parenting time, and ancillary matters.

On mis- and disinformation about domestic violence, claims of domestic and intimate partner violence and its deleterious effects on the victim, including minor children who may have been exposed to such violence, are often met with arguments such as: (1) Domestic violence only includes physical violence, (2) domestic violence is a private family matter, (3) domestic violence causes temporary distress and is inconsequential in the long run, (4) the victim provoked the violence, (5) victims can just leave an abusive environment, and (6) domestic violence is a poverty problem. And so, the propaganda of mis- and disinformation begins. To discharge its gatekeeping obligation, sometimes the trial court conducts an elaborate *Daubert* or *Frye* hearing before admitting expert testimony on domestic violence. On other occasions, the court may rule that abuse found in the case cannot be

---

1. Walter S. DeKeseredy, *Feminist Contributions to Understanding Woman Abuse: Myths, Controversies, and Realities*, 16(4) Aggression & Violent Behav. 297–302 (2011) ISSN 1359-1789, https://doi.org/10.1016/j.avb.2011.04.002.

2. *Id.*

3. DeKeseredy, *supra* note 1.

classified as domestic violence pursuant to the statutory definition of the jurisdiction, and the court would rather focus its attention on the behaviors of the parents and the best interests of the children. Often victims of domestic violence lack the tools to find and engage effective legal representation and advocacy, making it inherently problematic for them to navigate the legal evidentiary requirements to obtain protection for themselves and their dependents.

Commonly held myths and fallacies about family violence in general, and about domestic violence, child psychological maltreatment, and parental alienation in particular, continue to surface in family courts. These myths and fallacies gather momentum and morph into a propaganda of mis- and disinformation with the support of social media and special interests' groups that are ideologically driven. Whether these myths and fallacies are advanced by gender-focused activists, who argue that "domestic violence does not happen to men," or by individuals who, being willfully blind to the well-established research, argue "victims of domestic violence do not stay with their abusers," they result in significant harm to the victims.[4] This chapter attempts to address some common fallacies and misinformation regarding family violence that are commonly encountered in the country's family law courtrooms.

Domestic violence is not as nebulous as some detractors claim it to be. It can be identified with a careful, thoughtful, and methodical approach. As the scientific literature identifies, the key issues supporting the possible presence of domestic violence are gender inequality, power imbalances, and controlling behaviors within relationships.[5] The next task then is to determine how the power imbalance developed. Proper investigation and assessment are needed in all investigations and an investigation focused on domestic violence is no exception to the rule. Utilizing good data and technique, incorporating various sources of information, considering potential or real biases, implementing psychological testing and psychometric tools, and carefully considering the baseline family dynamic, along with following ethical principles and professional codes of conduct helps professionals formulate findings and opinions that are based on facts and science.

---

4. Demosthenes Lorandos, Preface, *in* PARENTAL ALIENATION: SCIENCE AND LAW, at xvii (Demosthenes Lorandos & William Bernet eds., 2020).

5. Janet Phillips & Anna Dunkley, *Parliamentary Library Information Analysis Advice, Research Paper Series*, Nov. 24, 2015.

Failure to confront, challenge, and debunk myths and fallacies surrounding family violence may lead to a compromised legal outcome that could be devastating not just for the victims of the violence but for society overall. Fortunately, practitioners can avail of recent, up-to-date, peer-reviewed literature to inform courts and to counter the fallacies surrounding domestic and intimate partner violence. For instance, in a recent 2023 peer-reviewed paper published in the *Journal of Interpersonal Violence*, a team of researchers focused their attention on the following myths and fallacies associated with domestic violence:[6] (1) Victims of abuse provoke abusive behavior; (2) victims of abuse have the ability to end the abuse by simply leaving the abuser; (3) some women are "masochistic and want to be beaten"; and (4) domestic violence is not abuse if used as a familial disciplinary measure.[7] The research study found that, while these beliefs are false and unsupported by science or research, they continue to persist and when experienced by a victim of abuse, they further the victimization. In that regard, the authors report that "victims tend to be revictimized by others' negative attitudes toward them, known as secondary victimization, and such negative attitudes reinforce the victim's self-blaming, making it extremely difficult to recover from the assault."[8] The researchers further observed that "[o]thers' negative attitudes not only discourage victims from seeking help to leave their abusers but may also actually encourage victims to return to their abusers by reducing their ability to recover from the assault, leading them to deal with the abuse on their own."[9]

Family law practitioners, including lawyers who represent the minor children's best interests in child custody litigation or assist the courts in the role of guardians ad litem must not only be cognizant of the myths and fallacies that surround the topic of family violence but also guard against such myths and fallacies from compromising outcomes in litigation. For instance, one myth that continues to derail legal outcomes for victims of abuse is the belief that if abuse was real, the victim would not have stayed with the abuser or, in some cases, returned to the abusive environment after having left it. People tend to "perceive the victim who decides to return to

---

6. Niwako Yamawaki et al., *Perceptions of Domestic Violence: The Effects of Domestic Violence Myths, Victim's Relationship with Her Abuser, and the Decision to Return to Her Abuser* 27(16) J. Interpersonal Violence 3195–212 (2023).

7. *Id.* at 3206.

8. *Id.*

9. *Id.*

her abuser as being responsible for and inciting the abuse and as having an unconscious desire to be abused, thus leading others to blame her."[10] In addition to peer-reviewed, up-to-date research in the field of social sciences, practitioners could also use other tools such as the Domestic Violence Myth Acceptance Scale (DVMAS), which was developed to "evaluate cultural beliefs that serve to legitimize and perpetuate violence in IPV."[11]

The DVMAS scale reviews the following aspects: *character blame* (e.g., "If a woman stays with the man who abused her, she basically deserves what she gets."), *behavior blame* (e.g., "Domestic violence occurs because women keep on arguing about things with their partners."), *exoneration of the perpetrator* (e.g., "Domestic violence results from a momentary loss of temper."), and *minimization of the violence* (e.g., "Domestic violence does not affect many people."). The use of this scale in determining myths that are prevalent regarding intimate partner violence has been determined to have internal consistency, making it an effective tool for further research and demonstration. The research regarding myths and fallacies associated with domestic violence has a critical part in seeking redressal for the victims of abuse, as it highlights the biases and false beliefs that members of our society operate under. These myths not only result in the victims of domestic violence failing to obtain proper redressal for their victimization, but they also "reduce social support for victims by transforming them from innocent victims of a potentially lethal crime to individuals who consciously or unconsciously decided to be battered."[12] These myths sustain the ideology that "the victim is not really a victim because she could have avoided the abuse, probably provoked it, and unconsciously desired it."[13] From a feminist vantage point, these myths "support both patriarchy and violence against women by reducing support for the victim, exonerating the perpetrator, and minimizing the seriousness of the crime."[14]

---

10. *Id.*

11. Vincenza Cinquegrana et al., *Psychological Abuse Is Not a Problem! Exploring the Role of Domestic Violence Myths in Psychological Revictimization*. Front. Psychology 14:1228822 (2023).

12. Jay Peters, *Measuring Myths About Domestic Violence: Development and Initial Validation of the Domestic Violence Myth Acceptance Scale* 16(1) J. Aggression, Maltreatment & Trauma (2008) DOI: 10.1080/10926770801917780.

13. *Id.* at 1-21.

14. *Id.*

Following are the myths and fallacies about family violence that are commonly encountered in family courts.

Domestic Violence Is Rarely Unprovoked

A principal myth surrounding all types of domestic violence is that the violence results from the victim's character or behavior. These myths blame the victim and exonerate the perpetrator. For example, those who perpetuate this myth hold the following beliefs:

Women like to be dominated.
She was asking for it.
Why does she push his buttons?
She should not have worn that short skirt.
She knew what she was getting into when she married him.

These myths perpetuate from a lack of understanding of how abuse occurs, how abuse affects a victim, and the abusive family dynamic. Research shows that women victims are often blamed for not exiting abusive relationships. For instance, "research on service providers has concluded that although this group holds husbands primarily responsible for abusing their wives, they do not hold victims altogether blameless."[15] Additionally, research also found that "38% of their sample of middle class, educated potential jurors held the wife 'at least somewhat responsible' for being abused in a hypothetical scenario, and about the same number believed that she would be 'at least somewhat masochistic' if she didn't leave in response to continued beating by her husband."[16] Between sexes, researchers found that both men and women engaged in character blaming of domestic violence victims—though for different reasons.[17] When men engaged in character blaming, it was second to exoneration.[18] When women engaged in character blaming, it was a way to eliminate threat.[19] For instance, women could disassociate themselves with the risk of violence by believing that a victim was at fault by not leaving. Perhaps it may be

15. Bonnie Carlson & Alissa Pollitz Worden, Public Opinion about Domestic Violence. National Institute of Justice (2002).

16. *Id.*

17. Peters, *supra* note 12, at 1-21.

18. *Id.*

19. *Id.*

easier to come to terms with the specter of violence by telling oneself, "If I were in that situation, I would just leave," without not really understanding how difficult it is for a victim of domestic violence to escape an abusive relationship. Courts that oversee cases involving domestic violence are not immune to discrediting victims for staying in an abusive relationship. Legal scholars report that "[j]udges tend to express their belief in the connection between women staying and story plausibility in less formal contexts, such as judicial training sessions and casual conversations outside of the courtroom. . .and this failure of understanding affects case outcomes."[20] The National Institute of Justice's Report on Public Opinion about Domestic Violence concluded that "a significant minority may continue to underestimate the difficulties women face in leaving violent relationships."[21]

Leaving an abusive relationship is a near impossible feat for many victims. There are psychological, emotional, and logistical implications that stall a victim's ability to escape. For instance, if the abuser is the primary wage earner for the family, the victim may lack resources to escape. This can become especially challenging if the victim has minor children. In that case, children's safety and their well-being upon a victim's leaving the abusive environment are extremely relevant factors and may cause the victim to reconsider exiting the situation. If the victim lacks financial autonomy in the relationship, the victim may have also been isolated from those social supports that could facilitate her escape. Even if the victim attempts to find gainful employment, the initial concern of safety may sabotage any effort by the victim to escape and establish themselves outside of the abusive home.

Additionally, the perpetual cycle of abuse traps the victim in a psychological trauma bond and enmeshment with the victim's abuser. The result is an "intermittent reinforcement of love and affection [which] can be very difficult to escape."[22] In fact, "[e]ven when survivors correctly identify the abuse and establish boundaries or leave the relationship, trauma bonding

20. Deborah Epstein & Lisa Goodman, *Discounting Women: Doubting Domestic Violence Survivors' Credibility and Dismissing Their Experiences* 167 Univ. Penn. L. Rev. 2, 399–461 (2019).

21. Carlson & Worden, *supra* note 15.

22. Zawn Villines, *When Family Relationships Become Toxic: The Trauma of Enmeshment*, GoodTherapy (Oct. 16, 2019), https://www.goodtherapy.org/blog/when-family-relationships-become-toxic-the-trauma-of-enmeshment-1016197#:~:text=Even%20when%20survivors%20correctly%20identify%20the%20abuse%20and,the%20person%E2%80%99s%20point%20of%20reference%20for%20a%20relationship.

and enmeshment can impact future relationships."[23] The victim may normalize the abuse because of intense feelings of shame, lack of identity, societal normalization, or feeling that they are at fault for the abuse. The victim may also use those feelings as a yardstick for every other relationship they enter.[24]

Domestic Violence Victims Lack Credibility

There appears to be a stereotype of a domestic violence victim—the victim must show proof of having been abused—in other words, show blood, bruises, or black eyes, report the abuse within a reasonable amount of time, and in a particular manner, all of which would go to show that it "really happened." If not, it is not a credible report.[25] In a law review article, *Discounting Women: Doubting Domestic Violence Survivors' Credibility and Dismissing Their Experiences*, legal scholars explain that domestic violence allegations sometimes lack internal and external consistency, which causes skepticism and distrust in the plausibility of the allegations. An example of the lack of internal consistency could be that professionals, including courts or law enforcement agents, "improperly discount as implausible women's stories of abuse, due to a failure to understand the symptoms arising from neurological and psychological trauma as well as the practical realities of survivors' lives."[26] While an example of the lack of external consistency could be that "courts and other legal actors are not always aware of how trauma can affect survivors' memory, testimony, and demeanor."[27] Psychological trauma can account for a victim's demeanor, dress, and tone in the courtroom; memory loss; dissociative flashbacks; and prolonged emotional responses.[28] A victim of domestic violence could have experienced post-traumatic stress disorder, whose symptoms "can influence demeanor in obvious ways," which may cause courts to "misinterpret—and, as a result, discount—the credibility of women who display each set of symptoms when telling their stories of abuse."[29] Further, traumatic memories "lack verbal narrative detail and con-

---

23. *Id.*
24. *Id.*
25. Epstein & Goodman, *supra* note 20.
26. Villines, *supra* note 22.
27. Carlson & Worden, *supra* note 15.
28. Epstein & Goodman, *supra* note 20.
29. *Id.*

text; they are encoded in the form of sensations, flashes, and images, often with little or no story."[30]

Additionally, physical abuse suffered by victims can lead to damage to their memory and behavior centers, causing "symptoms such as confusion, poor recall, inability to link parts of the story together or to articulate a logical sequence of events, uncertainty about detail, and even recanting of stories."[31] While domestic violence is not limited to physical abuse, physical violence is pervasive and a big component of domestic violence cases. A study of women in three New York domestic violence shelters found that "ninety-two percent of the women questioned had been hit in the head by their partners more than once; eighty-three percent had been hit in the head and shaken severely; and eight percent had been hit in the head over twenty times in the preceding year."[32] Also, societal expectations "about how survivors should appear and recount their abuse are based on unconscious norms that are gendered, racialized, and influenced by other dominant misconceptions."[33] This causes problems in external consistency and triggers biases that could skew an investigation or adjudication of domestic violence claims—the victim does not appear to be *what I would expect a victim to be*; therefore, the victim must not really be a victim.

Emotional or Psychological Abuse Is Not Real Abuse

As discussed earlier in this book, emotional or psychological abuse, including coercive control behavior, causes significant harm and is a type of family violence. Psychological abuse is defined as "actions aimed at preventing or controlling [a victim's] behavior, causing them emotional harm or fear."[34] Such abuse may be difficult to prove in litigation. While single acts of psychological abuse can demonstrate abuse, such as derogatory name calling, shaming, humiliating, and threatening, covert acts of psychological abuse may require documentation of patterns of these acts to demonstrate their intentionality and harm. Such covert patterns of abusive behavior may be hard to establish or prove in litigation.

30. *Id.*
31. *Id.*
32. *Id.*
33. Carlson & Worden, *supra* note 15.
34. Cinquegrana et al., *supra* note 11.

In fact, research has emphasized that "some forms of psychological violence can be subtler than others and difficult to recognize (i.e., manipulation or jealousy) [and] such subtler forms are typically perceived as less coercive and overtly violent than verbal abuse which is readily identifiable as an aggressive act."[35] Even professionals who undergo training in investigating domestic violence at times fail to see emotional or psychological abuse as "serious" domestic violence. For instance, "a recent English study found that police officers are more likely to mention physical assaults and injuries rather than psychological abuse when they are asked to evaluate whether an episode of [Intimate Partner Violence] is 'serious' or not."[36] Further complicating this dynamic, research suggests that even women victims of psychological abuse "did not describe the psychologically abusive behavior of their partner as violent, and, consequently, not worthy of attention from professionals."[37] As psychological abuse is often a precursor of physical and sexual abuse, it is critical that psychological abuse is recognized as a legitimate form of abuse in court.[38]

The scientific literature suggests that the prevalence of psychological abuse is undermined by the myths surrounding domestic violence.[39] These myths "were conceptually defined as stereotypical beliefs about domestic violence that are generally false but are widely and persistently held, and which serve to minimize, deny, or justify physical aggression against intimate partners."[40] There is a bifurcated problem here. On one hand, the victim experiencing psychological abuse may not present the abusive behavior as a problematic, reportable offense. On the other hand, laws governing domestic violence have taken a long time to recognize acts of psychological abuse as a form of abuse when deciding whether to prosecute acts of domestic violence. The myths perpetuate these false, "prejudicial and stereotypical beliefs about violence in intimate relationships that serve to deny, downplay justify, and legitimize [Intimate Partner Violence]."[41]

Research demonstrates that psychological abuse is no less harmful than physical abuse, and in some instances, could be more damaging than

35. *Id.*
36. *Id.*
37. *Id.*
38. *Id.*
39. *Id.*
40. Peters, *supra* note 12, at 1-21.
41. Cinquegrana et al., *supra* note 11.

physical abuse.[42] For instance, "women report that psychological abuse is by far the greatest source of their distress regardless of the frequency or severity of the physical harm they've experienced."[43] Because of the pervasiveness of psychological abuse, a victim's narrative may focus more on the psychological abuse the victim experienced.[44] "[S]urvivors often frame their courtroom stories in a way that fails to fit the expectations of most judges, and even of the law itself: what may feel to victims like the most insidious and intimate brand of abuse can come across to legal gatekeepers as something that really doesn't count as abuse at all."[45]

While several states include psychological abuse within the statutory definition of domestic violence, the majority continue to focus on physical abuse as being the key component of domestic violence. This leads to an anomaly where "the law tends to dictate psychic reality: what the law prohibits must be what is [truly] harmful. . . . The end result is that most judges assume that the way the world works, and therefore what is externally consistent, is that physical violence is far worse than psychological abuse."[46]

Courts, too, have been slow to adjudicate incidents of psychological abuse as constituting domestic violence. For instance, a Maryland court poignantly explained that, at least in cases involving at-fault divorce on grounds of cruelty, psychological abuse was often seen as inconsequential. Even instances of physical abuse were tolerated as the norm, if they were not too "serious." "Maryland's 'old' cruelty law and [] our precedent, unfortunately, shows 'remarkable tolerance for abusive behavior.'"[47] Maryland's "old cruelty law " is similar to early 20th century law through which a "husband's 'violent outbursts of temper, accompanied in some instances by his slapping' his wife did not constitute cruelty."[48] In fact, only in cases including "serious, continuous, corroborated physical abuse that indicated a likelihood of future abuse and public accusations of infidelity" would a Maryland court grant a divorce based on allegations of cruelty.[49]

---

42. Epstein & Goodman, *supra* note 20.

43. *Id.*

44. *Id.*

45. *Id.*

46. *Id.*

47. Frazelle-Foster v. Foster, 250 Md. App. 52, 68–72, 248 A.3d 1089, 1098–1100 (2021). *See* 133 Md. App. at 34, 754 A.2d 441.

48. *Id. See also* Bonwit v. Bonwit, 169 Md. 189, 193, 181 A. 237 (1935).

49. *Id.*

In another turn-of-the-century Maryland case, the court observed that:

> The wife testified that at various times her husband struck her, was excessively cruel to her, and that his cruel treatment consisted of repeated blows, threats to kill and shoot her, and other vicious conduct. On one occasion, he struck her in the back with his fist. At another time, he pointed a loaded pistol and threatened to shoot her. He threw her, when in a delicate condition, over a chair, and she fell to the floor. She further testified that he repeatedly threatened to kill her, and his threats became so frequent she believed he would do so, and also kill her child[.][50]

Maryland did not change this precedent until 1952, when it ruled that a husband who "invited his secretary, with whom he appeared to be conducting an affair, to live with them, and then kicked the wife out of the bedroom . . . used abusive language toward her, ridiculed her before their children, and hit her on multiple occasions" engaged in abusive conduct.[51] Citing a 1952 case, the Maryland court, in 2021, "announced that 'in Maryland physical violence is no longer essential to constitute cruelty of treatment. It is now accepted that cruelty as a cause for divorce includes any conduct on the part of husband or wife which is calculated to seriously impair the health or permanently destroy the happiness of the other.'"[52] The court underscored the harm associated with emotional injury and acknowledged how the courts of the past had failed to acknowledge this principle:

> The courts have seen the changing social sense of propriety, and now recognize that physical violence is not the most dreadful injury that can be inflicted upon persons of refined sensibility. In ancient days it was not understood that mental suffering had anything to do with bodily ills.[53]

Parental Alienation Is a Hoax and Not a Real Thing

A review of the family court decisions, both at the trial and appellate levels, across the United States over the past several decades demonstrates that the scientific theory of parental alienation has been acknowledged by the courts.

---

50. Sharp v. Sharp, 105 Md. 581, 582–83, 66 A. 463 (1907).

51. Frazelle-Foster v. Foster, 250 Md. App. 52, 68–72, 248 A.3d 1089, 1098–1100. *See also* Scheinin v. Scheinin, 200 Md. 282, 89 A.2d 609 (1952).

52. Frazelle-Foster v. Foster, 250 Md. App. 52, 68–72, 248 A.3d 1089, 1098–1100.

53. *Id.*

Family-court judges have acknowledged that not only "[is there] no doubt that parental alienation exists," but that it is "not a new phenomenon," and that "[a]nybody old enough to drink coffee knows that embittered parties to divorce can and do manipulate their children."[54]

According to one legal and mental health expert:

> What about the meme that PA does not exist? Reviewing the 3,555 cases the query for this research found lends itself to new conclusions about PA misinformation. It appears that most of the misinformation about the construct of PA comes from two sources: (1) legal professionals and law students without a scientific background challenging the validity of the science behind PA, and (2) other professionals and students, who lack a legal background, opining on evidence law. Together, they raise specious concerns about the materiality, relevancy, and admissibility of PA.[55]

In reducing needless distraction from the real issues at hand and to tamp down on unwarranted litigation, family courts have begun to focus more on parental alienating behaviors, rather than the phenomenon or theory of parental alienation "syndrome"—"whether or not a psychological 'syndrome' exists, parental alienation clearly does."[56] Judges, who are the triers of facts in most domestic relations litigation, have found that it is far more important and effective to focus on a parent's *behavior* rather than to go down the rabbit hole of chasing esoteric theories of a psychiatric disorder "syndrome" that may or may not exist. Behavior is discernible. It is not only easier for a practitioner or parent-litigant to focus the court's attention on a parent's alienating behavior, but focusing on behavior (instead of an abstract theory) may result in early legal and mental health interventions. Courts have found that while the scientific community may have disagreements on whether "parental alienation syndrome" exists, "there is no reasonable dispute that high-conflict custody disputes frequently involve acts by one parent designed to obstruct or sabotage the opposing parent's relationship with the child."[57]

Importantly, courts, legal scholars, and mental health experts have at times used different terms to describe the phenomenon of parental

54. J.F. v. D.F., 61 Misc. 3d 1226(A), 2018 N.Y. slip op. 51829(U), at *8 (2018).

55. Demosthenes Lorandos, *Parental Alienation in U.S. Courts, 1985 to 2018*, *in* Parental Alienation: Science and Law 378 (Demosthenes Lorandos & William Bernet, eds., 2020).

56. J.F. v. D.F., 61 Misc. 3d 1226(A), 2018 N.Y. slip op. 51829(U), at *8 (2018).

57. Martin v. Martin, Michigan Court of Appeals No. 349261 (Jan. 28, 2020), n. 2.

alienation and the associated behaviors. In their book *Children Held Hostage*, published by the ABA Section of Family Law, Stanley Clawar, a sociologist, and Brynne Rivlin, a social worker, used the terms "programming," "brainwashing," and "indoctrination" when describing the behaviors that cause children to reject a parent without a legitimate justification. Regardless of the different terms used to describe parental alienation, it is helpful to note the three key features underlying the phenomenon of parental alienation. First, it can be conceptualized as a belief system or mental condition present in the *child*, that is, the child has a distorted or false belief that the rejected or disfavored parent is "evil," "dangerous," or somehow unworthy of love or affection. Second, the child's rejection of the alienated or target parent is *without legitimate justification*. And this is the key distinction: If there is a documented or objectively verifiable history of the rejected parent being abusive or severely neglectful, the child's rejection of that parent could be legitimate, and, if so, it would not be a case of parental alienation. And finally, for a court to find that a family dynamic presents evidence of parental alienation there must be direct or indirect evidence of parental alienating behavior by the alienating or favored parent, which has influenced the child to reject the targeted parent. One should not simply *assume* that just because a child has demonstrated resistance toward or rejected a parent without apparent justification, the other parent must have engaged in parental alienating behavior.

As to *how* parental alienation takes place, in my prior book, *Litigating Parental Alienation: Evaluating and Presenting an Effective Case in Court*, I described the research conducted by Dr. Amy J. L. Baker and her colleagues by outlining the 17 alienating strategies that are commonly seen as alienating behaviors. They include badmouthing, limiting contact, confiding in the child, asking the child to spy on the target parent, referring to the target parent by first name, withholding important information from the target parent, and undermining the authority of the target parent.[58] These behaviors are not gender-specific; both fathers and mothers have been found to have engaged in these alienating behaviors. Take, for example, the behavior of a father who the Tennessee courts found to have engaged in severe parental alienation. His modus operandi consisted of brainwashing and programming his son by engaging in a pattern of behavior that included

58. Ashish Joshi, Litigating Parental Alienation: Evaluating and Presenting an Effective Case in Court 90–101 (ABA, 2021).

sending text messages to the minor child telling him that he had "a right to be ugly to [his] [Mother]," that his mother was "mentally ill" and "can't help the way [she] [was] born and created by God," that he had to visit his mother "because the law forces you to go," and that he "will never like her. Nobody likes her. It is impossible."[59] Subjected to such indoctrination and brainwashing, children may turn on the targeted parents, vilify them, reject them, and show no ambivalence or guilt in treating them in a most cruel fashion. The trauma is suffered not just by the rejected parent; the alienated and brainwashed children, too, are robbed of "a normal childhood, normal sibling relationships, and a normal relationship with [the] [targeted] [parent]."[60]

Therefore, it should not come as a surprise that family courts have found parental alienation to be "a form of emotional abuse that should not be tolerated."[61] To remediate such abuse, courts have realized that in severe cases of alienation it may be necessary to jettison the conservative approach of taking "baby steps" by ordering traditional psychotherapy while keeping the abused child in the custody of the alienator. For to do so will only result in a litigious "merry-go-round" that has neither worked in the past nor will "work in the future."[62] In some cases, courts have increasingly taken seemingly drastic but ultimately necessary steps of changing custody, ordering psycho-educational counseling for the alienating parent, ordering specialized reunification program for the targeted parent and the child, together with financial sanctions, reallocation of attorney fees and litigation costs, and, in severe cases, incarceration for repeated violation of court orders.

Parental alienation is by no means unique to the United States. Parental alienation has been described, discussed, and debated in the legal and scientific literature by numerous writers all over the world. It is addressed in thousands of court rulings outside of the United States: in Canada, United Kingdom, Brazil, Mexico, Israel, France, Spain, India, Australia, New Zealand, Hong Kong, the European Court of Human Rights, and other jurisdictions around the world.[63] This is not surprising, as it is an expression of human behavior, albeit pathological, that occurs worldwide with similar

59. McClain v. McClain, 539 S.W.3d 170, 194–95 (Tenn. Ct. App. 2017).

60. Matter of Marriage of Reichert, 2 Wash. App. 2d 1063, *2 (2018).

61. *McClain*, 539 S.W.3d at 200.

62. *Id.*

63. Joshi, *supra* note 58, at 197–227.

patterns. A parent who violates the boundaries by treating a child as a weapon in a divorce or custody litigation causes his or her child serious emotional harm.

Domestic Violence Must Be Ruled Out *Before* Considering Parental Alienation

Some commentators suggest that when dealing with issues of child custody and visitation, parental alienation should not be considered until the presence of domestic violence is effectively ruled out. For instance, the American Professional Society on the Abuse of Children (APSAC) states in a position paper that:

> In situations of marital/relationship dissolution, the allegation of interpersonal violence needs to be addressed before issues of custody and visitation can be addressed. . . . If interpersonal violence is determined to be unlikely, the best interest of the child in case specific factors should determine the custody and visitation arrangement.[64]

First, the term "interpersonal violence," could very well include parental alienating behavior by a parent if such behavior consists of weaponizing the children, threatening harm to the children and their loved ones, or using them as agents to perpetrate coercive controlling behaviors.

Second, it would be a mistake to deliberately delay the investigation of parental alienating behaviors or remain willfully blind to such evidence simply because the possibility of domestic violence, however small, has not been completely ruled out. Consider what Dr. Bradley W. Freeman, an associate professor of clinical psychiatry and behavioral sciences at Vanderbilt University Medical Center has written:

> While being vigilant about interpersonal violence is necessary in conducting parenting time evaluations, this can be accomplished in parallel to the overall evaluation. Proving something does not exist asserts the need to investigate and definitively determine the absence in all its forms, no matter how small or unlikely. A realistic approach to arriving at a conclusion regarding the presence or absence of domestic violence is being methodical and thorough. The evaluator should request and review police reports,

---

64. American Professional Society on the Abuse of Children, Position Paper on Allegations of Child Maltreatment and Intimate Partner Violence in Divorce/Parental Relationship Dissolution 2, 4 (2016).

court documents, medical documentation (psychological and physical), interview the parties, speak with collateral sources who know the parties in question, and review other pieces of information made available to them by the parties themselves.[65]

An evaluator should give more weight to *data*, which is less subjective and less likely to be biased. The systematic and methodical approach that Dr. Freeman recommends can help to uncover hidden patterns of abuse together with evidence of alienating behaviors or signs of alienation present in the children. Generating different and even conflicting hypotheses can be done in parallel by evaluators undertaking custody or visitation evaluations. The evaluator can thereby explore the evidence of domestic violence as well as gather information about alienating behaviors or signs of alienation present in the children *simultaneously*. Of course, the evaluator must come to a decision about the presence of domestic violence or abuse and the related safety factors before generating her final opinion concerning parental alienation. Experienced evaluators and professionals know that domestic violence or abuse can be difficult to discern yet can have a strong impact regarding the presence or absence of parental alienation. And, in some situations, an evaluator or a court could be confronted with a "hybrid" scenario where Parent A has engaged in instances of domestic abuse, while Parent B has demonstrated parental alienating behaviors.[66]

One Cannot Distinguish Alienation from Estrangement

Another common myth about parental alienation is a belief that alienation cannot be effectively distinguished from estrangement. For instance, consider what Dr. Robert Emery, a professor of psychology has to say in this regard:

> My experience tells me that some extremely angry parents alienate children from their other parent. My experience also tells me that some

65. Bradley W. Freeman, *The Psychosocial Assessment of Contact Refusal*, *in* Parental Alienation: Science and Law 75 (Demosthenes Lorandos & William Bernet eds., 2020), *citing* Peter G. Jaffe, Janet R. Johnston, Claire V. Crooks & Nicholas Bala, *Custody Disputes Involving Allegations of Domestic Violence: Toward a Differential Approach to Parenting Plans*, 46 Fam. Ct. Rev. 500 (2008).

66. *Martin*, Michigan Court of Appeals No. 349261 (Jan. 28, 2020), n. 2.

> self-absorbed parents use accusations of alienation to blame their former partner and excuse their selfish disregard of their children. . . . [However,] I do not have confidence in my own, or anyone else's, ability to discern truth in divisive divorces . . . and I would be greatly impressed if some investigator could punch a hole in my skepticism with research demonstrating reliable and valid discriminations between accurate and inaccurate accounts of his or her divorce.[67]

Other experts have disagreed with the opinion that it is impossible to differentiate estrangement from alienation. For instance, consider Dr. Bradley W. Freeman's analysis on this issue:

> The difference is straightforward: estrangement is a rational rejection of a parent while PA is based on an irrational rejection. For an experienced MHP [Mental Health Professional], the process of differentiating alienation from estrangement is analogous to diagnosing delusional disorder (i.e., distinguishing a rational from an irrational opinion) or a specific phobia (i.e., distinguishing a rational from an irrational fear). For example, one of the DSM-5 criteria for specific phobia is, "The fear or anxiety is out of proportion to the actual danger posed by the specific object or situation and to the sociocultural context."[68] Similarly, the basic premise of PA is that the child's rejection of the alienated parent is out of proportion to anything that parent has done.[69]

Courts appear to agree with Dr. Freeman's position and have been able to distinguish between cases where a child's rejection of a parent is premised on the parent's neglect or abusive behavior and where a parent's rejection is influenced by the other parent's alienating behavior. As a Tennessee court held:

> Alienation and estrangement, as psychological terms of art that may describe some of these family dynamics, are not interchangeable or synonymous concepts. The difference between estrangement and alienation resides in the presence vs absence of a reasonable objective basis for a child's severe and persistent rejection and denigration of a parent. Rejection and denigration of a parent with a reasonable objective basis is

---

67. Robert E. Emery, *Proponents Bear the Burden of Proof*, 43 Fam. Ct. Rev. 8, 9 (2005).

68. American Psychiatric Association, Diagnostic and Statistical Manual of Mental Disorders (5th ed. 2013)

69. Freeman, *supra* note 65.

estrangement; rejection and denigration without such a basis is parental alienation.[70]

The key issue supporting the possible presence of the parental alienation family dynamic is an irrational or frivolous excuse for the rejection of a parent. For instance, a teenager might say to an evaluator that she refuses to have any contact or relationship with her mother because the mother never listens to her and is too "controlling." The task for the evaluator then is to determine how the adolescent's perception of her mother developed and whether such belief was based in experiential reality of the parent-child contact or a result of a pattern of alienating behavior by the other parent, the father, or something else. To identify the presence of the alienation dynamic, some professionals adopt the Five-Factor Model, which has been described elsewhere in this book. The Five-Factor Model provides the evaluator with a methodology to follow. Once rejection of the parent or contact refusal is affirmed and maltreatment or neglect by the rejected parent is ruled out, the evaluator needs to consider three other factors. These include (1) a history of a previously positive relationship between the child and rejected parent, (2) the exhibition of alienating behaviors by the preferred or favored parent, and (3) the common symptoms of parental alienation in the child. While it is possible to distinguish alienation from estrangement, it is critical to do so since the effective therapeutic or mental health intervention differs greatly in cases involving alienation compared to those of estrangement. In fact, family courts and child custody evaluators do it all the time and are able to distinguish the estrangement dynamic from that of alienation.

Parental Alienation Cannot Be "Diagnosed" Because It Is Not in DSM-5

Some critics of the parental alienation theory have objected to the use of the word "diagnosis" in identifying the presence of parental alienation as a family dynamic in child custody litigation. This criticism is premised on the argument that parental alienation is not included as a specific mental disorder in the *Diagnostic and Statistical Manual of Mental Disorders* (DSM-5-TR or simply, DSM), published by the American Psychiatric Association. This criticism lacks merit for two reasons:

70. *McClain*, 539 S.W.3d at 194–95.

(1) Several well-known and widely accepted mental conditions have never been included in the DSM, such as "psychopathy," "complex posttraumatic stress disorder," "battered woman syndrome," "sexual addiction," and "pathological lying." Clinicians and researchers commonly refer to these conditions as "diagnoses."

(2) The DSM does not "own" the concept of diagnosing mental conditions. Other organizations have created their own systems of psychiatric nomenclature, including the National Institutes of Mental Health, which uses "Research Domain Criteria" (RDoC) instead of DSM diagnoses. The Group for the Advancement of Psychiatry (GAP), a large, influential organization, developed its own system of classification of mental conditions. And, of course, the World Health Organization uses the *International Classification of Diseases.*[71]

In addition, courts have interpreted the term *diagnosis* broadly and have permitted witnesses to testify about diagnoses even if these were not specifically included in the DSM. In an important case regarding pedophilia, the U.S. Supreme Court stated the general principle, "Legal definitions . . . need not mirror those advanced by the medical profession."[72] "More specifically, in two cases involving the diagnosis of hebephilia, federal appellate courts held that 'a mental disorder or defect need not necessarily be one so identified in the DSM in order to meet the statutory requirement [for testimony].'"[73]

A different but related fallacious argument focuses on dismissing the reality of the parental alienation phenomenon under the pretext that the term is not specifically mentioned in the DSM. This issue often arises in litigation, particularly when a litigant or his or her attorney is attempting to discredit the theory of parental alienation. Borrowing a page from actor Tom Cruise's antics in his role as the JAG Lieutenant Daniel Kaffee in *A Few Good Men*, attorneys attempt to cross-examine experts propounding the theory of parental alienation by handing them a copy of DSM and asking: "*Dr. Smith, would you turn to the page in this book that defines the term 'parental alienation,' please?*"

---

71. *Parental Alienation Theory: Official Synopsis* 41–42 (Parental Alienation Study Group, Inc., 2025), www.pasg.info/resources.

72. Kansas v. Hendricks, 521 U.S. 346 (1996).

73. *Parental Alienation Theory, supra* note 71, at 42, citing United States v. Carta, 592 F.3d 34 (1st Cir. 2010); United States v. Vandivere, 88 F.4th 481 (4th Cir. 2023).

The term *parental alienation* is not included in the DSM. Seizing this fact, critics of the parental alienation theory argue that the phenomenon lacks scientific support. In that regard, a team of professionals criticized that "[PAS] has not been accepted by any official organization. It is not in the American Psychiatric Association's DSM (not DSM-IV nor in the more recently published DSM-V); not in the International Classification of Diseases, nor is it adopted by any organization (e.g., the American Psychological Association)."[74] It is not just the detractors and opponents of parental alienation who make this incorrect argument. Even professionals who accept the concept of parental alienation commonly make the same mistake. Dr. William Bernet explains how writers who are friendly to the concept of parental alienation make this mistake:

> *Principles and Practice of Forensic Psychiatry* . . . made incorrect statements regarding P[arental] A[lienation]. *Role of the Psychiatric Evaluator in Child Custody Disputes* referred to "the controversial Parental Alienation Syndrome (PAS)," and then said, "PAS was ultimately not included as a mental disorder in the DSM-5, because it has never been shown to be both reliable and valid."[75] That statement was incorrect because the authors of DSM-5 never expressed doubt regarding the reliability and validity of PAS/PA. They simply said that PA should be considered a "mental condition," not a "mental disorder." When contacted about this error, the editors of *Principles and Practice of Forensic Psychiatry* readily agreed to correct it when the book is reprinted.[76]

The place of parental alienation in DSM is commonly misunderstood and misrepresented. The editors and authors of DSM-5 have *never* stated that they doubted the reality or importance of parental alienation.[77] Rather, they have explained that the phenomenon of parental alienation does meet their criteria for a "mental disorder" (the term used for diagnostic entities in the DSM-5 chapter, "Other Conditions That May Be a Focus of Clinical

---

74. William O'Donohue, Lorraine T. Benuto & Natalie Bennett, *Examining the Validity of Parental Alienation Syndrome,* 13 J. Child Custody 113, 120 (2016).

75. Steven J. Ciric et al., *Role of the Psychiatric Evaluator in Child Custody Disputes, in* Principles and Practice of Forensic Psychiatry 366 (Richard Rosner & Charles l. Scott eds., 3d. 2017).

76. William Bernet, *Recognition of Parental Alienation by Professional Organizations, in* Parental Alienation: Science and Law, at 275 (Demosthenes Lorandos & William Bernet eds., 2020).

77. *Id.*

Attention"). Although the *actual words*, "parental alienation," are not in the current version of DSM, DSM-5-TR, the *concept* of parental alienation is expressed in several official diagnoses. These diagnoses may be appropriate for clinicians to use in cases involving parental alienation, depending on the details of the clinical presentation and the focus of the practitioner's attention. For instance:

"**Parent–child relational problem (PCRP) (Z62.820).** The definition of this mental condition includes: '. . . negative attributions of the other's intentions, hostility toward . . . the other, and unwarranted feelings of estrangement.' The diagnosis of PCRP would be appropriate if the focus of clinical attention is on the relationship between the alienated child and the rejected parent.

Child affected by parental relationship distress (CAPRD) (Z62.898). The definition of CAPRD includes "negative effects of parental relationship discord (e.g., high levels of conflict, distress, or disparagement) on a child in the family[.]" The diagnosis of CAPRD would be appropriate if the focus of clinical attention is on the mental condition of the alienated child.

Child psychological abuse (T74.32X). The definition for this mental condition includes: "harming/abandoning people or things that the child cares about." The diagnosis of child psychological abuse can be given to the adult perpetrator of maltreatment or the child victim of maltreatment. This diagnosis would be appropriate if the focus of clinical attention is on the activities of an abusive, alienating parent.

Delusional symptoms in the context of relationship with an individual with prominent delusions (F28). This is DSM-5-TR terminology for the mental disorder that previously was called *folie à deux* and shared psychotic disorder. In severe cases of PA, the underlying explanation might be a delusional disorder in the favored parent. In such a case, it would be appropriate to diagnose the child with delusional symptoms in the context of relationship with an individual with prominent delusions.[78]

Factitious disorder imposed on another (F68.A). This is DSM-5-TR terminology for the mental disorder that previously was called "factitious disorder by proxy." In some cases of PA, the alienating parent might falsify physical or psychological signs or symptoms in order to cause the child to appear ill, injured, or abused. In such a case, it would be appropriate to

78. L.S. Tucker & T.P. Cornwall, *Mother-son folie a deux: a case of attempted patricide*, 134 J. Psychiatry 1146 (1977).

diagnose the perpetrator (not the child) with factitious disorder imposed on another.

Identity disturbance due to prolonged and intense coercive persuasion (F44.89). In some cases of parental alienation, the child who has been subjected to intense coercive persuasion (e.g., indoctrination, thought reform) may present with prolonged changes in, or conscious questioning of, their identity. In such a case, it would be appropriate to diagnose the child with identity disturbance due to prolonged and intense coercive persuasion."[79]

A clinician could select one or more of the preceding diagnoses, "depending on the focus of the practitioner's evaluation. If the focus is on the condition of the child, the clinician could use child affected by parental relationship distress; if the focus is on the relationship between the child and the rejected parent, they could use parent-child relational problem; if the focus is on the activities of the alienating parent, they could use child psychological abuse."[80]

The Concept of Weaponization of a Child by a Parent Has No Empirical Support

Some critics oppose the parental alienation theory or the concept of how a child could be weaponized by one parent against the other, and challenge the concept on the ground that it lacks empirical support. Often, attorneys that represent the favored or alienating parent, a guardian ad litem, or the counsel for a minor child who has been subjected to parental alienating behaviors make this argument. Some do it as a deliberate and calculative strategy in order to distract the court from the real issue at hand, that is, child psychological abuse. Others do it being willfully blind to the existing research in the field of social sciences. Regardless, this red herring of an argument continues to distract the courts and compromise outcomes in litigation.

At the outset, it is important to note that most of these arguments focus on parental alienation syndrome (PAS), as opposed to the parental alienation theory. For example, as one legal commentator wrote in 2013,

---

79. *Parental Alienation Theory: Official Synopsis*, *supra* note 71, at 13–14 (internal citations omitted).

80. Bernet, *supra* note 76, at 276.

"[w]hile Gardener and PAS have had many adherents, particularly among forensic evaluators and litigants, there is actually no empirical research validating the existence of PAS. And there is extensive empirical proof that the assumptions underlying the theory are false."[81] A similar sentiment has been echoed by others.[82]

The argument that the parental alienation theory lacks empirical support has no merit. In the book *Parental Alienation—Science and Law*, Dr. Amy J. L. Baker wrote an entire chapter on the theory of parental alienation and the empirical research in support of it. In her chapter, Dr. Baker describes numerous studies on parental alienation, which refute the argument that the theory lacks empirical support. As Dr. Baker explains:

> The numerous studies described in this chapter are offered as counter evidence. That is, in each study the measures of PA behaviors in the child and ABs [Alienating Behaviors] by the alienating parent were reliable and valid; objective, reliable and valid measures of other constructs were included (for example, measures of psychological maltreatment, parenting, depression, anxiety, and so forth); sample sizes were adequate; response rates were high; and statistically significant effects were found that support the foundational concept of PA theory: that exposure of children to ABs on the part of one parent are damaging to children and can interfere in their relationship with the other parent.[83]

Some critics of parental alienation have cited a 2016 book chapter authored by Dr. Michael Saini and his colleagues, which focused on a review of empirical research underpinning the parental alienation theory.[84] However, the chapter and its findings are often distorted, misrepresented, and taken out of context in litigation, which often attempts to find simplistic solutions to complex family dynamics. It is worthwhile to briefly discuss the argument presented in the Saini book chapter here and Dr. Baker's rejoinder to the argument. As Dr. Baker points out in her chapter on parental

---

81. Joan S. Meier, *Parental Alienation Syndrome and Parental Alienation: A Research Review*, Vawnet.org (Sep. 2013), https://vawnet.org/sites/default/files/materials/files/2016-09/AR_PASUpdate.pdf.

82. *See, e.g.*, Benjamin Garber et al., Family Evaluation in Custody Litigation: Promoting Optimal Outcomes and Reducing Ethical Risks 34 (2d ed. 2018).

83. Amy J. L. Baker, *Parental Alienation and Empirical Research*, *in* Parental Alienation: Science and Law 244 (Demosthenes Lorandos & William Bernet eds., 2020).

84. Michael Saini et al., *Empirical Studies of Alienation*, *in* Parenting Plan Evaluations: Applied Research for the Family Court 374 (Leslie Drozd et al. eds., 2d ed. 2016).

alienation and its empirical support, there are two notable problems with the critics' argument.[85]

First, the authors of the Saini book chapter reviewed and evaluated parental alienation research studies using what is known as the GRADE system, which stands for Grading of Recommendations Assessment, Development, and Evaluation.[86] However, the GRADE system was developed for a particular kind of medical research study known as a PICO study (Patient, Intervention, Comparator, Outcome). This means that the GRADE system was developed specifically to evaluate the quality of evidence in a *very specific type of study*, one in which patients with known medical conditions receive one of two comparable interventions, and outcomes are assessed to determine the relative effectiveness of each intervention. The GRADE system is not an appropriate tool to evaluate all types of parental alienation research studies. Dr. Baker further explained that of the studies that used the GRADE system, "most studies are given low marks because the samples were not randomly drawn from the population. However, most social science research employs samples of convenience and the ability to generalize is not considered compromised unless there is a specific reason to believe that the characteristics of the sample are different from the population in a way that would be related to the variables studied."[87]

The second problem with the argument presented in the Saini book chapter is that "the authors fail to provide information about inter-rater reliability in their coding of the studies reviewed. This is a notable problem because not only is it [a] standard practice in the field to provide the reader of a review article with information about the extent to which the reviewers agreed with their evaluations of the studies, but the GRADE system in particular has been difficult for coders to use reliably."[88] Even the creators of the GRADE system admitted having difficulty achieving reliability using their own system. Therefore, it would be even more important for the authors of the 2016 book chapter to provide that information about their coding of the parental alienation studies that they reviewed and evaluated.[89]

---

85. Baker, *supra* note 83, at 244–246.

86. David Atkins et al., *Systems for Grading the Quality of Evidence and the Strength of Recommendations I: Critical Appraisal of Existing Approaches,* 4 BMC Health Serv. Res. 38 (2004).

87. Baker, *supra* note 83, at 245.

88. *Id.*

89. *Id.*

The research studies described by Dr. Baker in her 2020 book chapter demonstrate that the theory of parental alienation has empirical support. It has been validated by using objective, reliable, and valid scientific measures. Recently, in 2022, Dr. Jennifer Harman and her colleagues published a peer-reviewed paper that discussed the scientific status of parental alienation. The results of their research "confirmed that the current state of parental alienation scholarship meets three criteria of a maturing field of scientific inquiry: an expanding literature, a shift toward quantitative studies, and a growing body of research that tests theory-generated hypotheses. [Further] [n]early 40% of the PA literature has been published since 2016, establishing that [parental alienation] research has moved beyond an early stage of scientific development and has produced a scientifically trustworthy knowledge base."[90]

Family Courts Have Rejected the Parental Alienation Theory

Family court judges often are asked to preclude all expert testimony regarding parental alienation on the ground that the testimony does not meet the *Frye* or *Daubert* or a particular jurisdiction's standard for admissibility of expert evidence. Often, a strawman argument is put forward challenging the validity and reliability of PAS (even though the issue before the court may concern a parent's alienating *behaviors* or symptoms of alienation manifested by the child without any reference to the "syndrome"). And after creating such a strawman, the detractors thereafter attempt to paint the controversy with the broadest possible brush strokes, equating PAS with parental alienation, and asking the court to rule that any/all evidence related to parental alienation be ruled inadmissible.

Even organizations that have unequivocally acknowledged parental alienating behaviors as being harmful to a child's cognitive, emotional, and psychological well-being are at times led to distance themselves from PAS. For example, a publication of the National Council of Juvenile and Family Court Judges (NCJFCJ) incorrectly states, "[t]he theory positing the existence of 'PAS' has been discredited by the scientific community."[91] The

90. Jennifer Harman et al., *Development Psychology and the Scientific Status of Parental Alienation*, Dev. Psych. (2022), http://dx.doi.org/10.1037/dev0001404.

91. Clare Dalton et al., Navigating Custody & Visitation Evaluations in Cases with Domestic Violence: A Judge's Guide 24 (2006).

argument is advanced further by arguing that parental alienation syndrome does not pass *Daubert* criteria, so, "[a]ny testimony that a party to a custody case suffers from the syndrome or 'parental alienation' should therefore be ruled inadmissible and/or stricken from the evaluation report[.]"[92] A practitioner should note how in one broad brush the proponent of this argument equated PAS with parental alienation, being willfully blind to a plethora of peer-reviewed literature demonstrating scientific and empirical support for parental alienation and parental alienating behaviors. Engaging in such strawman arguments also requires a litigant to turn a blind eye toward hundreds of judicial decisions from courts across the country that have acknowledged the theory of parental alienation and permitted expert evidence on the topic. Nevertheless, the strawman attacks continue and persist in their efforts to equate PAS with parental alienation.[93]

Like many simplistic but misleading arguments, absent a thorough understanding of the parental alienation construct together with a solid knowledge of the *Frye* and *Daubert* progeny of cases, it is easy to be distracted by the strawman argument that equates PAS with parental alienation. The rules for admissibility of expert evidence vary among jurisdictions, although they share the common goal that such evidence be useful and reliable.[94] The prevailing standards for admissibility of expert evidence have been articulated in two federal cases, *Frye* and *Daubert*, from which the states have derived their own variations. Most jurisdictions today follow a *Daubert*-leaning standard, while others lag with a *Frye*-leaning standard.[95]

Daubert imposes the gatekeeping obligation on the trial court and identifies the judge as the gatekeeper who before admitting expert testimony must determine that the evidence is not only relevant and helpful to the controversy at hand, but that the expert's methodology is based on a scientific method, "meaning that: (1) Hypotheses have been formulated and tested, (2) The results were subjected to peer review and published, (3) There is a known error rate, and (4) The methods in theory are generally accepted in the scientific community."[96]

---

92. *Id.*

93. Holly Smith, *Parental Alienation Syndrome: Fact or Fiction? The Problem with Its Use in Child Custody Cases*, 11 U. Mass. L.R. 64 (2016).

94. Daubert v. Merrell Dow Pharmaceuticals, Inc., 509 U.S. 579, 589 (1993).

95. Demosthenes Lorandos, *Admissibility of the Construct-Parental Alienation*, *in* Parental Alienation: Science and Law 326 (Demosthenes Lorandos & William Bernet eds., 2020).

96. Baker, *supra* note 83, at 246.

A proponent of the parental alienation theory or one who attempts to offer evidence of parental alienating behaviors would do well by reviewing the chapter authored by a legal and mental health expert, Dr. Demosthenes Lorandos: Admissibility of the Construct-Parental Alienation in the book, *Parental Alienation: Science and Law*.[97] This chapter examines the application of *Daubert* / *Frye* criteria to the parental alienation theory in greater detail, but suffice it to say here that the following points are established from the review of case law and professional literature.

First, Dr. Lorandos's research has found more than *1,000 cases* addressing parental alienation from 1985 through 2018, which clearly demonstrates that the courts have found the construct of parental alienation useful, reliable, and admissible.[98] Second, there is a plethora of scientific or medical literature including peer-reviewed literature to support parental alienation theory. Vanderbilt University's Center for Knowledge Management database contains citations to more than 1,000 treatises relevant to the parental alienation construct.[99] Third, hypotheses relevant to alienating behaviors have been generated and tested, which means that the theory is falsifiable.[100] Fourth, the research results on parental alienation have been repeatedly subjected to peer review and have been published in renowned peer-review journals.[101] Fifth, with respect to error rate—known or potential rate of error is an important factor in *Daubert* gatekeeping—both the qualitative and quantitative research housed at the Vanderbilt University's database demonstrates that all measures used in parental alienation research have known error rates. This demonstrates more than adequate reliability.[102] Finally, while there is a dispute amongst experts as to whether parental alienation should be considered a syndrome that resides within the child, there is widespread acceptance of the core concepts of the parental alienation theory, to wit: parents can engage in behaviors that can adversely affect a child's relationship with the other parent.

---

97. Lorandos, *supra* note 95, at 324–64.

98. *Id.* at 365–85.

99. *See* Vanderbilt University Medical Center, Center for Knowledge Management, https://www.ckm.vumc.org/ckm.

100. Baker, *supra* note 83, at 246.

101. *Id. See also* Parental Alienation: The Handbook for Mental Health and Legal Professionals, Eds. Lorandos, D., Bernet, W., and Sauber, S. R. (2013, Charles C. Thomas), which contains a bibliography with hundreds of peer-reviewed articles regarding the topic of parental alienation from more than 30 countries.

102. Baker, *supra* note 83, at 247.

Parental alienating behaviors should not be equated with PAS. When evidence of such behavior exists, a court should not waste its time and limited resources in holding a *Daubert* or *Frye* hearing to determine the scientific validity of a "syndrome," which has nothing to do with the concrete, observable, and ultimately provable evidence before the court. Perhaps in an attempt to refocus the courts and family law practitioners' attention to what really matters, the Association of Family and Conciliation Courts (AFCC) and NCJFCJ recently issued a *Joint Statement on Parent-Child Contact Problems*, which acknowledges the harm posed by "parental alienating behaviors" and recommends that family law practitioners receive regular and ongoing training in this area.[103]

Dads Do Not Alienate; Only Moms Do

The theory of parental alienation is often misrepresented—at times, deliberately, to create an unwarranted controversy—as a weapon to fan the flames of the gender war over children: Dads versus Moms. On one end of the spectrum, it is argued that alienation is a choice weapon of women to "get even" against men. At the other end of the spectrum, an argument is made that men accuse women of parental alienation to excuse or distract from their abusive conduct that is the root cause of the children's rejection.[104] Both arguments are ideologies masquerading as science.

Courts have acknowledged that the theory of parental alienation does not lend itself to a "simplistic analysis," where it is portrayed as a "gender war over the children."[105] However, statistics cannot be accused of being sexist and we do have to reckon with some interesting data. In 2010, a Canadian law professor and his colleagues published a paper that studied all reported Canadian cases between 1989 and 2008 that dealt with parental alienation claims.[106] The study found that between 1989 and 2008, alienation was found by Canadian courts in 106 out of 175 cases raising the

---

103. *See* National Council of Juvenile and Family Court Judges, Joint Statement of Parent-Child Contact Problems, available at https://www.ncjfcj.org/wp-content/uploads/2022/08/NCJFCJ-AFCC-Joint-Statement.pdf.

104. *See, e.g.*, Margaret Drew, *Collaboration and Intention: Making the Collaborative Family Law Process Safe(r)*, 32 Ohio St. J. on Disp. Resol. 373n (2017); Glenn, Current Legislation, 2017-2018, Father's Rights Movement, April 18, 2018.

105. J.F. v. D.F., 61 Misc. 3d 1226(A), 2018 N.Y. slip op. 51829(U).

106. Nicholas Bala et al., *Parental Alienation: Canadian Court Cases 1989—2008*, 48(1) Fam. Ct. Rev. 164–79 (Jan. 2010).

issue. Out of 106 cases, the mother was the alienating parent in 72 cases (68 percent), and the father was the alienating parent in 33 cases (31 percent). The Canadian study is not alone in finding mothers to be significantly more as the alienating parent. In the United States too, the statistics do indicate that the percentage of women who have been found or identified to have engaged in alienating behaviors outnumber men by three to one. The results of the Lorandos research project wherein he and his team analyzed over 1,000 cases involving parental alienation, demonstrate "that during 1985–2018, about 75% of the identified alienators were female and 25% were male. This proportion has remained approximately the same over the years."[107] However, to simply consider this statistic in a vacuum and rush to a conclusion that women alienate significantly more than men would be inappropriate. The "residual effects of patriarchy may account for some of the skew in the numbers of male to female alienators. According to a Pew Research Center analysis of median hourly earnings of both full-and part-time workers in the United States, women earned 82% of what men earned. Based on this estimate, it would take an extra 47 days of work each year for women to earn what men do. And in the process of a marital breakup, working males may have more access to ready cash. These differentials should be considered when reviewing the gender difference found in this research."[108] In other words, men, having more financial resources, may have been more willing to litigate cases involving parental alienation using skilled legal representation and top-notch mental health experts, as compared to women.

On the other end of spectrum, some critics of the parental alienation theory argue that the theory is misinterpreted and misused against women and mothers in child custody litigation. These critics have been vocal about not only challenging the validity of the parental alienation theory but also about avoiding the term *parental alienation* when women complain of being targeted parents of alienating behaviors. One group of domestic violence activists counsel women and mothers to "avoid the use of the term P[arental] A[lienation] or 'alienating behaviors[.]'"[109] These critics recom-

107. Lorandos, *supra* note 95, at 371–72.

108. *Id.* at 373–74 (citing Nikki Graf et al., *The Narrowing, but Persistent, Gender Gap in Pay, Facttank: News in the Numbers* (Apr. 9, 2018), http://www.pewresearch.org/fact-tank/2018/04/09/gender-pay-gap-facts.

109. Elizabeth Dalgarno, *From 'Parental Alienation' to [Abusers'] Child and Mother Sabotage (CAMS) as a Preferable Term for How Perpetrator Fathers Intentionally Sabotage the Child-Mother Connection* (Oct. 23, 2023), https://www.shera-research.com/latest-news

mend using the term, "'Child and Mother Sabotage' (CAMS) as a preferable term for how perpetrator fathers intentionally sabotage the child-mother connection."[110]

Setting the gender-focused inflammatory rhetoric aside, when we review the pertinent case law—judicial opinions from family courts around the country where courts have found parental alienation to exist—we find that neither gender has a monopoly on engaging in alienating behaviors. We find fathers and mothers behaving equally bad.[111]

Sub-Optimal Parenting Equals Parental Alienation: The Risk of False Positives

On occasions, evaluators—even the good, competent ones—may get it wrong. False positives of parental alienation in child custody cases fuel concerns about the application of the parental alienation theory in family law cases.[112] "False positive identifications of parental alienation can occur with respect to a parent's alienating behaviors, a child's alienation from a parent, or both."[113] For example, false positive identifications of a parent's alienating behaviors can occur when the parent's behavior is mistakenly interpreted as undermining or potentially undermining a child's positive regard for the other parent. In his peer-reviewed scientific paper, Dr. Richard Warshak provides an example of a situation where a simplistic understanding of the parental alienation theory may result in false positive conclusion about an alleged "alienating" behavior: A parent giving a child a cell phone and instructing the child to call when he or she feels like speaking.[114] The significance of this behavior depends on the context in which it occurs and how the child subsequently uses the phone given by the parent. For example, has the parent who provided the phone planted in the child a false belief that the other parent is dangerous? Has the parent instructed the child to call 911 if

---

/from-parental-alienation-to-abusers-child-and-mother-sabotage-cams-as-a-preferable-term-for-how-perpetrator-fathers-intentionally-sabotage-the-child-mother-connection.

110. *Id.*

111. *See* Appendix C, Cases Illustrative of Alienating Behaviors, *in* Parental Alienation: Science and Law 603–34 (Lorandos, & Bernet, eds., 2020).

112. Richard Warshak, *When Evaluators Get It Wrong: False Positive IDs and Parental Alienation*, 26(1) Psych., Pub. Pol'y, & Law 54–68 (2019).

113. *Id.* at 54.

114. *Id.* at 63.

the other parent did anything that the child did not like, such as disciplining the child for rude or disrespectful behavior? Has the parent instructed the child to use the phone to record the other parent? Has the parent repeatedly encroached on the child's time with the other parent by frequently calling and texting the child? Has the parent attempted to undermine the child's relationship with the other parent? If so, these would be examples of alienating behaviors and, in that context, providing the phone to the child would be a continuation of the pattern of alienating behaviors.[115] But if all that the parent did was to provide a cell phone to the child and instruct the child to call when he or she felt like speaking to the parent, that behavior by itself would not rise to the level of being an alienating behavior.

Of significance, the term "parental alienation refers either to the state of the relationship between a child and a parent whom the child rejects without good cause or to the child's attitudes and behaviors that reflect an unreasonable aversion to a parent with whom he or she formerly enjoyed normal relations."[116] However, it is possible that a parent can engage in negative, alienating behaviors—for example, persistently disparaging the other parent—without the child becoming alienated from the parent who is the target of such negative behavior. Alienating behaviors do not *always* result in parental alienation. For instance, in a New York case, the court rejected three experts' findings of parental alienation, concluding that "[t]here is not an iota of evidence that any one of three daughters are alienated from their father."[117] By the same token, another court in New York concluded that a child's rejection of a parent was a justified response and not due to parental alienation.[118]

A child's alienation from a parent can arise from factors independent of, or in combination with the favored parent's behavior. For instance, the child could be reacting to abuse, gross mistreatment, severe mental illness, witnessing domestic violence, or substance abuse.[119] Further, negative behavior toward a parent, such as denigrating, complaining, and resisting contact,

115. *See, e.g.*, McRoberts v. Superior Court of Los Angeles Cnty, B234877 (Cal. Ct. App. June 19, 2012).

116. Warshak, *supra* note 112, at 57.

117. J.F. v. D.F., 61 Misc. 3d 1226(A), 2018 N.Y. slip op. 51829(U).

118. A.E. v. S.E., NY Law Journal, Dec. 11, 1990 (No. O-1433-90, Fam. Ct. N.Y. Westchester County, Nov 19, 1990).

119. Warshak, *supra* note 112, at 57.

is insufficient *by itself* to identify a child as "alienated."[120] Experts identify seven criteria that distinguish negative behaviors of moderately or severely alienated children from negative behavior that does not indicate moderate or severe levels of parental alienation. A child with moderate or severe parental alienation displays negative behavior that meets all the following criteria:[121]

1. The behavior is chronic rather than temporary and short-lived.
2. The behavior is frequent rather than occasional.
3. The behavior occurs in most situations rather than only in certain situations.
4. The behavior occurs without displays of genuine love and affection toward the rejected parent.
5. The behavior is directed at only one parent.
6. The behavior does not reflect typical dynamics for the child's state of development.
7. The behavior is disproportionate to, and not justified by the rejected parent's past or current behavior.

Mis- and disinformation about family violence pose substantial societal challenges. They not only result in compromised outcomes in legal proceedings but may also deter victims of family violence from seeking the help that they desperately need to break the cycle of abuse. Spread of misinformation—in particular, intentional, and willful disinformation—leads to fear mongering and away from evidence-informed policymaking.[122] Family law practitioners who handle cases involving family violence must be prepared to counter the myths and fallacies that abound in this area of law. This may require a deliberate and persistent effort to separate the wheat from the chaff and to focus the courts' attention to what matters the most: *behaviors* and acts or omissions that constitute abuse—not abstract theories, stereotypes, and ideologies. In the end, family courts' primary focus in child custody litigation is to act in the best interests of the child. In cases involving family violence being distracted by the smoke and mirrors of the commonly held myths and fallacies could lead a court into committing catastrophic errors.

---

120. *Id.* at 58.

121. *Id.*

122. *See, e.g.,* Ashish Joshi & Petra Deeter, *Kayden's Law: Do Ends Justify the Means*, Mich. Fam. L.J. (Mar. 2025).

Chapter 7

Practice Pointers: Tips on Representing Victims of Family Violence

In the United States, there were three key movements across the country that revolutionized how law enforcement, prosecutors, victim advocates, family law practitioners, and courts address domestic violence (DV), including intimate partner violence (IPV). The first movement was the advent of High-Risk Teams within the DV agencies that try to quantify the dangerousness of any given DV/IPV situation, which is then used to customize safeguards around victims. The second was the 2002 opening of the family justice center, the country's first in San Diego, which brought all victim services under one roof: police, attorneys, victim compensation, counseling, education, and others. And the third was the Lethality Assessment Program, launched in 2005 in Maryland and later replicated in other jurisdictions, which addressed how law enforcement dealt with on-scene DV situations.[1]

For family law practitioners who handle family violence cases involving DV or IPV, it is important to not only understand the evolution of the terms and nomenclature used in the field, but also the unique nature of IPV, which sets it apart from other crimes:

> Domestic violence is like no other crime. It does not happen in a vacuum. It does not happen because someone is in the wrong place at the wrong time. Our homes and families are supposed to be sacred territory, the "haven in a heartless world.". . . This is part of what makes [DV] so untenable. It's violence from someone you know, from someone who claims

1. Rachel Louise Snyder, No Visible Bruises: What We Don't Know About Domestic Violence Can Kill Us 13 (2019).

> to love you. It is most often hidden from even one's closest confidantes, and on many occasions the physical violence is far less damaging than the emotional and verbal violence. I can't tell you how many abusers I've heard bemoaning their inability to stop loving the same women they assaulted so severely it landed them in prison. It is, perhaps, a powerful aphrodisiac, the idea that someone is gripped by love so intensely he or she is powerless in the face of it.[2]

Family law attorneys must have knowledge, skill, and training about the unique dynamics of DV and IPV, and should consider screening for the presence of these dynamics in the family law cases they are involved in.[3] This is because, while the presence of a DV or IPV dynamic may not be obvious, when it is present it affects all aspects of family law litigation, including "custody, relocation, parenting time, distribution of assets . . . and whether or not to participate in mediation."[4]

In fact, some have persuasively argued that the failure of a family law attorney to screen for and identify DV/IPV, and then properly counsel clients accordingly, is malpractice.[5] This is because DV/IPV victims face unique hurdles that are unlike other clients. For example, consider the pursuit of child support: Whereas a client who has not been victimized by IPV would generally fully pursue it, an IPV victim who has been subjected to or threatened with physical or other harm may prefer not to.[6]

To this end, the standards promulgated by the American Bar Association (ABA) for attorneys who represent DV/IPV victims require:

> Before representing a client in a civil protection order case, the lawyer should have competent knowledge of the dynamics of domestic violence, sexual assault, and/or stalking.
>
> In particular, the lawyer should understand the potential risk of escalated violence due to litigation, and how the experience of domestic violence, sexual assault and/or stalking may affect the client-lawyer

---

2. *Id.* at 10.

3. *Client Screening to Identify Domestic Violence Victimization*, Minnesota State Bar Association, at 3 (2013).

4. *Id.*

5. Margaret Drew, *Lawyer Malpractice and Domestic Violence: Are We Revictimizing Our Clients?* 39 Fam. L.Q. 7, 9 (2005).

6. *Id.* at 12.

relationship, including the process of establishing rapport with and gathering information, evidence, and case direction from the client.[7]

Furthermore, practitioners must understand that IPV perpetrators often exercise out-sized control over their victims, and, accordingly, it is imperative that the practitioner identify any such manipulation and employ strategies to combat it.[8] This dynamic frequently manifests with a cycle of separation and return as the abuser continues to control the victim, and attorneys are cautioned to "remain nonjudgmental toward clients who reunite with their perpetrators."[9]

Biases: We Do Not See Things as They Are, We See Them as We Are

Everyone has cognitive, affective, and other kinds of biases. No one is immune from them.[10] "Human nature confers a vulnerability to biases, blind spots, and self-enhancing illusions."[11] As Anaïs Nin aptly put it: We do not see things as they are, we see them as *we* are. Biases include "implicit biases which are immediate and unconscious beliefs, presumptions and assumptions based on the characteristics of people or groups of people," including "presumptions about people or groups of people based on their culture or ethnicity."[12]

Cognitive biases are closely related to heuristics, the latter of which are "simple, efficient rules that describe how people decide or reach conclusions when faced with complex problems."[13] Sometimes, heuristics are helpful (e.g., "rules of thumb"), but they "can also create errors in logical reasoning because they are shortcuts and templates, applied to situations for which

---

7. *Standards of Practice for Lawyers Representing Victims of Domestic Violence, Sexual Assault and Stalking in Civil Protection Order Cases*, American Bar Association, at 24 (2007).

8. *Client Screening to Identify Domestic Violence Victimization, supra* note 3, at 4.

9. *Standards of Practice for Lawyers, supra* note 7, at 25–26.

10. Joel Yager et al., *Clinicians' Cognitive and Affective Biases and the Practice of Psychology*, 74 Am. J. Psychotherapy (3) 119, 119 (2021).

11. *Id.*

12. Robert A. Simon & Philip M. Stahl, Forensic Psychology Consultation in Child Custody Litigation 58 (ABA, 2d ed., 2020).

13. *Id.* at 59.

a more *de novo* analysis is appropriate."[14] Thus, heuristics are problematic when they allow a person to ignore complex issues, relevant information, or parts of the problem; they are also problematic when they overemphasize some information, and/or minimize important factors.[15] Forensic professionals, such as child custody evaluators or court-appointed neutrals are especially required to consider and mitigate their biases, but even practitioners who are advocates for a party-litigant should consider their biases and try to mitigate their affect when dealing with an IPV victim or a case involving IPV.

Some of the well-known biases and heuristics include:[16]

- *Anchoring Bias.* Judgment is unduly influenced by initial information; often accompanied by inadequate adjustment when new information becomes available.
- *Availability Bias.* Making a judgment based on how readily information can be recalled from memory.
- *Confirmatory Bias.* A tendency to focus on evidence that might confirm a hypothesis while neglecting evidence that might refute it.
- *Hindsight Bias.* Making a judgment about a case based on the outcome of a previous case that involved similar allegations or behaviors, before gathering all the data.
- *Recency Bias.* Focusing on the most recent data one has heard and overweighing that data in reaching conclusions. Data gathered at the end of an evaluation process or a client interview is emphasized more than previous information received.
- *Stereotyping.* When an evaluator or an interviewer considers the characteristics of an individual rather than the data being collected.
- *The Dunning-Kruger Effect.* This occurs when an evaluator or a professional has an elevated level of confidence in their abilities and knowledge in a specific area. The over confidence and a lack of self-awareness prevent them from accurately assessing their skills, such as their ability to judge a parent's credibility.

---

14. *Id.*

15. *Id.* at 60.

16. Simon & Stahl, *supra* note 12, 58–69; *see also* Steven G. Miller, *Clinical Reasoning and Decision-Making, in* Working with Alienated Children and Families: A Clinical Guidebook 24–33 (Amy J. L. Baker & S. Richard Sauber eds., Routledge 2013).

- *Affiliative Bias or Dis-affiliative Bias.* The affiliative bias occurs when an evaluator or a professional such as a guardian ad litem is influenced by one parent that may have similar characteristics as themselves. Conversely, the dis-affiliative bias occurs when the professional and one parent have different characteristics that may cause a negative influence on the evaluator.
- *Pathology Bias.* When a professional relies on a mental health diagnosis to decide without exploring the relationship between the diagnosis and the diagnosed-parent's parenting and/or co-parenting.
- *Data Gathering Bias.* When an evaluator or a professional gives great weight to a specific method of gathering data and does not give enough weight to data that may have been collected in other ways.
- *Research Bias.* This occurs when one fails to properly cite their research that is being used to support an argument. Vaguely referencing research fails to inform the reader of important contextual information. This also occurs when one cites research that supports one position, while ignoring research that supports the opposite position.
- *"Truth Lies Somewhere in the Middle" Bias.* When an evaluator or a professional or, sometimes, even the court takes the stance that parents in conflict are contributing equally to the conflict. This perception assigns equal blame, where one parent may be more responsible for driving the conflict.
- *"Atilla the Hun Doesn't Marry Mother Teresa" Bias.* This perception presupposes that a psychologically healthy parent is not likely to marry and have children with someone that is much less psychologically healthy.
- *"For the Move" or "Against the Move" Bias.* When an evaluator is either totally against relocation or in favor of relocation, without considering all the factors in a case.
- *Personal Bias.* There are several different personal biases, such as sex, race, cultural, religious, sexual orientation, or being influenced by their own personal issues such as a divorce.
- *Representativeness Bias.* Making a judgment based on similarity, that is, on a stereotype.
- *Affect Bias.* Making a judgment based on an emotion or feeling—can lead to "emotional reasoning."
- *Premature Closure.* Making a diagnosis or other decision before obtaining and/or considering sufficient information.

- *Framing Errors*. Presenting identical information in a way that will lead to a different conclusion, depending on how it is presented.
- *The Fundamental Attribution Error*. Concluding that a behavior is dispositional when in fact it is situational.
- *Base Rate Neglect*. Failure to adequately consider the pre-test or prior probability that a hypothesis is correct when considering new evidence. Giving too much weight to clinical findings and not enough weight to prior probability.
- *Ecological Fallacy*. As used clinically, giving too much weight to group/epidemiological data and not enough weight to an individual patient's clinical findings.
- *Retention Bias*. This occurs when someone hires an individual such as a custody evaluator, who may be influenced due to their desire to please the retaining attorney.
- *"The Expert Will Figure It Out" Bias*. The assumption that because someone is an expert, they will have the correct answer and could not possibly be wrong.
- *"The Parent's Behavior in a Clinical Evaluation" Bias*. If a parent behaves in a certain way, such as being overly anxious or caring, the interviewer may assume that this is how they are all the time.
- *The Critical Parent Bias*. This occurs when a parent is critical of the other parent during an interview. The interviewer may assume that they must be critical of the other parent in front of the children as well.
- *"Both Parties Have Contributed" Bias*. This implies that all cases with child alignment issues are caused by both alienation and estrangement dynamics, meaning that both parents have played a role in the dynamic. For a professional operating under this bias, every case of child alignment is a "hybrid" case.
- *"If a Child Is Adamant, It Must Be True" Bias*. When a child is adamant that something occurred, some may falsely believe that it is true due to how consistent they are.
- *School Performance Bias*. This belief relies on a child's performance in school. If they are performing well, that must mean that their parent is doing a good job. If they are not performing well, it must therefore mean that the parent is not doing a good job.
- *"Time Heals All Wounds" Bias*. Some professionals or courts may believe or state—without evidence in support—that the child just needs time to heal, and they will resume a relationship with the other parent when they are ready to.

Biases are pervasive in family law and harmful. Presence of a bias can significantly undermine a practitioner's effective representation of a party-litigant. Bias could also affect and undermine judicial decision-making such that a court is influenced by a bias or may adopt findings and recommendations of a court-appointed professional whose work might have been undermined by the presence of a bias.[17] For example, a research study revealed that judges were no better at making factual determinations of demeanor evidence than random chance.[18] Other research has revealed that family law judges are remarkably biased in favor of following the recommendations of custody evaluators. Remarkably, they do so 85 percent of the time.[19] And one study also revealed that judges falsely believed that the longer they had been on the bench, the better they were at discerning the truth.[20] This type of overconfidence due to years in the field has been termed by one author as "professional narcissistic personality disorder" (PNPD).[21]

Family law practitioners, collectively, manifest all the biases just listed. For example, attorneys frequently discount the base rate, which is the prevalence of behavior in the population. Additionally, attorneys may conclude that a father is a bad father because the child returns to the mother after a weekend with the father being "defiant, difficult to manage, tired, and homework is not done."[22] But this wholly fails to consider that many children returning home from the less-seen parent may exhibit these traits or that the mother's reporting of the child's behavior may not be accurate and her perception of the situation may have been tainted by her underlying anxiety.

Bias could also cause a professional to deprive an IPV victim of his or her agency in how he or she wishes to litigate a case or approach a situation. For instance, consider the approach of the mainstream DV/IPV victim advocates who follow a carceral approach to address family violence. In a recent publication of investigative journalism, it was reported that some experts, including feminists, believe that the carceral approach is highly misguided.[23]

---

17. Mark B. Baer, *Unchecked Biases in Family Law Are Pervasive and Harmful*, 44(3) Fam. Advocate 6 (2022).

18. *Id.* at 12.

19. *Id.* at 14.

20. *Id.* at 12.

21. Kip Zirkel, *Mistakes Custody Evaluators (and GALs) Often Make and How to Control Them (to a Degree)*, (Unpublished White Paper, With Permission from the Author), at 1.

22. *Id.* at 3.

23. Sarah Lustbader, *The Feminist Law Professor Who Wants to Stop Arresting People for Domestic Violence*, The New Yorker, Mar. 9, 2025.

That locking up the DV/IPV perpetrators is not the only way to protect the victims, and these experts want to confront the racial, gender, and socioeconomic biases underlying the carceral approach and have law enforcement stop arresting people for having perpetrated DV/IPV. These experts have noticed a chasm between what IPV victims really need—a stable income, a place to live, a safe way to co-parent, an apology, family therapy, substance-use treatment for their partner, healthcare, childcare—and what the system offered: arrest, prosecution, and complete separation between the perpetrator and the victim. These experts complain about women who called in allegations of abuse only to be separated from their children by protective services. These victims of IPV also risked being jailed themselves for fighting back, for failing to protect their children, and, at times, for not testifying against their abusers. A bias in favor of a carceral approach to stop and remediate IPV, which is preferred by the mainstream white feminists, may not be the right approach for some victims. Research demonstrates that the carceral approach is not race-neutral—it never was—and it hurts Black and other minority victims, particularly women, who are at imminent risk of arrest, deportation, or losing their children to the foster care system.[24]

Biases also include thinking problems, such as mistaking correlation (two things happen at the same time) for causation (one thing caused the other to happened).[25] Overgeneralizing from incomplete data is also common; for example, one visit for one afternoon with a family may be insufficient information to decide as to the quality of the relationship or parenting.[26]

Attorneys who suffer burnout and vicarious trauma (discussed later) suffer from higher rates of cognitive bias.[27] But we need not remain victims of our biases. Experts have identified a process for being aware of one's biases, and attempting to mitigate their effects. It starts with:

- Becoming aware of the bias and why it exists;
- Having the motivation to overcome it;
- Being aware of the direction and magnitude of the bias; and
- Having the ability to apply an appropriate strategy to help reduce or otherwise manage the bias.[28]

---

24. *Id.*

25. Zirkel, *supra* note 21.

26. *Id.* at 4.

27. Jennifer Brobst, *The Impact of Secondary Traumatic Stress among Family Attorneys Working with Trauma-Exposed Clients: Implications for Practice and Professional Responsibility*, 10 J. Health & Biomedical L. 1, 19 (2014).

28. Baer, *supra* note 17, at 16.

Among the strategies for mitigating biases include the development of emotional self-awareness, by "reading one's own emotions and recognizing their impact."[29] Another is to consider all arguments, counterarguments, and alternatives *before* forming an opinion.[30] However, some experts have found such introspective strategies to be ineffective: "just thinking about how one might reduce the impact of bias; enumerating the various potential cognitive biases and vowing to control for them; and vowing to treat each parent equally. They simply don't work."[31] These experts instead recommend attending continuing education programs and professional courses that focus on debiasing strategies.[32] Likewise, changing internal systems, such as developing more comprehensive and systematic data-gathering methods, can also be helpful, as can instituting procedures such as checklists.[33] So is forcing oneself to develop multiple hypotheses, such as using checklists itemizing best interest factors in child custody statutory laws.[34]

One of the best debiasing strategies in family law matters is simply being curious.[35] Being genuinely curious with a scientific or investigative mindset that is geared toward systematic data collection and problem solving. To that end, ask open-ended questions, follow-up questions that are focused on obtaining information about actions, omissions, and behaviors, instead of rushing to "diagnose" a situation or to label or classify a particular set of family dynamic.

Managing Emotions When Representing Victims of Family Violence

Family law cases, even those that do not have a family violence component, are challenging. Handling a couple's separation, divorce, child custody, parenting plan disputes, mental health interventions, all require a practitioner to develop a skill set that is not necessarily required for other types of litigation: Namely, an attorney who represents such clients must be adept at

29. *Id.* at 16–17.
30. *Id.* at 17.
31. Simon & Stahl, *supra* note 12, at 70.
32. *Id.*
33. *Id.*
34. *Id.*
35. *Id.* at 73.

managing emotions—both the clients' and the attorney's.[36] "To ignore fear, anger, anxiety, sadness, denial, or any other psychological states of mind is to leave the client in a condition that makes rational informed decision-making difficult, if not impossible."[37] In cases involving family violence, the requirement that a practitioner be adept and skillful at managing the client's emotions as well as his or her own emotions is the key. It is not easy for a victim of family violence to tell his or her story and to provide all the relevant facts when attempting to obtain legal representation. In many cases, due to inappropriate, incomplete, or biased case intake or screening practices, practitioners may fail to obtain proper information. This could be for several reasons, including that the victim:

> (1) may not know why it might be in the interests of their children or themselves to disclose abuse; (2) may be unclear or concerned about the ramifications of disclosure; (3) may not trust [the attorney] with information about domestic abuse, in spite of your good intentions; and (4) may not perceive that their current level of risk warrants disclosure.[38]

In addition, a victim of IPV may not see himself or herself as a "victim" of abuse—it is not uncommon for some victims who have been subjected to childhood abuse to normalize abuse and see the abusive behavior as a normal family dynamic. Thus, "[a]dvising and representing individuals in planning and adjusting their family relationships requires excellent interpersonal communication skills."[39] Successful representation of family law clients in general, and DV/IPV clients in particular, necessitates that the attorneys become not only diligent advocates but also "empathic and sophisticated listeners, successful communicators, and effective translators of clients' emotions."[40]

While there are far fewer studies of male victims of DV/IPV, there are plenty that have helped to describe the characteristics of female victims. These have shown that female victims may have "avoidant, self-destructive,

---

36. Barbara Glesner Fines & Cathy Madsen, *Caring Too Little, Caring Too Much: Competence and the Family Law Attorney*, 75 UMKC L. Rev. 965, 968 (2007).

37. *Id.* at 982.

38. Gabrielle Davis et al., *Practice Guides for Family Court Decision-Making in Domestic Abuse-Related Child Custody Matters*, Battered Women's Justice Project, at 11 (2018).

39. Fines & Madsen, *supra* note 36, at 979.

40. *Id.*

borderline, and paranoid personality traits."[41] They have also, generally speaking, been found to "present with low self-esteem, insecurity, submissiveness, self-blame, increased social isolation, and financial and emotional dependence on their abusers."[42] Thus, competent representation of these clients requires the attorney to understand the associated characteristics and take them into consideration when crafting litigation strategy so that they don't "interfere with and undermine successful outcomes."[43]

Victims of DV/IPV often suffer from the interference of their tormentor in a number of areas, including (1) resources (e.g., money, bank accounts, food, housing, and transportation); (2) general freedom to manage their time and make decisions; (3) vocation and schooling; (4) daily needs (e.g., eating, sleeping, healthcare); (5) parenting; (6) social connections; and (7) general personal space.[44]

It is important to keep in mind that victims of DV/IPV reach out to attorneys while experiencing "the worst moments in their lives, when they felt vulnerable and alone."[45] Victims may display trauma in any of several ways, including either hostility or flat affect, over-reaction or lack of emotion, and vivid memories or a complete loss of memory regarding the abuse.[46] In such scenarios, an interaction with an attorney who is not knowledgeable, skilled, nor trained in handling IPV cases may result in the victim shutting down, losing trust in the legal system, or overall feeling hopeless. Attorneys who are ill-equipped to manage these troubled clients may end up doing damage, not just to the client but also to other victims as well who may interact with the client and whom the client may dissuade from seeking legal help. "[I]nterpersonally the lawyer-client relationship [can be] deeply troubled. All too often lawyers are thought to be inattentive, unresponsive, insensitive, non-empathetic, uncooperative, and arrogant."[47]

---

41. Teresa C. Silva, *Assessment of Credibility of Testimony in Alleged Intimate Partner Violence: A Case Report*, 22(1) J. Forensic Psych. Res. Practice 59 (2021).

42. *Id.* at 59–60.

43. Fines & Madsen, *supra* note 36, at 979.

44. SAFer, *Interference with Victim Detail,* Battered Women's Justice Project (2017).

45. Khadeeja Safdar, *The High-Pressure Tactics Attorney Gloria Allred Uses—On Her Own Clients*, Wall St. J., Mar. 9, 2025, at 3 of 28 (PDF version).

46. *Standards of Practice for Lawyers Representing Victims of Domestic Violence, Sexual Assault and Stalking in Civil Protection Order Cases*, American Bar Association, at 35 (2007).

47. Fines & Madsen, *supra* note 36, at 979–80.

A 2025 article in the *Wall Street Journal* illustrates both the frustration practitioners face when dealing with victims of physical and sexual abuse, including DV/IPV, as well as the emotional damage that an attorney can unwittingly inflict on his or her client.[48] For example, a woman who was allegedly raped by a Hollywood star and who "thought he was going to kill me," was berated by her attorney when she expressed that she was suffering panic attacks.[49] As per the client, when she shared her anxiety issues with her lawyer, the attorney said: "*How old are you? Get a hold of yourself.*"[50] Another, who was forced to sign a non-disclosure agreement (NDA), felt "isolated because she couldn't share what she was going through with friends or family."[51] And a third said "the experience with [her attorney] has worsened her trauma."[52]

Here, it is important to note that the goal of an IPV victim may be different from that of a typical civil litigant. For example, some IPV victims would choose to walk away from a cash settlement rather than agree to an NDA.[53] As one alleged victim said: "She [her attorney] told me she could have gotten me hush money. . . . That's the opposite of what I wanted."[54]

Some IPV victims point to the NDAs signed by early victims of Harvey Weinstein that prevented his victims and society from knowing the full extent of the sexual crimes for which he was convicted.[55] Those concerned with NDAs may also note the recent case of an alleged victim of author Neil Gaiman, who signed an NDA six weeks before another alleged victim filed a suit against the author for the same alleged behavior.[56] As an alleged victim of the celebrity golfer, Tiger Woods, said after she signed an NDA: "I feel like I helped create a monster."[57]

Practitioners who handle cases should recognize that aggressive and zealous advocacy is just one part of the job. The other part, which may be equally important (and which some fail to appreciate) is to actively listen

48. Safdar, *supra* note 45.
49. *Id.*
50. *Id.*
51. *Id.*
52. *Id.*
53. *Id.*
54. *Id.*
55. *Id.*
56. *Id.*
57. *Id.*

to the client, allow them to have agency in the handling of their case, and provide emotional support when needed. Victims of family violence consistently gave high marks to "attorneys [who] provided emotional support in the forms of calming and listening to them, and encouraging them to feel less helpless."[58]

Like adults, children, too, suffer from family violence, both directly and indirectly. And their abuse can begin while they are in utero if their mother is a victim.[59] In addition to suffering direct physical and verbal abuse, children may also be "caught in the crossfire" of their parent's abuse, or simply observe it.[60] In addition, children are sometimes enlisted by the abusive parent to participate in perpetrating abuse, which they may do in order to protect themselves.[61] Long-term, child-sufferers of family violence may have parental and/or separation anxiety, broken social ties, loss of trust, chaos, and disruption of their lives.[62]

Screening for Abuse or Violence

IPV Victims Are Unlike Other Reporters of Violence

Cases involving allegations of IPV like other controversies often turn on the credibility of the alleged victim. A trier of fact, whether he or she is a family court judge or a forensic child custody evaluator making determinations regarding allegations of IPV, may look at the following factors when assessing credibility of a witness:

1. the consistency of the witness's statement with what is agreed or clearly shown to have occurred by available evidence,
2. the coherence among all the pieces of witness's evidence,
3. the compatibility among witness's several statements or depositions,
4. the credibility of the witness regarding matters not related to the litigation, and 5. the behavior of the witness.[63]

---

58. Fines & Madsen, *supra* note 36, at 980.

59. SAFeR, *Children's Experience of IPV*, Battered Women's Justice Project (2017).

60. *Id.*

61. *Id.*

62. *Id.*

63. Teresa C. Silva, *Assessment of Credibility of Testimony in Alleged Intimate Partner Violence: A Case Report*, 22(1) J. Forensic Psych. Res. Practice 58 (2021).

These factors may be sufficient in cases where there is no evidence of family violence, including IPV. However, these factors may be insufficient when dealing with IPV cases, which also require "consideration of the perpetrator's and victim's psychological, behavioral and attitudinal attributes . . . especially when the available evidence is limited and testimonies are contradictory."[64]

As is well-known:

> It is important to understand that trauma might affect a client's ability to remember and that the story might change from one interview to the next, not because they are lying but because they are confused.[65]

Applying generalized guidelines that assess credibility of a witness to a case involving IPV may result in the victim being discredited, not believed, or even accused of making false allegations of abuse to obtain an advantage in the battle over child custody. A practitioner who is not knowledgeable, skilled, and trained in IPV may mistake a sign of trauma or anxiety—for instance, incoherence of the narrative of abuse—as lack of credibility. Therefore, it is vital for practitioners to seek help from DV advocates or to associate themselves with professionals who are experienced in handling cases involving family violence.

Gaining the Cooperation of IPV Victims

Victims of family violence may not be forthcoming in describing the abuse that they have endured. Some may not be aware of their victimization and may blame themselves for the violence or abuse that they were subjected to. Others have inherent distrust of the legal system, law enforcement, and legal professionals and may not volunteer or provide the information that may be required to obtain protective safeguards. Many may have suffered trauma due to physical violence, sexual violence, or being subjected to years of coercive controlling behaviors. Working with these victims is a challenge. Working with clients who have been traumatized by IPV significantly increases the difficulty of case preparation. It takes time to get the cooperation of a client who has been traumatized by IPV or other form of family violence.

---

64. *Id.* at 59.

65. Lisa Morgillo, *Do Not Make Their Trauma Your Trauma: Coping with Burnout as a Family Law Attorney*, 53(3) Fam. Ct. Rev. 456, 461 (2015).

"Many traumatized clients avoid discussing traumatic events at all costs."[66] Others may minimize abusive behavior or hold back on providing details of the abuse endured by them due to the fear of retaliation. Some may have temporarily escaped the abusive environment but have no permanent place to go. And some may have left their loved ones—children or pets—behind in the abusive environment, who they are afraid of hurting by disclosing abuse.

Thus, it can be difficult to convince victims of domestic abuse to cooperate with a screening because the victims: (1) may not know why it might be in the interests of their children or themselves to disclose abuse; (2) may be unclear or concerned about the ramifications of disclosure; (3) may not trust the attorney or DV professional with the information, or (4) may not perceive that their current level of risk warrants disclosure.[67]

However, it is also important that a practitioner allows an IPV victim to have agency in making relevant decisions, including a decision on whether to report abuse to law enforcement or disclose it in court filings. To obtain "safe and informed disclosure for domestic abuse" the practitioner must:

> [E]xplain to the people you screen why you are asking about abuse, how you will use the information they provide, who will have access to it, and where it might show up later in the family court process.[68]

As one survey revealed, clients in family law cases, generally, need "information and guidelines about what to expect from the legal process, and wanted their attorneys to serve as 'interpreters' of the system's unfamiliar language and procedures."[69] And as many practitioners have learned, IPV victims "may require a heightened level of patience and assurance," before they will divulge essential information.[70]

It is also helpful to explain the "professional standards that guide your work," and to clearly identify the "specific role and function" the screener has in the process.[71] This includes information on how the professional came onto the case (appointed, hired, referred) and the process that will

66. *Id.* at 459.
67. Davis et al., *supra* note 38, at 11.
68. *Id.* at 4.
69. Fines & Madsen, *supra* note 36, at 980.
70. *Standards of Practice for Lawyers, supra* note 46, at 25.
71. Davis et al., *supra* note 38, at 7.

be employed by the professional in handling the case.[72] In addition, prior to utilizing a screening tool(s), a practitioner should explain precisely what will (and won't) be shared with the court and opposing parties, and whether any information will appear in the record or some other type of report.[73] Likewise, the scope and limits of confidentiality, and the duty to report suspected child abuse and crimes must also be discussed.[74]

There are a variety of tools available to assist with screening for domestic abuse or IPV. "Different tools look for different things for different reasons,"[75] and it may be necessary to use more than one tool or to amalgamate separate screening tools to obtain all the required information.

Screening Tools

There are several screening tools available to family law practitioners and professionals involved with the family courts to effectively screen for presence of IPV. It is essential that practitioners use evidence-informed practices to screen for IPV. Following is a checklist of best practices when screening for IPV, as suggested by a team of psychiatrists and psychologists:[76]

1. Use a standardized screening instrument that has undergone empirical testing;
2. Use behaviorally specific questions to ask about IPV;
3. Ask about a wide range of IPV behaviors;
4. Inquire about IPV-related fear and injury;
5. Inquire about severity and time frame of IPV behaviors;
6. Conduct consistent and frequent administration of IPV screening;
7. Ask IPV screening questions in a confidential manner and in private location; and
8. Determine the purpose for which IPV screening is being conducted.

---

72. *Id.*

73. SAFeR, *Practitioner's Manual*, at 10.

74. Davis et al., *supra* note 38, at 7.

75. *Id.* at 4.

76. Fernanda S. Rossi et al., *Intimate Partner Violence Screening for Separating or Divorcing Parents: An Introduction to the Mediator's Assessment of Safety Issues and Concerns-Short (MASIC-S)*, Fam. Ct. Rev. (2023), DOI: 10.1111/fcre.12762.

Initial Domestic Abuse Screening Guide

This is perhaps the simplest of the screening tools, and it starts with eight overarching questions with follow-up options.[77] It is recommended when a less-than comprehensive screening is sufficient.

Its initial rubric has two columns—questions on the left, and "what to listen for" on the right.[78] The areas covered in the overarching questions are personal interactions, everyday decision-making, control of everyday life, physical violence, emotional well-being, sexual autonomy, fear of physical or psychological harm, and parental decision-making.[79] For instance, here's an example of a screening question for the left column: *When you look back over time, how were practical, everyday decisions made in your relationship?* Such a question could be divided into sub-questions: *How did you arrive at that arrangement? Are you comfortable with that? What happened when disagreements arose?* In the right column, the answer to the screening question could lead to an assessment of the family dynamics, which could range from being "Equal" to "Dominating"; "Cooperative" to "Coercive"; "Responsible" to "Irresponsible"; and "Fair" to "Manipulative."

Following these questions is a four-column check-a-box questionnaire with approximately 100 different behaviors, broken down into the following categories:

- Physical/Sexual Abuse,
- Emotional Abuse
- Control of Daily Life
- Economic Abuse[80]

Examples of Physical/Sexual Abuse include hitting, kicking, striking, forced sex, and spitting on.

Examples of Emotional Abuse include threats of harm to the adult or child, humiliation, mind games, and accusations of infidelity.

Examples of Control of Daily Life include examining mail and phone records, stalking and following, accessing email, invading privacy, and punishing for disobedience.

---

77. Davis et al., *supra* note 38, at 7.
78. *Id.* at 9–10.
79. *Id.*
80. *Id.* at 10.

Finally, examples of Economic Abuse include refusing money and to pay debts, hiding assets, destroying credit and canceling credit cards, and litigation abuse.

Similar to the screening used for adults, information regarding children should be assessed across eight areas: (1) physical/sexual abuse, (2) emotional abuse, (3) economic abuse, (4) using the child as a tool of DV/IPV, (5) denying the impact of DV/IPV on the child, (6) ignoring the child's needs, (7) undermining the other parent's relationship, and (8) relentless harassment.[81] Questions for children seek to identify (or eliminate) use of force and restraint, deprivation, intimidation, threats, denial or interference with support, harassment, manipulation, rationalizing behavior, lack of consideration of child's separate needs, withholding the child from the other parent, and constant disruption of the child's life.[82]

National Council of Juvenile and Family Court Judges Screening Tool

While this screening tool is designed for judges, attorneys, particularly those serving in the role of a child's legal representative or guardian ad litem, may find this simple screening tool helpful as well. As with other screening tools, it has check-a-box options, broken down by topics, including children, abuse and custody, emotional control, financial control, physical control, and sexual control.[83] It also provides helpful advice on how to sift through contradictory evidence and testimony.[84]

Domestic Abuse Interview Guide

The Guidelines formulated by the Battered Women's Justice Project/SAFeR is yet another source that offers a helpful screening tool. This comprehensive questionnaire is intended to assist in identifying domestic abuse and coercive controlling behaviors.[85] It offers a framework to help a practitioner gather, organize, synthesize, assess, and analyze information related to domestic abuse or violence, and thereby offers opportunities for making informed decisions. The framework consists of four parts:

---

81. SAFeR, *Parenting by Abuser-Parent*, Battered Women's Justice Project (2017).

82. *Id.*

83. Mary V. Mentaberry et al., *A Judicial Guide to Child Safety in Custody Cases*, National Council of Juvenile and Family Court Judges, at 58–60 (2008).

84. *Id.* at 60.

85. Davis et al., *supra* note 38, at 11.

1. Screen for Domestic Abuse
2. Assess the Nature and Context of Abuse
3. Focus on the Effects of Abuse
4. Respond to Abuse in Actions and Decisions

The Guidelines offer detailed examples of basic screening questions and offer tips on discussion areas and "what to listen for" when screening a client who has complained of being abused or who may have undergone abuse.[86] The Guidelines offer seven broad topic areas on which a professional can collect information. They include personal interaction, access to resources, children and parenting, control of daily life, emotional abuse, physical abuse, and sexual abuse. The questions suggested by the Guidelines are "behaviorally specific," which has been found to be an effective method for screening for IPV.[87]

When answers to these questions reveal a possibility of domestic abuse or violence, the discussion areas assist in gaining a more thorough understanding of the "nature, context, severity and implications" of domestic abuse, including coercive control.[88] The "what to listen for" identifies "concepts, behaviors, and dynamics" that could be instructive in identifying—or eliminating—concerns regarding DV/IPV.[89]

The Guidelines also include a rubric to assist in identifying safety concerns and specific types of risks.[90]

Six-Factor Test

This tool could be helpful in situations where there is no legal substantiation of the alleged violence.[91] The factors are as follows:[92]

- Objective Verification: The screener should "observe[] the frequency and severity of data in police complaints, medical records, or other observations by neutral third parties."
- Pattern of Abuse Complaints. The practitioner "considers official reports and unofficial complaints to others."

---

86. *Id.* at 13.
87. *Id.* at 11.
88. *Id.*
89. *Id.*
90. *Id.* at 19.
91. Silva, *supra* note 41, at 66.
92. *Id.* at 66–67.

- Corroboration by Credible Others. The assessor "analyzes information collected by credible (i.e. neutral) third parties." This ideally does not include family and friends who are far more likely to be biased.
- Absence of Disconfirming Verbal Reports. Under this factor, the practitioner "considers whether third parties who had ample opportunity to observe or interact with the couple provide information that disconfirms the abuse allegations."
- Alleged Abuser Psychological Profile and Past History of Abusive Behavior. The screener uses a risk assessment approach such as the B-SAFER tool. This considers ten risk factors, split into two groups: antisocial characteristics and historical psychological and social functioning.[93] The B-SAFER risk factors are:[94]
  - Serious physical violence and the history of abuse of current and former partners;
  - Serious violent threat, ideation, intent, which includes credible threats, stalking, and harassment;
  - Escalation of violence or threats, asking if they have "increased in frequency or severity over time";
  - Violations of civil or criminal court orders, particularly regarding DV/IPV behaviors;
  - Negative attitudes about spousal assault, including possessiveness, sexual jealousy, and misogyny;
  - Other serious criminality, unrelated to DV/IPV;
  - Relationship problems, such as marital discord, constant arguments, and fights;
  - Employment and/or financial problems, including poor job performance, frequent job changes, long-term unemployment, and absenteeism;
  - Substance abuse;
  - Mental disorder, which considers everything from depression and anxiety to personality disorders and toxic traits.
- Alleged Victim Psychological Status. The assessor should look for the psychological characteristics of suffering DV/IPV, such as "anxiety, depression, posttraumatic stress disorder, and substance use disorder."

---

93. *Id.* at 67.
94. *Id.* at 67–68.

Minnesota Attorney Screening Guide

The Domestic Abuse Committee of the Family Law Section of the Minnesota State Bar Association has created a screening guide for lawyers to implement, particularly prior to engaging in mediation.[95]

Similar to the SAFeR Domestic Violence Screening Guide, the Minnesota tool is broken down into questions in one column and "what to listen for" in the other.[96] The screening tool has questions in categories that include employment, finances, relationship, children and parenting, coercive control, physical violence, alcohol, drugs, mental health, and summary.[97]

If abuse is disclosed or suspected, the tool also has a risk assessment questionnaire, as well as a detailed danger assessment.[98]

Keeping an Open Mind

Screening tools are just that—tools. Even the best screening tool will only reveal so much, so it is important for the screener to remain cognizant of all possible inferences from any given observation.[99] For example, a victim's account may change over and again; this could indicate they are lying, but it could also be that they are simply afraid or that the trauma affects their memory and recollection of events.[100] The same is true if the victim is hostile to the screening; again, they could be lying, but they could also simply be naturally hostile or scared.[101] How the screener forms questions is critical, because follow up questions could explore and reveal certain situations or issues. For instance, a victim of IPV may not report that he or she was "terrorized" and may not "check the box" for being subjected to "intimidating" or "controlling" behavior. However, upon being asked open-ended questions and follow-up questions, he or she may provide information that leaves little doubt that the victim was subjected to hair-raising psychological violence. That kind of violence is exemplified by the following narrative of domestic

95. *Client Screening to Identify Domestic Violence Victimization*, Minnesota State Bar Association, at 3 (2013).

96. *Id.* at 10.

97. *Id.* at 10–15.

98. *Id.* at 15–18.

99. *Id.* at 20.

100. Davis et al., *supra* note 38, at 20.

101. *Id.*

abuse reported by associate professor Rachel Louise Snyder in her book *No Visible Bruises: What We Don't Know About Domestic Violence Can Kill Us*:

> That night was the first time Sally heard about a rattlesnake Rocky had recently acquired from somewhere and kept in a cage in their living room. Michelle was terrified. He told her he would put it in her bed while she slept or sneak it into the shower with her. A murder that would look like a freak accident. Sally understood immediately that her daughter's situation was far beyond her own casual acquaintance with domestic violence.[102]

Beware of False Positives

IPV is such a widely discussed topic that it is not uncommon for someone to create a story that is fake but convincing.[103] Common characteristics of abusers, such as jealously, callousness, and drug and alcohol abuse are well known, as are the settings in which abuse is alleged to occur, such as via coercive control and victim isolation.[104] So how to tell a real narrative of IPV from a lie? There are no hard and fast rules, but remaining aware of the biases at play, attempting to mitigate them, and using a structured screening tool to systematically obtain and analyze information could help separate fact from fiction. Look for the specific types of psychological harm that are "almost impossible to reproduce" if they have not been experienced; this includes fear in unrelated environments,[105] as well as "anxiety, depression, posttraumatic stress disorder, and substance use disorder."[106]

If IPV Is Found

Once IPV is identified, there are several steps the screener should take:

1. Obtain as much information as possible in order to fully understand the context and implications of the abuse;
2. Conduct a thorough domestic abuse risk assessment or refer the person to a qualified risk assessment specialist; and
3. Refer the person to a qualified domestic abuse advocate for safety planning assistance.[107]

---

102. Snyder, *supra* note 1, at 51.
103. Silva, *supra* note 41, at 60.
104. *Id.*
105. *Id.*
106. *Id.* at 67.
107. SAFeR, *Practitioner's Manual*, Battered Women's Justice Project, at 10 (2020).

The ABA Standards of Practice also directs that attorneys who work with IPV victims "ensure that comprehensive lethality assessment and safety planning" occurs.[108] Practitioners may not only have to assist and represent a victim in obtaining protective measures such as a personal protective order, but also obtain protective safeguards for the minor children or pets and protect the victim and his or her loved ones from retaliation by the perpetrator.

Recommendations for Professionals Who Handle Cases Involving Family Violence

Legal professionals who work in the high-stress field of family violence, including IPV, face a risk of becoming burned out, succumbing to alcohol or substance abuse, or developing secondary trauma (i.e., vicarious trauma). "Burnout is defined as a physical, emotional, or psychological exhaustion caused by continued exposure to occupational stressors."[109] It is frequently "caused by responsibility overload, inadequate or imbalanced rewards, and time pressures."[110] Other causes include "lack of respect or inequity at the workplace, lack of community at the workplace, few financial or emotional rewards with the work, little control of quality of services provided, and conflict between individual values and organizational goals and demands."[111]

"There are three sub-components to burnout—emotional exhaustion, depersonalization and reduced personal accomplishment."[112] The first "refers to feelings of being overextended and depleted of emotional resources."[113] Depersonalization is characterized by "a loss of idealism and increase in detached responses to others."[114] This could also result in being desensitized to abusive behaviors and violence. The third manifests as "a self-evaluation dimension and includes a decline in perceived occupational competence and productivity."[115] While burnout, alone, does not cause many of the symptoms of vicarious trauma (discussed next), it "can lead to an increased

---

108. *Standards of Practice for Lawyers, supra* note 46, at 33.

109. Charles P. Edwards & Monica K. Miller, *An Assessment of Judges' Self-Reported Experiences of Secondary Traumatic Stress*, 70(2) Juv. & Fam. Ct. J. 7, 10 (2019).

110. *Id.*

111. Lisa Morgillo, *Do Not Make Their Trauma Your Trauma: Coping with Burnout As a Family Law Attorney*, 53(3) Fam. Ct. Rev. 456, 457 (2015).

112. Edwards & Miller, *supra* note 109, at 10.

113. *Id.*

114. *Id.*

115. *Id.* at 10–11.

vulnerability to developing vicarious traumatization by diminishing an individual's personal resources to effectively resist the impact of vicarious traumatization."[116]

Vicarious trauma, also known as secondhand or secondary trauma, is different from burnout. Where burnout happens when the attorney is "overloaded resulting from working with difficult clients," and stems from "a perceived discrepancy between an individual's effort . . . and the reward received for that work," vicarious trauma is due to a "specific reaction to particular information presented by the client."[117]

Given the unique relationship between an IPV victim and their attorney, the possibility that clients' "emotional traumas become the attorneys' own personal and professional crises" is significant.[118] "Wanting to help can have negative emotional, psychological, and physical effects on the attorney."[119]

Thus, vicarious trauma is "a well-recognized phenomenon among helping professionals,"[120] and has been defined as "a transformation in the self of a trauma worker . . . that results from empathic engagement with traumatized clients and their reports of traumatic experiences."[121] That is, practitioners working with DV/IPV victims may develop symptoms and behaviors similar to their clients.[122]

The condition develops during representation where the attorney is "privy to traumatic material through client narratives and case discovery."[123] It is "rooted in, the open engagement of empathy, or the connection with the client that is inherent in helping relationships."[124] Social isolation and social and family instability can contribute to the development of vicarious trauma.[125]

---

116. Fines & Madsen, *supra* note 36, at 990.

117. *Id.* at 989.

118. *Id.* at 984.

119. Morgillo, *supra* note 65, at 457.

120. *Standards of Practice for Lawyers, supra* note 46, at 35.

121. Tina M. Mattison, *Vicarious Trauma: The Silent Stressor*, Institute for Court Management, at 5 (2012).

122. *Standards of Practice for Lawyers, supra* note 46, at 35.

123. Fines & Madsen, *supra* note 36, at 988.

124. *Id.* at 990.

125. Jennifer Brobst, *The Impact of Secondary Traumatic Stress among Family Attorneys Working with Trauma-Exposed Clients: Implications for Practice and Professional Responsibility*, 10 J. Health & Biomedical L. 1, 22–23 (2014).

Akin to PTSD, vicarious trauma symptoms include "feelings of fear, sadness, horror, helplessness, anger, mood swings, grief, guilt, and anxiety."[126] Some experience "recurrent, upsetting thoughts, ruminative thoughts about the traumatic event, nightmares, flashbacks, difficulty concentrating, confusion and forgetfulness."[127] Vicarious trauma victims may have "changes in appetite, loss of energy, withdrawing socially, increased use of alcohol and/or drugs, restlessness, agitation, and/or difficulty relaxing, gastrointestinal distress, nausea, dizziness, rapid heartbeat, trembling, muscle tension, increased startle response, and difficulty meeting school, work [and] social responsibilities."[128]

A 2003 survey revealed that "attorneys [suffering from vicarious trauma] demonstrated higher levels of intrusive recollection of trauma material; avoidance of reminders of the material; diminished pleasure and interest in activities; and difficulties with sleep, irritability, and concentration."[129]

Likewise, those affected may suffer from an inability to "think clearly, to modulate emotions, to feel effective, or to maintain hope."[130] They may also "react defensively by avoiding cases with traumatic content, downplaying a case's degree of severity, and rationalizing the case's destructive impact."[131] "On the other hand, defensive reactions might manifest in the form of over-involvement and efforts to rescue a client."[132]

Some "develop a pattern of learned helplessness . . . a condition in which one feels little control over his or her situation and efforts to correct the situation are futile."[133] Moreover, "[g]uilt is one of the strongest signs of a trauma exposure," whereby the sufferer blocks "any experience of pleasure, peace, or happiness."[134]

Long-term effects include fatigue, impaired immune system, eating disorders, job dissatisfaction/low morale/poor performance, high absenteeism,

---

126. Tina M. Mattison, *Vicarious Trauma: The Silent Stressor*, Institute for Court Management, at 6 (2012).

127. *Id.*

128. *Id.*

129. Morgillo, *supra* note 65, at 461.

130. Fines & Madsen, *supra* note 36, at 988.

131. *Id.*

132. *Id.*

133. *Id.* at 991.

134. Morgillo, *supra* note 65, at 459.

staff conflicts, depression, poor self-care, chronic physical ailments, substance abuse, and heart failure or stroke.[135] As one person described it:

> There is a difference between feeling tired because you put in a hard day's work and feeling fatigued in every cell of your being. . . . The kind of tired that results from having a trauma exposure response is a bone-tired, soul-tired, heart-tired kind of exhaustion—your body is tired, your mind is tired, your spirit is tired, your people are tired. You can't remember a time when you weren't tired.[136]

Formal options for addressing vicarious trauma include the Minnesota Divorce Camp offered by the Minnesota Chapter of the American Academy of Matrimonial Lawyers.[137] Another has been created by the Wisconsin State Bar Lawyers Assistance Program that includes proactive strategies for firms that feature regular debriefing, reducing caseloads for trauma-related cases, and checklists for self-assessment.[138]

In addition, many state bar associations also provide assistance.[139] Moreover, law schools have begun offering formal classes in representing trauma victims.[140]

There are also several less formal recommendations that may help prevent vicarious trauma, including notably, "balance," that is "managing one's caseload to include a diversity of clients (e.g., non-traumatized clients)."[141] Likewise, creating a culture within your organization that supports workers and addresses "the effects in personal and work lives," such as providing "counselors to talk in an open and nonjudgmental context about their experiences."[142] This "provides an empathic connection and supports clear thinking."[143]

---

135. Mattison, *supra* note 121, at 7–8.

136. Morgillo, *supra* note 65, at 459.

137. *Id.* at 463. *See also* AAML-MN's 2025 Divorce Camp, https://aamlmn.org/divorce-camp/ (last visited Apr. 12, 2025).

138. Jennifer Brobst, *The Impact of Secondary Traumatic Stress among Family Attorneys Working with Trauma-Exposed Clients: Implications for Practice and Professional Responsibility*, 10 J. Health & Biomedical L. 1, 42 (2014).

139. Morgillo, *supra* not 65, at 463.

140. *Id.* at 464.

141. Fines & Madsen, *supra* note 36, at 993.

142. *Id.* at 993–94.

143. *Id.* at 994.

Setting appropriate boundaries is also recommended.[144] These include "structural boundaries of space and time (not giving out home phone numbers, considering carefully where one will meet clients, etc.) to the more permeable boundary of emotional distance and connection."[145] Thus "proper boundaries provide a foundation for the attorney-client relationship by fostering a sense of safety and the belief that the professional will always act in the client's best interests," while also lessening "the risk for potential misinterpretations of communication and motives."[146]

Some also recommend being clear-eyed about the attorney's role and skills, and making referrals for those tangential areas where others are available to help—such as with housing and employment.[147] Others suggest requiring trauma-victim clients to have some sort of separate support system, such as a 12-step program or a shelter.[148]

One final recommendation is self-care: "finding creative outlets or spiritual practices that replenish the helping professional," as well as "systematically monitoring one's own emotional and mental health."[149]

---

144. *Id.* at 995.
145. *Id.* at 996.
146. *Id.*
147. Morgillo, *supra* note 65, at 458.
148. *Id.*
149. Fines & Madsen, *supra* note 36, at 997.

TABLE OF CASES

INDEX